EXAMINATION OF BASIC WEAKNESSES OF INCOME AS THE MAJOR FEDERAL TAX BASE

Edited by

Richard W. Lindholm

PRAEGER

New York
Westport, Connecticut
London

Library of Congress Cataloging-in-Publication Data
Main entry under title:

Examination of basic weaknesses of income as the major
  federal tax base.

  Includes index.
  1. Income tax – United States – Addresses, essays,
lectures. I. Lindholm, Richard Wadsworth, 1914–
HJ4652.E9 1986   336.24′0973   86-518
ISBN 0-275-92148-4 (alk. paper)

Library of Congress Catalog Card Number: 86-518
ISBN: 0-275-92148-4

First published in 1986

Praeger Publishers, 521 Fifth Avenue, New York, NY 10175
A division of Greenwood Press, Inc.

Printed in the United States of America

The paper used in this book complies with the Permanent Paper Standard issued by the
National Information Standards Organization (Z39.48-1984).

10 9 8 7 6 5 4 3 2 1

PREFACE

The basic aim of the research reported in this volume is to identify the seriousness of the breakdown of the federal tax system. However, the goal does not end with identifying weaknesses of a federal tax system based on profits and income; the next step is also taken: reform possibilities are considered by both practitioners and academic fiscal analysts.

The result is a group of recommendations and findings solidly based in the roots out of which the current federal tax system grew. The current system was all fine and good as long as the taxes required by the federal government were relatively minor--a condition no longer existing. Honest fiscal researchers now dig into the relationship that has developed out of big-time federal spending when using a revenue system aimed at taxation of surpluses, and therefore forced to apply high rates to a base possessing considerable potential for evasion, bribery, and instability of collection levels plus causing a reduction of available capital for investment.

This approach identifies current fiscal characteristics that demonstrate great instability and an inability to face up to the requirements of changing conditions. The chapters of this volume examine these sources of economic instability and inefficiency. The instability and revenue-raising characteristics are serious enough to deserve the descriptive term "debacle."

ACKNOWLEDGMENTS

Each contributor to this volume examined in-depth the functioning of a portion of our federal fiscal system. The U.S. fiscal system has become the world's largest creator and user of funds. However, it continues to look for its financing to institutions—established over 100 years ago—that show many signs of the institutional procedures under which they were spawned, as well as the impact of current operational pressures. We acknowledge the genius of those originators of the system under which we function, but at the same time we must move forward so that the huge government-financing requirements are met efficiently within the bounds of democratic decision-making.

My secretary Heidi Holling, an undergraduate student of the College of Business Administration at the University of Oregon, performed magnificently under conditions that were often uncertain at best. David Pollack assisted tremendously in editing the final drafts.

The analyses of each of the chapter-authors and my participation as editor and coordinator were made possible through funds provided by the Weingart Foundation of San Diego and Los Angeles and the Sol Price Foundation of San Diego.

The University of Oregon was most cooperative in providing housing and research facilities. Also, I have appreciated the various chapter analysts who have used me as a consultant in their preparatory efforts to describe the fiscal problems of our federal government as they have developed through the years and as they exist today. The aim of the analyses is to identify and examine the characteristics developing out of the existing mismatch between the income sources of our federal government and its spending and management needs.

CONTENTS

LIST OF TABLES

LIST OF FIGURES

INTRODUCTION

This study consists of eleven chapters, each prepared by experts selected by the editor because of their knowledge and interest in the areas analyzed in this book. Examination of Basic Weaknesses of Income as the Major Federal Tax Base provides an analysis in some depth of an area identified as being basic to change and a source of difficulties that arise out of the functioning of the federal income tax.

Each of these selected areas of active, current development requires considerable management shifting, individual stimulus to efficiency, and the creation of long-term plans. These three facets of development also are employed in the investment of savings and in the monitoring of efficiency and economic growth. The intensive use of income as the tax base reduces the ability of a welfare democracy to operate in the same fashion, which is, of course, the way private enterprise organizes capital and labor to carry out production projects.

1

The Growth and Failure of the Income Tax

Douglas Y. Thorson

The income tax made its debut in the United States over a century ago. It was ushered in on a wave of high expectation by some, skepticism by others, and doctrinaire opposition by still others. After a long history of experience, it is time for an appraisal. The keynote of our conclusion is that while this tax had met some important fiscal and social needs in the past, in our own time the income tax has become a debacle. It is inefficient, inequitable, and complex. We will identify the roots of this failure as we trace its history, and we will examine the details of current problems as our history carries to the present day. The unifying theme of our chapter is the concept of taxable income under the income tax.

The plan of our chapter is to begin with the early federal experiences with the income tax. The specific years we will examine are the 1860s, 1894, and 1913. These were formative years; many of the troublesome structural features of taxable income adopted in these early years continue to the present day. Next, we will briefly survey the voluminous theoretical work on defining personal income. While there have been a number of theories and partial theories of income, the concept of net accretions of current income, on the one hand, and the concept of lifetime income, on the other hand, have been the two main rival theories of personal income. (Until coming under serious challenge during the past two decades, the former served as the rallying point for those who sought to reform the income tax.) Following this, we will look at the erosion of the income tax that took place in the 50 years after its passage in 1913. Then, we will look at how the concept of tax expenditures developed in the 1960s and how the income tax ceased to be viewed primarily as a fiscal instrument for generating revenue. In particular, we will critically examine the ideas of Fessendon and Senator Sherman. Next the ideas of David Wells, a government economist, are considered. Also, the first and second commissioners of internal revenue, Boutwell and Lewis, who contributed both through their revenue rulings and through their testimony before Congress. Contemporary American economists such as Amasa Walker (elected to Congress in 1862) and Arthur Perry supported the income tax.

What makes the deliberations and actions of this group interesting is that they approached the income tax de novo. They lacked experience to know what could not be done, so they concentrated on what they thought ought to be done. They were inclined to make the definition of income inclusive, to consider gain whether realized or accrued and whether monetized or in kind. In fact, they supported the income tax because of its potential for uniformly reaching income regardless of source. They also were guided in their actions by an awareness that people often arranged their affairs to avoid paying taxes.

The first federal income tax statute was passed in 1861; it was revised in 1862 before being put into practice. The statute specified that income was to include "the annual gains, profits, or income of every person residing in the United States, whether derived from any kind of property, rents, interests, dividends, salaries, or from any profession, trade, employment, or vocation carried on in the United States or elsewhere or from any other source whatever except as hereinafter mentioned" (13 U.S. Statutes at Large, 281). While the concept of income essentially was periodic net money receipts, the exceptions to this principle are more interesting and important than the rule itself. The efforts to extend to income tax to all income proved to be administratively unfeasible, but the beguiling compulsion to do so was present even at this early date.

Several characteristics of taxable income in these statutes should be noted. First, no distinction was made between individual income and corporate income. In this difficult aspect of income taxation, undistributed corporate profits were taxed to the individual. Also, the tax on corporate interest and on dividends was withheld for a certain class of taxpayer. Second, realized capital gains were taxed in full. Eventually a time limit, first of one year and then of three years, was set for capital gains to be taxable. The complexity of this form of income had begun already to surface. Third, accrued income and income in kind were a matter of concern and dilemma. Both those who designed the laws and those who administered them tried to cope with this momentous issue, but with little success. Initially, both realized and accrued interest were designated as taxable, as were unrealized gains on farm crops. But this approach had to be abandoned since it was administratively unfeasible. An especially troubling case was that of imputed income on owner-occupied homes. The commissioner of internal revenue wanted to tax this income; instead, Congress allowed tenants to deduct rent as a way of establishing equality between owners and renters. Thus, the precedent for subsidizing residential construction started early. Fourth, all factor payments (wages as well as interest) by state and local government were taxable. This area of current preferential treatment had not yet begun.

Business deductions and personal deductions were limited, but each is of interest. Congress was reluctant to limit explicitly the income tax to net income. It was aware that a hard and clear line did not exist between business expense and personal expense. It permitted deductions for casualty losses, bad debts, and repairs. However, it hesitated over deductions for depreciation. Concern was expressed that such an allowance would be abused. This is an interesting anticipation of later major problems with the income tax. Some personal deducations were allowed. All state and local taxes could be deducted. The concern at the time was over multiple taxation, and this deduction was a concession to duplication of taxes. Interest on loans was deducted only to the extent that it was attributable to an income-producing loan. Hence, an effort was made to avoid preferential treatment on consumer durable goods and arbitrage. As stated earlier, however, house rent was deductible. Regardless of motivation, this clearly was a preferential item.

In terms of revenue, the Civil War income tax was successful during the war years. From 1863 to 1865, income tax revenues amounted to $84 million, about 20 percent of internal revenue. This revenue came from the top 20 to 30 percent of householders. Actually, two types of income tax were enacted during the Civil War. One was the general income tax; the other was a special income tax applied to certain kinds of income at a flat rate withheld at the source. It applied to the income of a designated group of financial, transportation, and turnpike companies as well as the salaries of federal government employees. Except for the latter, the income taxed was that of dividends and interest. These special income taxes, for the years 1863 to 1865, accounted for about one-fourth of the income tax revenues. Administratively at least, they were the most successful part of Civil War income taxation.

After the Civil War, serious problems with the general income tax surfaced. These problems caused a decline in its acceptability, leading to repeal in 1872. First, there was the problem of the definition of taxable income. The income tax had been chosen because of its potential for reaching all individuals regardless of income source. However, once those responsible for the income tax began to confront the complex issues of the definition of income, they discovered that no clear guidelines existed. Furthermore, when efforts were made to extend taxable income beyond periodic, realized money income, grave administrative difficulties were encountered. Finally, the use of self-assessment in the collection of the general income tax resulted in sweeping evasion and placed the Internal Revenue Service in an unpopular adversarial relationship with taxpayers. This combination of problems created an image of the income tax as arbitrary in its definition of income, inquisitorial in its collection, and capricious in deciding who paid.

In conclusion, the Civil War experience is instructive though not conclusive. The promise that the income tax would reach all sources of income and treat them uniformly was enticing in a democracy that embraces equal contributions by equals. It was discovered that even designing such a concept of income is elusive, at best. To make the ideal actually work proved impossible. The experience was foreboding, but this was a war period during which the entire internal revenue system was assembled from scratch. The real test of the income tax had to wait for peacetime.

The next experience with a federal income tax was a brief one in 1894. Unlike the Civil War income tax that was legislated out of a broad-based political compromise, the income tax of 1894 was the product of a partisan political movement fueled especially by small farmers. Congress passed an income tax statute in 1894, and it was declared unconstitutional shortly thereafter. Thus, there was scant opportunity for statutory development of the income concept. Nonetheless, this law is interesting in several respects. First, though the statute borrowed most of its content from its Civil War predecessor, it added a provision that was particularly beneficial to the farmers who sponsored it. It included in its base gifts and bequests of personal property but not of real property. Second, home produced and consumed food was explicitly excluded from the base. Third, the personal exemption was set at $4,000. These three features made the income tax a class tax upon a small group of financial and industrial capitalists. All but the most exceptional farmer was excluded from paying income taxes.

Because the income tax had become the instrument of a partisan political movement, many who had supported the Civil War income tax opposed the income tax of 1894 (Wells, 236). Though the Supreme Court declared the tax unconstitutional on technical grounds, the justices viewed the statute as a dangerous precedent and a direct threat to property (Ratner, 203). The experience reveals a potential danger of the income tax. In its theoretical conception, the income tax was to apply to clear income. When this idea is put into practice through a personal exemption, it means that for a country in its early or middle stages of development a majority of the population will be exempted from tax. In a democracy the possibility exists for a partisan majority to impose a tax upon an unwilling minority. Some of this element was present in 1894, but with the Supreme Court decision there was no opportunity to observe whether a self-correcting bipartisan consensus would have emerged in Congress to modify the tax.

With the income tax of 1894 declared unconstitutional, the income tax question was put aside for over a decade. After the turn of the century, interest in the income tax resumed. This interest and support culminated in the corporate income tax in 1909 and the Sixteenth Amendment in 1913, which permitted an individual income tax.

By 1913, a broad political consensus had developed in support of income taxation. Representative Cordell Hull assumed an important role in Congress in the drafting of an income tax statute. He had devoted years of study to the income tax experience of the United States and other countries. He was correctly perceived in both houses of the Congress as an income tax expert. In the drafting of an income tax statute, he balanced the desire to avoid tax loopholes with an equal desire to draft a statute that could be administered and that would be held constitutional. Several features characterize the statutory definition of income under the 1913 law.

First, the statute explicitly specified net income, allowing for the deduction not only of business expenses and losses, but also of capital costs. In addition, it permitted deductions for interest paid on indebtedness; national, state, and local taxes; uncompensated casualty losses; and bad debts. Furthermore, in 1917 deduction for charitable contributions was allowed. Second, realized capital gains were included as fully taxable. No maximum holding period for taxability was included as under early laws. Provision for the deduction of capital losses was made in 1916 and 1918. Third, the law provided that individuals could deduct from taxable income the amount of corporate dividends on which tax already had been paid by corporations. Thus, relief for double taxation of corporate income was provided at the individual level. Fourth, it was decided not to extend the definition of income to accrued income, income in kind, or gifts and inheritances. The administrative failures of the earlier attempts to include these items were keenly felt and there was a desire not to repeat past mistakes. Fifth, due to prior Supreme Court decisions, all income paid by state and local instrumentalities--salaries as well as interest--was excluded from taxation. Although one line of legal opinion maintained that these sources of income could be taxed, the framers of the law did not want to jeopardize the entire statute. It was hoped that the law would later be amended to include incomes received from state and local governments.

In summary, a serious effort was made in the 1913 statute to enact as comprehensive a definition of income as was consistent with administrative and constitutional constraints. The personal exemption was set at $4,000 for a married couple and at $3,000 for a single person. The level of personal exemptions restricted the income tax to about the top quintile of the population. The generous personal exemptions coincided with a widely held view of the time that a minimum of comfortable existence ought to be exempted from income taxation. Thus, this was a consensus level for personal exemptions, not a narrow partisan view.

In conclusion, this is a good point at which to take stock of our concept of taxable income as we approach the modern era of federal income taxation. Though interest groups had not yet succeeded in making a substantial impact upon the base, several significant gaps already existed in taxable income. These gaps were the harbinger of later developments that led to the current debacle of the income tax. First, under the immunity doctrine, interest on state and local bonds as well as salaries of state and local employees were exempt from federal taxation. The former continues to this day as a serious loophole. Second, owner-occupied housing was granted the full set of tax preferences that it continues to enjoy. Thus, a significant subsidy for residential construction existed from the beginning. It has caused much overallocation of resources to this area of the economy. Third, national taxes were deductible, along with all state and local taxes. Deductibility of taxes has been a costly subtraction from the tax base. Fourth, all interest expense was deductible. This feature has subsidized durable consumption goods and tax arbitrage. Fifth, although capital gains were taxable in full, no provision existed for taxing unrealized capital gains. Sixth, charitable contributions were deductible.

In retrospect, the modern problem of income tax loopholes has existed from the beginning. They were introduced into the tax statute by a group of dedicated and public-spirited members of Congress for reasons beyond their control. This group led by Cordell Hull did the best they could. Nonetheless, these loopholes created conditions for inequity, inefficiency, and complexity under the income tax. With the low marginal rates of tax and with a response not fully developed, problems of avoidance had not yet become severe. In addition, there was hope on the part of the original framers of the law that the base would be broadened and that the income tax would be improved over time. But the beginnings of erosion of the income tax base had taken form already. As we will observe, this erosion was extended in each succeeding decade. Even at this early date, taxpayers had an incentive to lower their marginal and average rate of tax by investing in housing, durable goods, tax-exempt bonds, or by leveraging for investment. In the process, a misallocation of resources resulted, horizontal and vertical inequity developed, and complexity was added. The great tax scholar of the time, E. R. A. Seligman, was aware of the limitations and vulnerability of the income tax. He cautioned that "the success of an income tax depends . . . upon administrative machinery" (Seligman, 673). He also was skeptical of how far one could go in practice in implementing the principles of income taxation. "Simply to adopt the principle of an income tax and to enact a law providing for its imposition is by no means adequate. . . . We must decide between ideal perfection of theory which cannot be made to work in real life, and a less ambitious, but more realizable, programme of practical efficiency" (Seligman, 673). He had the prescience to see that the income tax was considerably more attractive as an ideal than as a reality.

THE DEFINITION OF TAXABLE INCOME

The income tax was in the air in the late nineteenth and early twentieth centuries in the United States and Europe. It was a part of political platforms and of legislative action. It was also a subject of study by tax scholars. In this time frame, thousands of articles and books were written on the income tax.

Early in the century, Irving Fisher commented that while the layperson thinks of the meaning of income as obvious, it is in fact the most difficult of concepts to define (Fisher, 379). Henry Simons, writing in the 1930s, observed that while reams had been written on defining personal income, most of it was not worth reading (Simons, 42). Numerous theories and theory fragments were developed to define personal income (Wueller). It would be an unwarranted digression to summarize this voluminous literature. Nonetheless, two concepts are basic to our topic: the net accretion concept of income and the disposition concept of income.

The former is associated with the early work in the field. It is important as it provided the theoretical underpinning for the ideal of legislating a comprehensive income tax in the United States. According to the Schanz, Haig, and Simons (S-H-S) definition of income, all gain accruing to an individual between two points of time constitutes income, regardless of source. The gain represents income whether it is consumed or saved. It is the capacity of the individual to command goods that is being measured. It does not matter whether the gains are realized or unrealized, factor income or transfer payments, regular or irregular, monetized or in kind. Of course, a distinction came to be drawn between what constituted income in principle and what could realistically be taxed given the constraints of administration. Thus, two emphases developed, one a theoretical definition of income and the other a policy strategy. For example, annual unrealized capital gains constituted income in principle, but in practice it was agreed that they could not be estimated and taxed except upon the death of the individual.

Henry Simons was candid and explicit in his economic philosophy and his long-run economic goals. For example, he objected to the degree of inequality in the distribution of income in the United States. He held there was too much inequality and that the income tax ought to serve the end of a more equal distribution of income. Those who have accepted Simons' definition of taxable income have chosen to be less explicit about their own views on the distribution of income and have, instead, endorsed the more general objectives of horizontal equity and vertical equity. They are comfortable, however, with a progressive rate structure for the income tax.

The work of Simons has served as the rallying point for the true believers in the income tax. In the post-World War II period, they concentrated on the policy strategy for income tax reform and the passage of a comprehensive definition of income. Some of the most prominent of this group are Joseph Pechman, Richard Goode, and Richard Musgrave. Apart from lack of policy success, the most troublesome aspects of this theoretical guideline have been inflationary adjustments, taxing income in kind, averaging irregular income, drawing a conceptual line between a business expense and a personal expense, a strategy for taxing unrealized gains, and how to treat capital gains created by interest rate changes (Goode, 10-29). Those responsible for the passage of the 1913 income tax law hoped that the concept of taxable income would be extended with time. The S-H-S definition of income provided a basis upon which this statutory definition of income could be extended. We will examine the extent to which this in fact occurred. In doing so, we will find that the drift of policy has been away from rather than toward the comprehensive definition of personal income advocated by Simons.

Before turning back to the policy history, one other definition of income should be noted. Early in this century, there were many contentious issues in the definition of income. In retrospect, the most interesting rival of the S–H–S definition was the disposition concept of income. This rivalry continues to the present time, and has in fact intensified (Wueller, 570-72). The advocates of the disposition concept included such Italian economists as Einaudi, but the most prominent enthusiast was the American economist Irving Fisher. This group chose to emphasize the disposition of income rather than its accrual. Fisher defined real income as the utility we derive from consumption. Thus, current consumption became the proper measure of income. By taxing current consumption, we tax lifetime income. The income tax of 1913, however, enacted a statute in the spirit of the S–H–S definition of income. Nonetheless, the drift of tax policy and of tax thinking over the past decade has been away from Simons and toward Fisher. We will return to this theme later.

THE EROSION OF THE INDIVIDUAL INCOME TAX

In 1957 Joseph Pechman published a paper entitled "The Erosion of the Individual Income Tax." In it he quantified the extent to which tax preferences had reduced the individual income tax base and the consequences of this erosion. He estimated that if the bulk of these tax preferences were repealed and a comprehensive definition of income established, marginal rates of tax could be reduced by 25 percent while still raising the same amount of revenue. As we have seen, some of these tax preferences were present from the beginning, and many others were added later. We will now take account of how these tax preferences spread.

The drift to expand tax preferential treatment of income began in the 1920s. From 1913 to 1921, capital gains had been taxed as ordinary income. However, starting in 1921, a lower rate of tax was applied to long-term capital gains. This was a concession to the bunching of a capital gain and taxation at high marginal rates after a long gestation period. This created an incentive for taxpayers to find ways of receiving income in the form of capital gains rather than ordinary income. This along with progressivity created an important impetus to tax avoidance and tax complexity. In 1926 another important tax precedent was set: a tax subsidy was granted to the oil and gas industry in the form of percentage depletion. It was rationalized on the grounds that incentives were necessary to discover and develop new oil and gas deposits. This began an infamous chapter in income tax history that has had implications beyond one industry. It is a common pattern that once a special tax privilege is granted in our democratic form of government, this creates a precedent and motivation for others to seek that same privilege. As an example, in the 1930s percentage depletion was extended to sulfur, metals, and coal. Eventually, almost all extractive industries enjoyed percentage depletion.

In the 1930s another area of tax preference developed, that of public transfer payments and fringe benefits. The system of public transfers was virtually nonexistent in 1913, but some extensive beginnings were developed in a variety of directions during the 1930s. Social Security and Aid to Families with Dependent Children are examples of only two of the well-known programs. Private health and life insurance programs and annuity programs also developed, concomitant with social insurance and public welfare programs. Transfer payments and fringe-benefit programs paid by the employer were excluded from the income tax base. So also was interest in life insurance reserves. After World War II, this network of public and private programs became a rapid growth industry, and progressively siphoned off an increasing share of personal income not included in the tax base.

In addition, the marginal rewards for tax avoidance were substantially increased during the 1930s and 1940s. The top marginal rate was raised to 70 percent in the late 1930s and to 91 percent in 1944. A very lucrative economic game was created, that of rearranging one's activities so as to divert income to a zero tax rate, a capital gains tax rate, or to a lower rate by splitting into multiple taxing units.

After 1945 other avenues of tax avoidance were opened. Accelerated depreciation was introduced in 1954 and the investment tax credit in 1962. The subsidization of capital that was started in the 1920s was extended. As discussed, this subsidization was continually enriched in subsequent years, and the debacle was well on its way.

Still another facet of tax preference was created in the 1970s, the decade of new social regulations: energy conservation, protecting the environment, and aiding those facing hardship. The income tax was turned to as a vehicle for facilitating these changes.

Another factor began affecting thinking on the income tax in the early 1970s--inflation. According to the accretions theory, taxable income was supposed to be independent of price-level changes. As inflation became double digit, price-induced distortions became a matter of serious concern. Bracket creep was considered to be a problem. Even more anxiety was expressed over capital income being inflated and overtaxed. The clamor reached a peak early in 1980 as the Wall Street Journal began a three-part series with the first article entitled "Popular Support Fades for U.S. Income Taxes as Inflation Lifts Rates." The changes made by the 1981 Recovery Tax Act in part were motivated by a decade of deliberation over the effects of inflation upon income taxation.

The result of these seven decades of multiplying tax preferences and inflation-induced changes is a maze of statutes, regulations, special rulings, and court cases through which a huge industry of tax services roam, selling their services to taxpayers while reaping a good profit. We will return to this problem again after reviewing some of the theoretical turmoil over the proper definition of personal income.

NET ACCRETIONS DEFINITION OF INCOME ON THE DEFENSIVE

At some point in the 1960s the status of the net accretions concept shifted from an undistributed norm toward which we were striving to reform taxable income, to a defensive position as it came under theoretical attack. On the political front, no progress had been made in eliminating tax preferences, but this by itself did not pose a serious challenge to this policy ideal.

Actually, there were two significant critiques of the principles of income taxation in the 1950s: The Uneasy Case for Progressive Taxation (1953) by Blum and Kalven and The Expenditure Tax (1955) by Kaldor. The former dealt primarily with the principles underlying a progressive rate structure for an income tax. The latter presented an unequivocal case in support of an expenditure tax upon consumption. It did at one point, however, offer a theoretical criticism of the net accretions concept. Kaldor argued that changes in interest rates make the "problem of defining individual income . . . in principle insoluble" (70). Defenders of the net accretions concept acknowledged this to be a difficult issue. However, the critique of this concept did not build at this time.

The most devastating critique came from those who challenged the very foundation of the income tax--the net accretions concept of income. Three forays in particular deserve mention, those of Bittker, Feldstein, and Andrews. In 1967 Bittker criticized what he referred to as the arbitrary selection by the net accretions advocates of what to include as taxable income under their practical policy guidelines. He points out that the difference between ideal taxable income and practical taxable income is substantial, and that this discrepancy leaves the concept devoid of use in solving policy problems. "In short, they harbor, in my opinion, the same attitude toward the Haig-Simons definition of income that Congress is said to exhibit toward our progressive rate schedule: a declaration of faith, combined with advocacy or tolerance of numerous exceptions, each of which inures to the benefit of a 'special' group of taxpayers" (981-82).

An even more serious criticism was levied by Martin Feldstein in 1975, when he argued that, even in theory, the net accretions concept is deficient as an index of welfare. He pointed out that the net accretions theorists have excluded leisure and have not taken into account differences in tastes among individuals. The latter give rise to differences in utility due to differences in job satisfaction among individuals, or to differences in utility from the consumption of an equivalent bundle of economic goods (82-83, 86-89).

Andrews offered still another type of critique in 1972. He observed that Simons emphasized the disposition side of income, consumption plus accumulation, when defining personal income. He argued that it is more useful to make refinements on the disposition side than on the sources side. He favored excluding expenditures on charitable contributions and medical services. In addition, he questioned the merit of including saving. He indicated that the law has already moved in this direction and that a good strategy would be to refine a tendency already in process. Thus, his critique leads to an advocacy of an expenditure-type tax upon consumption.

Still another line of criticism has been by those who note the distorting effects of inflation upon personal income. Many of these critics advocate a spendings tax on consumption that circumvents this problem (Bradford, in Pechman, 1980, 57).

Those who defend the net accretions concept have answered this criticism. In response to Bittker, Musgrave argues that just because a rule is not 100 percent effective in solving all problems does not negate the importance of policy ideals in constructing an equitable income tax (1967, 449-51). In response to Feldstein's criticism, Musgrave indicates that net accretions theorists have neglected to include certain factors in their definition of personal income. He indicates that the accretions concept can be revised to include leisure, but that it is conceptually impossible to include differences in tastes (1976, 4-9). As to those who advocate consumption as the base, Goode has asserted that individuals ought to be taxed upon their full capacity, both actual and potential consumption (Goode, in Pechman, 1980, 36). They also argue that the income tax can be adjusted to correct for inflation.

Though those who favor an income tax continue to defend the net accretions concept, they have been placed upon the defensive. A comprehensive individual income tax as a compelling and realizable ideal—though still with defenders—is no longer an unquestioned goal of tax policy. Among policymakers, the ideal has become even more shaky.

FROM TAX PREFERENCES TO TAX EXPENDITURES

We have seen that the legislative intent of the 1913 income tax was that of a comprehensive definition of personal income, even though that ideal was not attained in practice. The expectation was that with time the base would be broadened. This had also been the expectation of tax scholars who supported an income tax. History, however, moved in the opposite direction. A point was reached when the ideal itself came under strong question.

"Tax loophole" or "tax preference" is a pejorative term. It implies a deviation from the norm that requires correction. To the extent that the income tax is a fiscal device for raising revenue, the concern is that the base meet criteria of equity and efficiency. Deviations have no place. However, as a growing stream of tax preferences was added to the income tax code, it became clear that the income tax—by design or by chance—was also an instrument of subsidization. As this became the rule rather than the exception and as the tax preferences took on permanence, the income tax could no longer be judged solely as a fiscal instrument. The subsidies themselves had to be appraised in a manner similar to budget expenditures.

The concept of tax expenditures was developed to appraise the tax subsidies. An early formulation of this idea was provided by Joseph McKenna in the March 1963 issue of the National Tax Journal: "An effective approach to eliminating tax loopholes must start by considering all deductions in the full context of government fiscal activities. An accounting procedure which treats them as expenditures would be an invaluable first step" (67). In 1967 Stanley S. Surrey, while assistant secretary of the treasury for tax policy, further developed the idea and carried it forward as a policy recommendation for a tax expenditure budget. He explained that we need this technique because "through deliberate departures from accepted concepts of net income and through various special exemptions, deductions and credits, our tax system does operate to affect the private economy in ways that are usually accomplished by expenditures—in effect to produce an expenditure system described in tax language. . . . It can be suggested therefore that we need a full accounting for these effects of the tax system. The approach would be to explore the possibility of describing in the Federal Budget the expenditure equivalents of tax benefit provisions" (3-4).

Congress acted upon this recommendation in 1974. The Congressional Budget Act of 1974 requires a listing of tax expenditues in each budget, and directs all congressional committees to identify any changes made in them by new legislation. The 1974 act defines tax expenditures as "revenue losses attributable to provisions of the federal tax laws which allow a special exclusion, exemption, or deduction from gross income or which provide a special credit, a preferential rate of tax, or a deferral of tax liability" (Pechman, 1983, 341).

These tax preferences that translate into tax expenditures include such familiar items as expensing of exploration costs, accelerated depreciation, the investment tax credit, and capital gains, and such lesser known features as the alcohol fuel credit, tax incentives for preservation of historic structures, the targeted jobs credit, and tax credit for orphan drug research.

Tax expenditures constitute about 46 percent of budget outlays, and in recent years they have grown faster than budget outlays (Pechman, 1983, 343). Once these tax preferences are identified as forms of public expenditure, certain stock budget questions follow. Is it desirable to provide this financial assistance at all? Is the program doing well? How do benefits compare with costs? Who is actually being assisted by the program, and is that assistance too much or too little? Furthermore, if it be conceded that these are appropriate subjects for public outlay, is tax expenditures the best form of subsidy or should the activity be subsidized by direct government expenditures? Subsidies through tax expenditures are dispensed only to taxpayers and with progressively more assistance as income increases.

In summary, if tax preferences are to be justified, they must stand the test of tax expenditures. The benefits must exceed the costs. The costs include not only the revenue foregone but also the well-known economic inefficiency caused by resulting higher marginal rates of tax and complexity to the tax code. We will now analyze two of the most costly tax expenditures: accelerated depreciation and the investment tax credit.

INVESTMENT TAX SUBSIDIES

Saving and investment enjoy numerous tax preferences under individual and corporate income taxes. These preferences include reduced rates of tax on capital gains, subsidization of residential investment, exemption of state and municipal bond interest, favored treatment of certain industries such as oil, exclusion of interest income on life insurance, and the postponement of tax on most income designated for retirement saving. However, the two most visible and costly tax expenditures on investment are accelerated depreciation (AD) and the investment tax credit (ITC). Total tax expenditures on AD, ITC, and safe harbor leasing (SHL) in 1982 were $29.4 billion. This constituted 8.7 percent of total tax expenditures and 4 percent of budget outlays. The ITC was the most costly at $19.3 billion. With this high level of expenditure, it is appropriate to ask whether they are necessary and if their benefits compare favorably with their costs.

Accelerated depreciation began in 1954. Previously, only straight-line depreciation was allowed. The principle had been economic depreciation. But extractive industries had long received subsidies for investment, and manufacturing industries lobbied for parallel benefits. In 1954 two new methods of depreciation were allowed: declining balance and sum of the digits. These methods permitted a faster write-off in the early years of the asset, and thus an interest-free loan from the government. In 1962 the investment incentive was enhanced. Under the advanced recovery system (ARS) introduced in this year, the number of years in which assets could be written off was considerably reduced. Also in this year, the investment tax credit was introduced. It was suspended in 1966-67 and 1969-71 due to inflationary pressures. In 1969 ARS was modified as it applied to real estate. However, in the Tax Reform Act of 1981, investment tax expenditures were substantially increased. The investment tax credit was enlarged, categories of assets were developed at considerably reduced service lives, and the SHL provision was added so that new firms and firms with substantial losses could sell their unused tax losses. The liberalized depreciation was called the accelerated cost recovery system (ACRS).

With the liberalization of investment tax incentives in the 1980s, we are subsidizing investment at a rate of over $30 billion through AD, ITC, and SHL alone. Some fundamental questions are in order. Is it necessary or desirable to alter the rate of capital formation set by the market? Do we understand how taxes affect investment? How well have the investment subsidies accomplished their objective? Have there been costs in addition to the lost revenue? Are these the best techniques for subsidizing investment?

The rate of economic growth slowed in the 1970s. Though there has been much study of this slowdown, no consensus exists on the primary cause. Less than half of the decline is explainable by a reduction in capital and labor inputs. Yet it is agreed that an increase in the rate of investment would speed economic growth. "If the net investment share were raised from 4 percent of GNP to 5 percent of GNP (a 25 percent increase), net output per worker would be raised in the long run by 5 to 6 percent and the growth rate would be accelerated by 0.1 to 0.2 percent annually in the decade following the change"

(Bosworth, 58). Thus, if there is an effective policy program to speed investment, there has long been a consensus supporting encouragement of capital formation.

But here is where consensus stops and where policy becomes problematic. Economists are not in agreement on investment theory either at the theoretical or the empirical level. One group emphasizes the rental price of capital as the determinant of investment; another group stresses the relationship between investment and changes in output.

Concerning the former, substitution of capital for labor occurs when the rental price of capital is reduced. Thus, under this formulation, tax investment incentives that reduce this rental price of capital are effective in increasing investment demand. However, for the second group, government can influence investment only by affecting output. As a consequence, the ITC and AD will affect investment only insofar as they affect aggregate demand and thereby output in the economy. More than a decade of empirical studies have not resolved the disagreements between these two groups.

Uncertainty over investment theory is hardly an acceptable basis from which to launch a massive investment subsidy program, but this is what was done with the help of armies of corporate lobbyists. It should be added, however, that there is a consensus among economists that with sufficient time--about five years--investment tax incentives tend to increase investment by an amount equal to the loss in tax revenue (Bosworth, 128). The complication is that investment is also keenly influenced by other variables, such as changes in output and interest rates. Thus, the positive effects of AD and ITC upon investment can easily be canceled by adverse movements of other variables. Some of these variables are potentially controllable through appropriate policy actions; others are not. This is a serious limitation of investment tax incentives. For instance, interest rates have been high during the 1980s and a recession set in early 1981. Investment tax incentives are not effective in this type of economic climate.

Another serious failure of our investment tax incentives has been the unintended differential impact they have had upon different types of investments and industries. For example, equipment is favored over industrial structures, and manufacturing industries receive considerably more benefits than service industries.

The specific problems and limitations of our investment tax incentives can be particularized by a review of the 1981 and 1982 tax acts and their effects. As stated, the 1981 Economic Recovery Act liberalized AD, increased the ITC, and provided for SHL. Personal income tax rates were cut, but the statutory rate of the corporate income tax was not changed. The effect of the ACRC and the ITC is roughly equivalent to expensing capital assets, and deductibility of interest makes this into a subsidy. Revenues from the corporate income tax started declining in the 1960s as a share of total federal revenues. With the 1981 act they declined absolutely as well as relatively. Corporate tax revenues as a percentage of total revenues were 23 percent in 1960, 17 percent in 1970, 12 percent in 1980, and 6 percent in 1983 (Aronson, 431).

Tax expenditures through AD and the ITC increased substantially during the 1980s. They increased from $23.5 billion in 1980, to $29.4 billion in 1981, to $32.8 billion in 1982, and to $40 billion in 1983 (Pechman, 345). Thus, these investment tax expenditures increased 70 percent from 1980 to 1983. Looking directly at particulars, Citizens for Tax Justice (CTJ) studied 250 profitable companies between 1981 and 1983 and found that 128 (51 percent) paid no federal income taxes or less in at least one of the three years, while earning profits of $57.1 billion (CTJ, 1984, 2).

What have we gotten in return for these tax subsidies? Let us look first at the CTJ study. CTJ found that 50 corporations with the lowest tax rates, −8.4 percent (a net public subsidy), reduced their investment over the period by −21.6 percent while raising their dividends by 14.1 percent. By contrast, 50 corporations with the highest tax rate, 33.1 percent, increased their investment by 4.3 percent while increasing their dividends by only 10.7 percent. The five corporations claiming the largest tax benefits between 1981 and 1983 were General Electric, Boeing, Dow Chemical, Tenneco, and Santa Fe Southern Pacific. Their tax rates ranged from −4.3 percent (General Electric) to −28.7 percent (Dow Chemical). All decreased their investment from −15.0 percent for General to −59.1 percent for Boeing. On the other hand, all increased their dividends, from 0.7 percent for Boeing to 19.2 percent for General Electric.

Overall, the 238 nonfinancial companies included in the study had an effective tax rate of only 14.3 percent, far below the 46 percent corporate tax rate on incomes over $100,000. In exchange for the reduced effective tax rates, these companies reduced new investment by 15.5 percent and increased dividends by 17 percent. Adjusted for inflation in plant and equipment prices, investment by this group fell by 17.6 percent. This is a worse performance than for the economy as a whole, where plant and equipment spending for these recession years (1981-83) fell by 8.8 percent in constant dollars (CTJ, 1985, 9).

Many of these companies explained their cutbacks in investment in terms of weakness in demand for their product. This is consistent with the economic theory summarized earlier. For reasons such as this, the tax breaks did not increase corporate investment, but they did increase after-tax profits. This added cash flow may be used to increase dividends, expand cash reserves, fund mergers or acquisitions, raise executive pay, or increase advertising budgets. The study confirmed that dividends indeed were increased between 1981 and 1983. Also, many companies noted in their annual reports that they had added greatly to their cash reserves and reported substantial use of funds to acquire other firms (CTJ, 1985, 14-15).

In summary, the findings of CTJ show no response of investment to AD and the ITC. The tax breaks financed dividends, liquidity, and mergers. Of course it must be remembered that 1981 to 1983 was a time of recession and slack in the economy. In addition, taxes were cut on both personal and corporate income without any corresponding reduction in budget outlays contributing to higher interest rates with corresponding negative effects upon investment. Nonetheless, this brings out the point that several variables are strategic to investment. If tax breaks are to work, the overall economic climate must be reinforcing. Otherwise the tax breaks will be negated by adverse factors as in this period. Investment tax expenditures will not work unless demand conditions and interest rates are also favorable.

For purposes of analysis, if we ignore the findings of the CTJ study and assume that tax incentives increase investment over time, how strong is the case? We believe the case fails on several counts. First, recent studies indicate that the marginal tax rate on corporate investment and the rental price of capital have been tending downward since the 1950s (Bosworth, 104). The main exception is the late 1960s and early 1970s, when inflation forced the effective rate of tax on corporate income upward. Thus, the corporate tax rate is not a serious deterrent to investment and the tax breaks of the 1980s were unnecessary. Second, if tax rates are lowered on corporate income, they will have to be raised elsewhere to compensate for the revenue loss. If, as a consequence, there is an increased tax on labor income, this will cause disincentives to work and to human capital formation. Thus, an incentive at one point must be balanced by the adverse effects of disincentives at another point. Third, and very important, tax breaks such as AD and the ITC have caused a divergence in tax treatment of different types of capital. There is no rationale for this divergence; it was not anticipated and thought through. This variability causes inefficiency in the capital mix and deserves additional examination.

The variability in tax treatment of capital assets stems from a number of sources. Tax breaks, such as AD and the ITC, are uneven in their impact upon firms. The ITC, for example, applies only to equipment and not to structures. On the other hand, AD can be applied to both. But the time set for recovery periods is arbitrary. Under ACRS there are four recovery periods, depending upon capital asset. The length of these periods is shorter than for economic depreciation, thus providing a subsidy. The amount of the subsidy varies with type of capital asset. In contrast with equipment and structures served by AD and the ITC, there is no special tax treatment for inventories and land. At the other extreme, owner-occupied housing pays neither a personal nor a corporate income tax, and interest costs are deductible. It pays only a property tax. Other features of our tax structure further enhance this variability, as for example the variance in our treatment of alternative methods of financing. The difference in treatment of equity and debt financing is one source, and another is the treatment of dividends as compared to retained earnings. Tax exemption is another source of variability, as in the case of state and municipal bonds or tax-exempt institutions, and adds to the tax debacle.

With this diverse pattern of tax treatment of capital assets and alternative methods of financing, it is not surprising that empirical studies have revealed a great divergence in effective rates of tax. Fullerton and Henderson found effective marginal rates of tax on corporate capital for 1982 varying from -4 percent on equipment to over 30 percent for other capital assets. For structures and land it was 38 percent and 40 percent, respectively. For non-corporate capital, they found the same divergence. In the noncorporate sector, the rate for equipment was -5.6 percent, while the rates for structures, public utilities, residential structures, inventories, land, and residential land were 29, 33, 33, 36, and 41 percent, respectively (Fullerton and Henderson, in Bosworth, 118-19). The 1982 Economic Report of the President presented data on this uneven impact of taxes by industry. Certain industries paid negative or very low taxes, such as motor vehicles, mining, paper and pulp, transportation services, petroleum refining, chemicals, and primary metals. Other industries—such as services, trade, and utilities—paid effective rates of tax over 30 percent. Still other industries such as agriculture, machinery, instruments, and communications paid at rates midway between the other two extremes. Industries that are equipment-intensive are favored by ACRS and the ITC. The effect of the tax breaks varies because each industry uses a different mix of capital. Industries with a high concentration of short-lived equipment will face low effective tax rates, while industries that are non-capital-intensive will face high effective rates (Council of Economic Advisers, 124).

In conclusion, AD and the ITC are the most costly of the tax expenditures. They are not refinements in the definition of taxable income, but subsidies. As subsidies, they ought to be judged by the rules of all budget outlays. They should meet a clearly defined need; they should be effective in meeting this need; the benefits generated ought to exceed the costs; and this means of subsidy should be superior to alternatives.

None of these conditions holds. Investment is only one of many factors that determine economic growth. It is not clear why it should be selected for subsidy above other factors such as education, research and development, or labor. In addition, there is no agreement on how taxes affect investment. The best guess is that they affect investment both through the rental price of capital, and on the demand side through output. If it is agreed that investment ought to be singled out for special inducement, there should be a policy that coordinates all variables that affect investment. Such has not been the case. While tax policy has encouraged investment, monetary and budget policy have discouraged it by keeping interest rates high.

As a consequence, the subsidies have shown up primarily in increased dividends, liquidity, and acquisitions. Finally, the subsidies have been dispensed very unevenly over alternative capital assets and various industries. Some industries and some types of capital have been encouraged while others have not. There is no justification for this. It is an unintended by-product and cost in the form of inefficiency in resource allocation. This tax variability is an indirect cost beyond the revenues lost. Another indirect cost is the complexity added to the code by AD and the ITC, along with the boost these provisions have given to the growing tax-shelter industry with its huge staffs of accountants, lawyers, and lobbyists.

Two other subjects need attention. First, in order for there to be investment, there must also be saving. Thus, policy interest has focused not only on increasing investment but in increasing saving. Some saving incentives were added by the 1982 Economic Recovery Tax Act. However, a common view is that the net effect of our saving incentives is the change the composition of household assets, not the saving rate. In addition, the availability of interest deductibility encourages tax arbitrage, which negatively affects saving. Furthermore, the large deficits constitute negative saving. Thus, though actions have been taken to encourage saving as a complement to investment incentives, we do not have a coherent and effective policy of saving inducement. This is another instance where though the existence of tax expenditures implies and necessitates an economic plan, there is no plan and program that will stand the test of analytical scrutiny.

Second, from the work of public choice theorists and political analysts, we know more about the workings of the democratic political process and the tax legislative process. We know there is a tendency for special benefit legislation to expand over general benefit legislation. Such has been the case with investment tax incentives. Manufacturing corporations were successful in their lobbying efforts to obtain a substantial lowering of their taxes in 1981. They took advantage of a mood of concern over .growth and investment, along with the economic philosophy of the administration that emphasized supply-side economics and lower taxes. A well-thought-out, coordinated, and coherent saving-investment policy was not forthcoming. Instead, the income tax code was further emasculated. Additional departures from a defensible concept of taxable income occurred without any compensating benefits. Thus, two of the most costly of tax expenditures do not stand up under close examination. It is doubtful if very many of them could.

INVESTMENT TAX INCENTIVES
IN OTHER COUNTRIES

Having studied the definition of taxable income and investment tax incentives in the United States, it is appropriate to extend our view to other countries. Have the experiences of other countries been similar, or is the United States unique in the problems it has encountered? We will review tax structures in the United Kingdom, Sweden, West Germany, and Japan. Then we will consider studies that have been made of the use of investment tax incentives in these countries.

In the United Kingdom, taxes on personal income constituted about 31 percent of revenue for 1979. This percentage has trended upward since 1960. The corporate income tax yielded 7.6 percent for 1979, and has edged down since 1960. A value-added tax was passed in 1963, and it yields about 10 percent of total receipts.

The United Kingdom goes further than any other developed country in relieving capital income from income taxation, and in providing protection from inflation-imposed burdens. Expensing of machinery for industrial corporations is allowed, along with greatly accelerated depreciation on structures. Nominal interest is deductible. LIFO accounting is permitted and investment grants are available. Imputed income on owner-occupied housing is not taxed, but interest payments on the first £25,000 of a home loan are deductible. Capital gains in excess of £3,000 are taxed at a 30 percent rate, and the base is indexed for inflation. A grossed-up dividend-received credit is provided to remove double taxation of dividends. Fewer personal deductions are permitted than in the United States.

In Sweden, taxes on personal income made up about 42 percent of total revenue in 1979, and have declined from 1960 when the share was even higher. Revenues from the corporate income tax constitute 3 percent of total revenues and have declined. A value-added tax was passed in 1959. It provided 13 percent of total receipts in 1979.

Corporations are allowed generous accelerated depreciation schedules. There is also a longstanding investment fund system that has been used to promote investment almost continuously over the past decade. Only FIFO accounting is permitted, so inventories are not protected from inflation. Long-term capital gains are taxed, but the inclusion rate varies with type of property. It varies from zero on personal property, to 40 percent on stocks, and 100 percent on real estate. Capital assets are not indexed. Income is imputed to owner-occupied homes and taxed, with capital gains on these homes fully taxable. Interest expense is deductible with no upper limit. Tax concessions are made to specific forms of household saving. There is a partial mitigation of double taxation of dividends.

In West Germany, personal income taxes as a share of government receipts were about 29 percent in 1979, higher as a percentage than in 1960. The corporate income tax provided 6 percent of total income, and has trended down since 1960. West Germany passed a value-added tax in 1968. It provided 16 percent of total receipts in 1979.

Depreciation allowances were liberalized in 1977 and 1981. Also, investment grants are given to certain designated types of investment. West Germany uses its own compromise between FIFO and LIFO accounting. Inflation has not been as much of a problem in its economy. Withholding is applied to capital income as well as to wage income. Double taxation of dividends is completely alleviated at the individual level. Capital gains are not taxed if the holding period exceeds six months for securities and two years for real property. Interest payments on mortgages or consumer loans are not deductible. Imputed income from single family owner-occupied homes is not taxed, but if there are two or more families, it is. Household saving subsidies were repealed in 1980. Many deductions are granted for work-related expenses.

In Japan, tax receipts from personal income taxes constituted 38 percent of government revenue in 1980. For the corporate income tax, this percentage is 25.5. Japan at this time does not have a value-added tax, though it is up for consideration.

Accelerated depreciation and the investment tax credit are permitted for assets and industries that the government desires to promote. Capital gains are taxed as ordinary income, but security sales are tax exempt.

Tax concessions are made to certain forms of household saving. Mortgage interest and interest on consumer loans are not deductible. Japan has many of the same personal deductions as the United States, such as for the handicapped, the elderly, for extraordinary medical expenses, and for charitable contributions.

In summary, several points emerge as we compare income taxation in the above countries. First, as in the United States, the income tax laws in these countries have undergone much change over the past four decades. After World War II, the concern had at first been with general income taxation, equity, and redistribution. But in the 1970s the concern shifted to economic growth and a favorable tax climate for saving and investment. Tax concessions were made to capital income. Second, tax incentives have not been shared evenly among different types of saving and investment. For example, residential construction and machinery are favored over structures. Also, debt financing is favored over equity financing. This uneven impact has been more an unintended effect than a conscious design of the government. In Japan, however, planning has been more deliberate. Third, certain countries, such as the United Kingdom and Sweden, have gone further in extending their tax preferences to capital income than have West Germany or Japan.

There have been several comparative studies of the income tax in developed countries. Vito Tanzi published one in 1969. His conclusion is that the adverse effect of the income tax upon economic growth is more a function of particular aspects of income tax laws than of the level of reliance upon this tax. He observes that the income tax is quite suitable to the taxation of wage and salary income among countries, but that the tax is not well suited to the taxation of nonwage income. He cites empirical evidence from a number of developed economies that substantiate this point. The proportion of wage and salary income taxed is considerably higher than is nonwage income. The latter rate is particularly low for France and Italy. Countries compensate for this differential by a higher statutory rate of tax upon nonwage income. Tanzi maintains that it is this higher rate along with variance of treatment of different industries and assets that is the most damaging to economic growth.

A 1984 study conducted by a team of researchers from four countries examined the marginal effective tax

rate upon corporate investment in the United States, the
United Kingdom, Sweden, and West Germany (King and
Fullerton). All taxes that affected capital income were
included. The following average effective tax rates upon
capital income were found: United Kingdom 3.7 percent,
Sweden 35.6 percent, Germany 48.1 percent, and United
States 37.2 percent.

The study provided much information on comparative
levels of taxation on capital income and how effective
rates were affected by inflation. However, more striking
was the information provided on the variability of effective
rates among project types. This variability was present
in all countries and occurred among different assets, industries, sources of finance, and types of owners.

For assets, typically machinery was taxed the lowest and inventories were taxed the highest, with buildings
a close second. The range in effective rates between machinery and inventories was United Kingdom –37 to 40 percent, Sweden 0.2 to 69 percent, West Germany 45 to 59 percent, West Germany 45 to 59 percent, and United States 18
to 47 percent. The variation was also considerable among
industries. The pattern of this variation differed among
countries. For example, the manufacturing industry is
taxed at the lowest rates in the United Kingdom and Sweden,
whereas in West Germany the lowest taxed industry is commerce, and in the United States the "other industry" category (transportation, construction, communication, and utilities) is lowest. As to variation by source of finance, it is
extreme, with debt being favored in all of the countries.
When variation is studied by different combinations and
configurations of assets, industries, finance, and owner,
the variation becomes even greater.

In summary, the coefficient of variation in effective
rates ranges from 2314.9 in the United Kingdom, 232.7 in
Sweden, 140.9 in the United States, and 111.2 in West Germany. The authors offer the following comment in interpretation of this variation. They state that

> the taxation of the return to investment is
> governed in all four countries by extremely
> complex rules. The primary basis for taxa-
> tion is "income" in name only. Taxes inter-
> vene between the social yield on an invest-
> ment and the return obtained by the saver,
> and these taxes are influenced by a variety

of provisions that diverge widely from those required to tax real income. Some divergences are explicitly designed to encourage investment. Others reflect particular political interests. Still others arise from the sheer practical difficulty of identifying and measuring income, especially in time of inflation (King and Fullerton, 303).

Our look at the income tax experience of other developed countries reveals that their problems are similar to those in the United States. In particular, their efforts to use the income tax to encourage saving and investment have not been successful. The extreme variability of marginal tax rates among types of investment has not been planned. It comes out of difficulties in making the income tax work in practice. The effects of this variation are costly. As is well known, such variation causes inefficiency in resource allocation. The country in our survey that had the lowest growth rate, the United Kingdom, had the greatest variability in effective rate of tax on investment. The country that had the highest growth rate, West Germany, had the least variability in effective tax rate. It is not likely that these relationships are coincidental.

CONCLUSION

This examination of the concept of taxable income under the income tax has been in theory and practice. The use of departures from taxable income as incentive devices for attaining national objectives has also been considered. In conclusion, our study has revealed several lessons.

First, those responsible for the Civil War Income Tax and the Income Tax of 1913 were strongly committed to a broad-based, comprehensive, personal income tax. They did not, however, succeed in realizing their ambitions due to administrative, political, and constitutional limitations. Thus, some of our primary loopholes have been present from the beginning. They are a generic defect of the income tax in practice.

Second, until recently there has been optimism that the income tax could be improved with time. The accretions concept of income provided a theoretical base and a policy strategy. But the march of events after seven decades has not brought about a comprehensive base; instead, the income base has steadily eroded. Despite the improved research and writings of accretions theorists and journalists, and despite different political strategies to eliminate loopholes, the trend of erosion has not reversed. As inflation added to the problem, both public and professional support for the income tax declined.

Third, the theoretical consensus built around the accretions concept has dissolved. Opinion is now split. Some still advocate a comprhesive income tax; others favor a personal consumption tax; still others favor a value-added tax. At best, advocates of the income tax have been placed on the defensive.

Fourth, the effort to treat loopholes as tax expenditures and subject them to tough-minded budget scrutiny has failed. Though Congress has acted to place tax expenditures in the budget, they serve as an embellishment and are not a part of the process and scrutiny reserved for usual budget outlays. Tax expenditures as budget outlays are not taken seriously, and tend to be looked upon as harmless and costless incentives. As a case in point, we discovered that the massive tax incentives given to corporate investment have not brought the results promised, and have indeed contributed to serious economic inefficiencies and complexity. In other words, they have been a failure.

Fifth, our experience with the ineffectiveness and perversity of the income tax as an incentive device for controlling and managing the economy is not unique. It is an experience shared with other developed economies. They are in the process of reducing and eliminating these tax incentives. Also, they have supplemented the income tax with a value-added tax.

In closing, we must be honest and admit that the income tax has become a debacle. It has served useful purposes in the past and has been girded by hope, idealism, and public support. But its evolution has been cruel to it. It has steadily departed from its norms; its supporters have not been able to alter the erosion of its base; and the social purposes for which it was most needed, such as income and wealth redistribution, are now of lesser importance and are met in other ways. It is time to think of other revenue sources to supplement or replace it.

REFERENCES

Andrews, William D. 1972. Personal Deductions in an Ideal Income Tax. Harvard Law Review 86:309–85.

Aronson, J. Richard. 1985. Public Finance. New York: McGraw-Hill.

Bittker, Boris I. 1967. A "Comprehensive Tax Base" as a Goal of Income Tax Reform. Harvard Law Review 80: 925–79.

Blakey, Roy G., and Gladys C. Blakey. 1940. The Federal Income Tax. London: Longmans, Green.

Blum, Walter J., and Harry Kalven, Jr. 1953. The Uneasy Case for Progressive Taxation. Chicago: University of Chicago Press.

Bosworth, Barry P. 1984. Tax Incentives and Economic Growth. Washington, D.C.: Brookings.

Citizens for Tax Justice. 1984. Corporate Income Taxes in the Reagan Years. Washington, D.C.

_____. 1985. The Failure of Corporate Tax Incentives. Washington, D.C.

Council of Economic Advisers. 1982. Economic Report of the President. Washington, D.C.: Government Printing Office.

Feldstein, Martin. 1976. On the Theory of Tax Reform. Journal of Public Economics 6:77–104.

Fisher, Irving. 1937. A Practical Schedule for an Income Tax. Tax Magazine 15:379–490,438.

Foster, Roger, and Everett V. Abbot. 1895. A Treatise on the Federal Income Tax. Boston: Boston Book Company.

Goode, Richard. 1977. The Economic Definition of Income. In Comprehensive Income Taxation, ed. Joseph Pechman. Washington, D.C.: Brookings.

_____. 1980. The Superiority of the Income Tax. In What Should Be Taxed: Income or Expenditure, ed. Joseph Pechman. Washington, D.C.: Brookings.

Haig, Robert Murray. 1921. The Concept of Income—Economic and Legal Aspects. In Readings in the Economics of Taxation, ed. Richard Musgrave and Carl S. Shoup. Homewood, Ill.: Irwin.

Howett, William Wallace. 1925. The Concept of Income in Federal Taxation. Journal of Political Economy 33:155-76.

_____. 1925. The Definition of Income and Its Application in Federal Taxation. Philadelphia: Westbrook Publishing.

Kaldor, Nicholas. 1955. An Expenditure Tax. London: George Allen.

King, Mervyn A., and Don Fullerton. 1984. The Taxation of Income from Capital. Chicago: University of Chicago Press.

Lindholm, Richard W. 1984. A New Federal Tax System. New York: Praeger.

McKenna, Joseph P. 1963. Tax Loopholes: A Procedural Proposal. National Tax Journal 16:63-67.

Musgrave, Richard A. 1967. In Defense of an Income Concept. Harvard Law Review 81:44-62.

_____. 1976. ET, OR and SBT. Journal of Public Economics 6:3-16.

Pechman, Joseph A. 1957. Erosion of the Individual Income Tax. National Tax Journal 10:1-23.

_____. 1983. Federal Tax Policy. Washington, D.C.: Brookings.

Rater, Sidney. 1967. Taxation and Democracy in America. New York: Wiley.

Seligman, Edwin R. A. 1914. The Income Tax. New York: Augustus M. Kelley.

Simons, Henry C. 1938. Personal Income Taxation. Chicago: University of Chicago Press.

Surrey, Stanley S. 1973. Pathways to Tax Reform. Cambridge, Mass.: Harvard University Press.

Tanzi, Vito. 1969. The Individual Income Tax and Economic Growth. Baltimore: Johns Hopkins Press.

Wall Street Journal. 1980a. April 22.

_____. 1980b. May 2.

_____. 1980c. May 14.

Wells, David. 1880. The Communism of a Discriminating Income Tax. North American Review 130:236-46.

Wueller, Paul A. 1938. Concepts of Taxable Income. Political Science Quarterly 53:83-110, 557-83.

_____. 1939. Concepts of Taxable Income. Political Science Quarterly 54:555-75.

2

Federal Individual Income Tax Collection Costs: The Burden of Compliance and Administration

John L. Mikesell

Economy of collection has been revived as a significant criterion for tax policy. Adam Smith included it as one of the four maxims proposed in Wealth of Nations, but it drifted out of importance over the years. Smith's maxim of economy of collection states, "Every tax ought to be contrived as both to take out and to keep out of the pockets of the people as little as possible, over and above what it brings into public treasury of the state."[1] Any difference between private economic welfare before the tax and private economic welfare after the tax not accounted for by treasury receipts (or harm done by a public spending program) is a waste of resources that should be minimized. Unfortunately, modern tax systems do not function without substantial resource costs. One of these costs, the distortions economists term "excess burden," is outside the scope of this chapter. The other two, administrative cost and compliance cost, are the present focus.

Total collection cost for any tax equals cost incurred by the government (administrative cost) plus cost incurred by the public (compliance cost) in satisfying legal requirements of that tax, beyond the tax liability. Both administrative and compliance costs are real burdens on society and ought, within the constraint of satisfactory equity in administration, to be kept at the lowest level

---

*Jacqueline Thiell assisted with data collection for this chapter.

needed to produce intended revenue. Administrative cost sometimes may be reduced simply by shifting more of the collection activities to private individuals or firms; when this occurs, the government's cost may substantially under-state the total cost of collection. Agency costs clearly are important to the governmental unit, but to gauge the effect of taxes upon society--and the total sacrifice im-posed upon the populace--total collection cost (compliance plus administration) is the important basis for comparison.

The share of collection cost made up by each of its components depends on the nature of the administration of the tax. Carl Shoup identifies six types of tax adminis-tration:

1. The taxpayer is wholly passive.
2. The taxpayer has right of appeal, but is wholly passive at initial assessment.
3. The taxpayer is passive, but third parties must supply certain information to tax authorities as an aid to them in assessing the tax.
4. The taxpayer must file a return to provide tax authorities information for computing tax due.
5. The taxpayer's agent computes tax liability and files a return with payment to the tax authority.
6. The taxpayer assesses the tax.[2]

The income tax in the United States--federal, state, and local--is one of the few in the world using the sixth sys-tem for individuals. Some elements of that structure do, of course, involve effort by third parties--particularly the employer withholding system and the 1099 information re-ports for interest and dividends--but they do not alter the basic point that collection cost will be heavily from com-pliance, not administration, for the individual income tax. Low administrative cost by itself is of no special advan-tage for society, even as it makes life easier for tax offi-cials; the important question is the level of combined ad-ministrative and compliance cost.

The combined costs are particularly critical for self-declared taxes like the U.S. individual income tax: the individual or firm maintains records of potentially taxable transactions and other events that influence the tax base, computes the tax base and the appropriate tax liability, and makes payments at appropriate times. The crucial government activity, besides distribution of necessary forms and instructions to payers, is the audit of selected taxpayers to insure substantial compliance with the law. In a properly functioning system, direct audit revenue will be only a small percentage of tax revenue, because audits are performed to stimulate compliance, not to produce revenue. Under this structure, much of the cost of collection rests with the taxpayer. Is it any wonder that the Internal Revenue Service can report collections of $680 billion at an operating cost of less than 50 cents per $100 collected?[3]

The predominant resource cost of collection appears in the expense records of the private sector--the taxpayer, the taxpayer's employer, and those paying the taxpayer interest, dividends, and royalties--so low administrative cost will not portray actual collection cost. A tax structure should attain the lowest collection cost consistent with equity in the generation of intended tax revenue, defined to mean an absence of systematic patterns of tax errors left uncorrected by enforcement. Cheap administration by itself is not a satisfactory target. It is well to keep in mind the Harold Groves reminder, "That a tax which is ideal in other respects can produce weird and perverse results if badly administered is a precept often enough propounded but nevertheless frequently ignored."[4] Federal tax reform cannot ignore this precept. For a self-declared tax, low administration cost can be associated with bad administration as easily as it can be associated with efficiency. Accepted standards of administration equity cannot be disregarded.

ADMINISTRATIVE COST

With that background about the nature of collection, a more detailed examination of collection costs is possible. Administrative costs, the direct costs to the government, cannot be judged as anything but low for the federal income tax. Table 2.1 recounts the cost data presented by the Internal Revenue Service. Those data unfortunately include all taxes the service administers, not just the individual income tax. Thus, operating cost does not separate cost from that tax from cost for the corporation income tax, the employment taxes, the selective excise taxes, and so forth. Because the individual income tax is such a critical element in the system, however, and most functions

Table 2.1

Internal Revenue Service Administrative Cost, 1965-84

Year	Operating Cost	Number of Return	Collections	Population (thousand)	Collected (per $100)	Per Capita	Per Return	Per Capita* (deflated)	Per Return* (deflated)
1965	597,387,471	102,492,000	114,434,633,721	194,303	0.52	3.07	5.83	--	--
1970	886,159,162	113,078,185	195,722,096,497	204,878	0.45	4.33	7.84	--	--
1972	1,127,390,411	112,000,449	209,855,736,878	208,846	0.54	5.40	10.07	5.40	10.07
1974	1,312,894,661	121,609,260	268,952,253,663	211,901	0.49	6.20	10.80	5.43	9.46
1976	1,667,331,689	127,348,211	302,519,791,922	215,142	0.56	7.75	13.09	5.71	9.65
1978	1,962,129,287	136,718,328	399,776,389,362	219,033	0.49	8.96	14.35	5.77	9.24
1980	2,280,838,622	143,445,842	519,375,273,361	223,383	0.44	10.21	15.90	5.65	8.79
1982	2,626,338,036	170,369,266	632,240,505,595	232,634	0.42	11.29	15.42	5.38	7.35
1984	3,279,067,495	172,512,069	680,475,229,453	237,051	0.48	13.83	19.01	6.15	8.46

*1972 = 100.

Sources: Annual Reports of Commissioner of Internal Revenue Service, National Income and Products Accounts, and Survey of Current Business.

are directed toward its operation, it is not inappropriate to look at the total operations of the service as an indication of cost of that tax.

Administrative cost in relation to revenue collected is only 48 cents per $100 of revenue in 1984. The cost is slightly above that of the earlier 1980s, but below that of earlier periods. More important, however, is the fact that the cost is incredibly low. As a comparison, Due and Mikesell find an average administrative cost in 1979–81 of 73 cents per $100 of general sales tax revenue.[5] Furthermore, that cost is low in comparison with administration costs as a percentage of collections in other countries. Some reported costs in recent years include: 1.71 percent in the United Kingdom (1973), 1.87 percent in Japan (1973), 1.10 in the Philippines (1976–77), and 0.96 in Australia (1976–77).[6] None of these other countries has quite the same system that the United States has, particularly the degree of self-declaration, so little can be made of the comparison except to note that the figure for the IRS is indeed low.

One may quarrel, however, that any cost comparison with revenue is not germane, because the functions that require administrative expenditure are little related to dollar collections. Instead, they are related to numbers of returns, population covered, and so on. Table 2.1 presents per capita and per return operating cost data for the years examined. While both measures have increased dramatically, roughly doubling over the past dozen years, much of that change has been the result of higher prices, not greater input usage. When the cost measures are deflated by the implicit price deflator for federal nondefense purchases, per capita cost shows only moderate change, discounting a sizable increase in 1984 (from $5.38 in 1982 to $6.15 in 1984).[7] Real cost per return is probably more meaningful for analysis. That cost in 1972 prices has trended downward in the recent past, from $10.07 in 1972 to $8.46 in 1984, a 15 percent reduction over those years.

Regardless of the way in which one considers administrative cost, it must be concluded that cost of administration is low. But it would be remarkable if that cost were not low because the heart of the system--prepayment of tax owed on wage and salary income through the employer withholding system--insures both that income earned gets reported and that the individual files a return. For tax year 1982 (returns filed in calendar 1983), withheld tax exceeded income tax due for the aggregate of both 1040A and 1040EZ returns; even for those filing itemized returns, withholding was 90 percent of tax due. Similar numbers apply for return filing: 71 percent of itemized filers, 88 percent of 1040A filers, and 94 percent of 1040EZ filers had overpayments refunded.[8] That reduces agency cost and simplifies administration, as overwithholding creates a powerful incentive for return filing.

The withholding structures also apparently induce a high degree of compliance with the tax law. IRS estimates from the Taxpayer Compliance Measurement Program indicate a reporting compliance rate of 97 to 98 percent for wages and salaries, as shown in Table 2.2. (The IRS estimates that around 75 percent of the individual income tax liability gap for legal sector activity comes from unreported income, rather than deduction or business expense overstatement or other evasion.[9]) Compliance rates are high for interest and dividend income, both covered to a large degree by information reporting, but not as high as for wages and salaries. The rates are far lower for other forms of income. That is quite consistent with the principle that third-party reporting and tax prepayment are valuable devices for revenue collection at low administrative cost.[10] Indeed, they are likely the elements that make the broad individual income tax economically feasible.

To make voluntary compliance a reasonable taxpayer response, administration must insure an adequate probability that the tax evader will be found and subjected to sufficient penalty that evasion would not ordinarily be profitable. Otherwise the honest taxpayer will be at a competitive disadvantage, compared to the dishonest. Table 2.3 presents the pattern of return examination coverage for filing years from 1973 through 1983 by classes of examination. In general, audits by revenue agent are done at the taxpayer's place of business, tax auditor examinations are done in an IRS office with taxpayer records, and service center examinations are by correspondence. The profile is one of declining coverage: in 1984 the IRS could cover by one form of examination or another only 1.27 percent of individual returns and 2.66 percent coverage of corporate returns, compared with 2.13 percent and 6.76 percent in 1974. Unless the IRS has made remarkable improvements in coverage targeting, it is not a desirable profile to encourage voluntary compliance. At least in the short run, one could argue that overall revenue system performance would be improved with somewhat higher administrative

Table 2.2

Estimated Amount of Unreported Income from 1976 as Percent of
Reportable Amount, by Type of Income (in billions)

	Amount of Income[a]		
	Reportable on	Reported on Tax Returns	
	Tax Returns	Total[b]	As % of Amount
Type of Income	(in $)	(in $)	Reportable
Legal-source incomes			
Self-employment	93–99	60	60–64
Wages and salaries	902–908	881	97–98
Interest	54–58	49	84–90
Dividends[c]	27–30	25	84–92
Rents and royalties	9–12	6	50–65
Pensions, annuities,			
estates, and trusts	31–33	27	84–88
Capital gains	22–24	19	78–83
Other	9–10	7	70–75
Total	1148–1172	1073	92–94

[a]Sum of components may not add to totals due to rounding.
Percents of amounts reportable were computed from unrounded
figures.

[b]A small amount of illegal-source incomes are included
in the figures below. These inclusions will not significantly
affect the percentages shown in the right-hand column.

[c]Dividends include an estimated portion of distributed
net profits of qualified small business corporations.

Source: Internal Revenue Service, Department of Treasury. Estimates of Income Unreported on Individual Income Tax
Returns. Publication 1104 (9-79).

costs than at present. One should note, however, that taxpayers do have perceptions of audit coverage that favor the
IRS: A Yankelovich, Skelly, and White survey in 1984 found
that taxpayers believed on average that the IRS audited
12.3 percent of returns, a percentage ten times higher than
the actual.[11] So long as that misperception can be maintained, low actual coverage may not be devastating—but
experience does eventually change perception.

Table 2.3

Return Examination Coverage Rates, 1974–84

| | Returns Filed | Revenue Agent | Returns Examined (percent) | | |
			Tax Auditor	Service Center	Total
1984 Individual	95,541,300	276,182	859,351	80,394	1,215,927
(CY 83 filed)		(0.29)	(0.90)	(0.08)	(1.27)
Corporation	2,475,330	65,803	--	--	65,803
		(2.66)			(2.66)
1982 Individual	94,013,000	285,526	1,066,557	103,173	1,455,256
(CY 81 filed)		(0.30)	(1.13)	(0.11)	(1.55)
Corporation	2,279,000	107,705	--	--	107,705
		(4.73)			(4.73)
1980 Individual	90,727,115	292,465	1,346,320	195,073	1,833,858
(CY 79 filed)		(0.32)	(1.48)	(0.22)	(2.02)
Corporation	2,061,672	133,593	--	--	133,593
					(6.48)
1978 Individual	85,623,810	306,433	1,369,419	169,390	1,845,242
(CY 77 filed)		(0.36)	(1.60)	(0.20)	(2.16)
Corporation	1,839,364	147,273	67	--	147,340
		(8.01)	(0.00)		(8.01)
1976 Individual	83,913,057	326,951	1,560,449	--	1,887,400
(CY 75 filed)		(0.39)	(1.86)		(2.25)
Corporation	1,765,539	166,709	1,044	--	167,753
		(9.44)	(0.06)	--	(9.56)
1974 Individual	83,029,000	311,000	1,455,000	--	1,767,000
(CY 73 filed)		(0.37)	(1.75)	--	(2.13)
Corporation	1,981,000	134,000			134,000
		(6.76)			(6.76)

Source: Annual Reports of the Commissioner of the Internal Revenue Service, various years.

COMPLIANCE COST

The compliance cost of the individual income tax does not appear in the federal budget as a cost of raising revenue. Rather, it is the cost that individuals, their employers, their financial institutions, and the like bear in fulfilling their legal recordkeeping and reporting obligations. Those costs are dispersed throughout the economy and, even when they involve payments to a tax preparer, are not tallied in the way that spending by the Internal Revenue System is. Accordingly, reports of compliance cost are somewhat fragmentary. In dealing with the issue, three separate questions must be confronted: how taxpayers perceive the compliance process, how taxpayers respond to that perception, and what compliance cost thereby results. Each will be noted in turn.

In analyzing this portion of collection cost, it is well to recall the Willis Committee admonition pronounced more than 20 years ago: "It would seem that any ratio [of compliance cost to tax liability] is too high if it indicates unnecessary cost. While it is true that no cost could be considered unnecessary if a less expensive way of collecting the tax did not exist, the high cost itself would seem to present a challenge to the fundamental soundness of the system which requires it."[12] Not only are compliance costs real, they merit attention directed toward their reduction.

Despite IRS attempts to explain the federal tax system in clearer fashion and development of a simple form available for those with uncomplicated tax affairs (the 1040EZ used by 16 percent of calendar 1983 filers), taxpayers perceive the system to be complicated, according to recent public opinion polls. A 1984 poll commissioned by the IRS asked, with regard to filling out the tax form, "How complicated do you think our federal income tax laws and rules are for your particular income situation?" Responses were from 6 (not at all complicated) to 1 (extremely complicated and very difficult to understand). Thirty-six percent of respondents replied with 1 or 2 (21 percent with 1), compared to 26 percent replying with 5 or 6. On that basis, one would conclude that a substantial number of taxpayers have difficulty with the form they fill out.[13] A more recent Newsweek survey (1985) asked those interviewed, "How easy is it for the average citizen to understand the tax system?" Seventy-one percent replied that

the system was "Not too easy" (42 percent) or "Not at all
easy" (29 percent).[14] That response provides strong evidence of a perception that the system is not simple to understand, a stronger reaction than perceived complexity
with one's own tax form, as noted in the prior survey.

How do U.S. taxpayers respond to system complexity?
Table 2.4 shows that in the most recent year for which
data are available (1982), 40 percent of all returns had
been prepared by a paid preparer. Of the 1040 returns,
the percentage ranged from 53 to 63 percent in adjusted
gross income (AGI) classes, with 56.8 percent overall. Of
the 1040A returns, the percentage by AGI class ranged
from 13 to 25 percent, or 22.1 percent overall. For the
latter returns, there is some tendency for the percent of
returns with paid preparers to decline with AGI; there is
no such pattern apparent for the 1040 returns. Surprisingly
enough, 3.3 percent of 1040EZ returns showed a paid preparer. Many more taxpayers undoubtedly received assistance that was unpaid, ranging from informal hints to com-
pletion of the return by a family member or friend.[15]

Table 2.4

Use of Paid Tax Preparers Classified by Return Type and Size
of Adjusted Gross Income, 1982 Tax Year

Size of AGI	All Returns % with Paid Preparer	1040 % with Paid Preparer	1040A % with Paid Preparer	1040EZ % with Paid Preparer
Under 5,000	24.1	58.9	22.0	2.7
5,000–10,000	36.9	63.0	25.3	4.5
10,000–15,000	38.0	60.0	24.4	2.8
15,000–20,000	41.0	56.3	18.6	3.6
20,000–30,000	46.4	53.3	17.1	3.6
30,000–50,000	51.9	53.6	13.3	--
Over 50,000	60.8	60.8	--	--
Total	40.1	56.8	22.1	3.3

Source: Dorthea Riley, "Individual Income Tax Returns:
Selected Characteristics from the 1982 Taxpayer Usage Study,"
Statistics of Income Bulletin 3 (Summer 1983):52.

Income tax preparation services for individuals exist largely because people feel unable to complete their own returns. Donald Alexander, former commissioner of the IRS, argues a linkage between the tax system and tax prepara- tions firms: "It's a huge industry, thriving on complexity. Complexity is its goal, more and more. The more complex the individual tax obligation, the bigger the profits."[16] While the firms may not directly encourage complexity, they undoubtedly do gain from it and the significance of com- mercial preparers should not be ignored. H & R Block, incorporated in 1955, is the largest single preparer of fed- eral income tax returns for individuals, preparing 9.6 percent of all such returns in the 1983 tax season. In mid-April 1984, the company operated 4,154 offices; 4,853 more offices were operated by franchisees. Although analy- sis is complicated by company diversification into other areas, total company revenue rose from $114.1 million in 1975 to $415.6 million in 1984 (May 1 fiscal year start). The price of company stock has moved generally upward, as market highs and lows for recent years show: 1980: 36 1/4 - 22 1/8; 1981: 39 - 28 3/4; 1982: 43 3/4 - 25 1/4; 1983: 49 1/8 - 35 1/2; and 1984: 50 - 37 3/4. On June 20, 1985, the stock closed at 56 1/2, close to the top of its 52-week range (58 3/8 - 38 1/2).[17] Investors do not ap- pear convinced that current simplification proposals will drastically harm the tax preparer market—or, possibly, they are not convinced that simplification will pass.

Two other patterns of return utilization emerging from taxpayer compliance appear in Tables 2.5 and 2.6. Table 2.5 shows the distribution of individual returns by type of form used from 1975 through 1984, with a projection for 1985. Although usage of the 1040 long form is not now as great as it was in 1975 (before liberalization of the standard deduction reduced the advantage of itemization for many taxpayers), there has been a gradual increase in relative use of that form through the 1980s. Use of the short form, 1040A, has accordingly declined. As would be anticipated, the 1040EZ option substantially reduced the use of the short form. For the 1982 tax year, 35.07 per- cent of all returns used itemized deductions, up from 33.09 percent in the prior year. That continues an upward trend in itemization that began in 1978, after a decline in itemi- zation through the earlier portion of the 1970s.[18] That pattern indicates, on the whole, an increase in compliance cost with the greater recordkeeping and complexity of the long form and of itemization.

Table 2.5

Individual Income Tax by Form of Return, 1975–85

Calendar Year	Percent 1040	Percent 1040A	Percent 1040EZ*
1975	73.13	26.73	--
1980	59.40	40.44	--
1981	60.63	39.22	--
1982	60.48	39.36	--
1983	62.26	21.99	15.59
1984 preliminary	62.96	20.48	16.40
1985 projected	62.45	20.40	16.99

*Form 1040EZ not available in 1975, 1980, 1981, and 1982.
Source: Statistics of Income Bulletin.

Table 2.6

Distribution of Returns by Type of Return and Adjusted Gross Income, 1983 (percent)

Size of AGI	Form 1040	Form 1040A*	Form 1040EZ	Total
Under $5,000	8.64	21.65	43.74	17.39
5,000–10,000	11.93	24.93	29.30	17.65
10,000–15,000	12.60	19.42	14.86	14.43
15,000–20,000	11.43	14.82	7.96	11.55
20,000–30,000	22.83	15.39	3.82	18.01
30,000–50,000	25.23	3.70	0.32	16.42
50,000–100,000	6.19	0.00	0.00	3.82
100,000 and over	1.15	0.08	0.00	0.73

*A reporting error; the 1040A cannot be used for such income.
Source: Dorthea Riley, "Individual Income Tax Returns: Selected Characteristics from the 1983 Taxpayer Usage Study," Statistics of Income Bulletin 4 (Summer 1984):52.

Table 2.6 presents the distribution of return types by AGI class. It shows the concentration of 1040EZ utilization in income classes below $10,000 AGI, significant utilization of the 1040A through the $30,000 AGI level, and particularly significant use of the 1040 return in the $20,000 to $50,000 AGI range. As would be expected, the 1040EZ is especially beneficial to lower income filers and, presuming such individuals can rule out the advantage of itemization without substantial calculation, would substantially reduce their compliance cost. The 1040-1040A choice may be more difficult for a tax minimizer, but there are undoubtedly many filers up to $20,000 who save much compliance expense from that option. The numbers would increase with increased zero-bracket amounts. Simplified itemization would benefit the 35 percent or so who itemize, primarily higher income taxpayers, although simplified itemization might tempt some 1040A filers into that option.[19]

From those perceptions and responses, what compliance cost results? That includes "all those costs incurred by taxpayers or by third parties in complying with the requirements of the tax system, over and above the tax payments themselves."[20] Components are the value of the taxpayer's own time and effort in maintaining records and in handling tax computation and reporting, the amounts taxpayers pay accountants, lawyers, tax services, and the like to do tax preparation work, and the cost to the taxpayer's employer, bank, and others of complying with the W-2, 1099, and other reporting or withholding requirements imposed on them by the tax law. Unfortunately, no full estimate of this total cost is available, even if one ignores the need to examine only the incremental cost produced by the tax system. The best that can be done is to piece together the available fragments to obtain as reasonable an estimate as possible of this existing administrative debacle.

Four studies, none entirely satisfactory for the issue at hand, present the best pattern of income tax compliance cost estimates for use here.

On the basis of a survey questionnaire distributed through economics students to their parents, John Wicks estimated in 1966 that the average Montana taxpayer spent $88 in time and money in complying with the federal income tax, or 11.5 percent of revenue produced.[21]

The Commission on Federal Paperwork devoted one report volume to federal taxation. Their estimate of the cost of collecting and maintaining necessary records, reading and understanding instructions, and completing tax forms equaled $4.6 billion for individual income tax returns in 1977, an amount equal to 3 percent of revenue.[22] That estimate was based on the fees charged by commercial tax preparation firms. It does not include compliance cost borne by third parties (withholding by employers, information returns, and so forth). If costs increased since then at the same rate as the implicit price deflator for services of this type, the cost would be around $8 billion in 1985.[23]

Shortly after the filing deadline for 1982 calendar returns, Slemrod and Sorum mailed a survey to a sample of Minnesota householders to identify time spent by the taxpayer and expenditure on assistance in complying with the income tax.[24] On the basis of their responses, they estimated for the nation as a whole that two billion hours of taxpayer time was spent on returns, along with $3 billion spent on professional assistance. They concluded that the compliance cost was between $17 and $27 billion. That estimate does not include third party costs.

The Paperwork Reduction Act of 1980 requires the Office of Management and Budget to present annually to Congress an information-collection budget that indicates "the estimated reporting hours imposed by the information collections of each Federal agency." Of the 1,923.6 million hours required by federal programs, more than 25 percent are associated with the individual income tax (see Table 2.7).[25]

Table 2.7

Estimated Reporting Hours Required to Collect Individual Income Tax Information

Income Tax Forms	Reporting Hours (in millions)
Form 1040 and related schedules	261.4
W-2, W-3	104.2
Travel, entertainment, and gift expense reporting	52.5
Form 1040A	23.6
Form 1099 (interest)	23.2
Employer's quarterly tax return (941)	18.6
Partnership return (1065)	14.8
Total	498.3

If those hours are valued at the national average hourly earning rate ($8.54 in March 1985), the value of these hours would be $4.3 billion.[26] That figure excludes most labor fringe benefits as well as all nonlabor costs associated with compliance. It also excludes cost associated with the 1040EZ (16 percent of all returns expected in 1985) and other forms not directly included here.

The lowest cost estimate is 30 percent higher than IRS operating cost; the highest, 8.2 times as large. Furthermore, none of the estimates even attempts to include all costs of compliance! Beyond any shadow of doubt, cost of compliance should be the predominant concern in any effort to improve the economy of tax collection. Simplification or other reforms to reduce the compliance portion of collection cost should be a reasonable first order of tax reform aimed at reducing the federal income tax debacle.

CONCLUSION

The evidence examined here is clear. Taxpayers view the current tax system as difficult to understand. Many respond to that difficulty by hiring tax preparers; others spend many hours preparing the returns themselves. Furthermore, the employers and financial institutions used by the taxpayer face significant reporting responsibilities on behalf of the taxpayer. Although administrative cost of the system is quite low, compliance cost is much larger and there are systematic differences in that burden across taxpayer classes. It is reasonable to consider taxpayer compliance cost to be a significant problem with the current federal income tax.

NOTES

1. Adam Smith, The Wealth of Nations (New York: Random House, 1937), p. 778.

2. Carl Shoup, Public Finance (Chicago: Aldine, 1969), pp. 429–30.

3. 1984 Annual Report of the Commissioner and Chief Counsel of the Internal Revenue Service, p. 71.

4. Harold Groves, "Income–Tax Administration," National Tax Journal 12 (March 1959):37.

5.   John F. Due and John L. Mikesell, Sales Taxation, State and Local Structure and Administration (Baltimore: Johns Hopkins University Press, 1983), p. 324.

6.   U.S. Congress, House, Committee on Ways and Means, Subcommittee on Oversight, Underground Economy Hearings, 96th Congress, 1st Sess., July 16, September 10, October 9 and 11, 1979 (Washington, D.C.:   U.S. Government Printing Office, 1980), p. 125.

7.   Implicit price deflator for federal nondefense service purchases, reported in Survey of Current Business (1972 = 100.)

8.   Internal Revenue Service, Statistics of Income—Individual Income Tax Returns, 1982.   Forms are as follows: 1040, the long form used by itemizers and others with more complex tax conditions and all with taxable income over $50,000; 1040A, the short form used by nonitemizers not eligible for the simpler form; and 1040EZ, the form for single taxpayers claiming no other exemptions, having only wage, salary, and tip income and no more than $400 interest income, and taxable income less than $50,000.

9.   Office of the Assistant Commissioner (Planning, Finance, and Research), Research Division, Internal Revenue Service, Department of Treasury, Income Tax Compliance Research: Estimates for 1973–1981 (July 1983), p. 3.

10.   Reka P. Hoff, "Tax Withholding at Source Would Reduce Underreporting of Income on False Returns," Tax Notes (February 22, 1982):443–50.

11.   Public Opinion, February/March 1985, p. 25.

12.   U.S. House of Representatives, State Taxation of Interstate Commerce, Report of the Special Subcommittee of State Taxation of Interstate Commerce of the Committee on the Judiciary, Vol. 1, June 15, 1964, p. 364.

13.   Yankelovich, Skelly, and White survey, May-June 1984, for the Internal Revenue Service, reported in Public Opinion, February/March 1985, p. 25.

14.   Gallup organization telephone interviews on May 29 and 30, 1985.   Reported in Newsweek, June 10, 1985.

15.   A Roper Organization poll in 1983 found that a total of 57 percent of all respondents received help from an accountant/accounting firm, an income tax service, a family member, a lawyer, or the IRS.   Because their poll included those who did not file and those not receiving payment, the higher overall percentage that Roper found is not inconsistent with the IRS's 1982 Taxpayer Usage Study data

reported in Table 2.4 (Roper data from Public Opinion, February/March 1985, p. 25). IRS taxpayer assistance in the 1983 tax year included: 1,264,000 returns prepared/reviewed, 285,000 returns prepared in the Volunteer Income Tax Assistance program, and 185,000 returns prepared in the Tax Counseling for the Elderly program. SOI Bulletin (Winter 1984-85):85.

16. Mary Williams Walsh, "Preparers' Views Mixed on Tax Plan," Wall Street Journal, December 4, 1984.

17. Data compiled from Moody's and Standard & Poor's publications.

18. I.R.S., Statistics of Income-Individual Return, 1982.

19. Fear of audit may, however, reduce some switching: an IRS poll done by Yankelovich, Skelly, and White in 1984 showed that 81 percent of respondents believed that claiming expenses, deductions, and exemptions increased audit chances. Public Opinion, February/March 1985, p. 25.

20. Joel Slemrod and Nikki Sorum, "The Compliance Cost of the U.S. Individual Income Tax System," National Tax Journal 37 (December 1984):461.

21. John Wicks, "Taxpayers' Compliance Costs from Personal Income Taxation," Iowa Business Digest (August 1966):16-21.

22. Report of the Commission on Federal Paperwork: Taxation (June 10, 1977):13.

23. Implicit price deflator for other service in personal consumption expenditure from Survey of Current Business.

24. Slemrod and Sorum, "Compliance Cost."

25. Office of Management and Budget, Information Collection Budget of the United States Government, Fiscal Year 1985 (April 12, 1985), p. 20. Two other tax compliance burdens: corporate income tax, 22.8 million hours, and FICA/Railroad Retirement, 30.3 million hours.

26. Average hourly earnings from Monthly Labor Review.

3

Complexity, Verbosity, and Progressivity

Howard Gensler

The complexity of the Internal Revenue Code has grown to infamous proportions. The density of the prose makes the style of Cicero and John Stuart Mill appear to be as light as greeting card inscriptions. The text of the law alone dwarfs any novel by Melville, Dostoevski, or Tolstoy. The regulations and rules are encyclopedic in scope. The adage that only two things in life are certain—death and taxes—is only partially true. It is certain that there will be taxes. However, the actual amount of tax is highly uncertain. If the tax code had been presented in its current form as the work of a single person, the inescapable conclusion would be that the author was either a madman or a demon.

However, if mere complexity were the only flaw in this diabolical system, it would be of little concern to anyone. Accounting, banking, and insurance are governed by impervious principles of stultifying magnitude, but there is no great public outcry against these institutions—only sympathy for the dreary victims who must practice these mortifying arts. If the tax law were just a very complicated discipline, its practitioners would be admired as sophisticated, intelligent, and painstaking professionals worthy of the respect that is properly due professors, doctors of medicine, scientists, and other learned individuals. But the tax law has become one of the greatest national concerns because the complexity of the law is unfair, makes both business and personal planning uncertain, modifies the actions of individuals against their will, and hovers over the citizenry like the Sword of Damocles.

The greatest crime of the tax code is that the complexity is an unnecessary result of an unnecessarily complicated fundamental device. The complicated progressive marginal rate structure of the tax code provides a powerful incentive to individuals to divide income. Accordingly, much of the tax law is merely a response to counteract this incentive. The chilling realization is that the capital gains provisions are an ameliorative response to the progressive rate structure, and the most insidious provisions of the code are counteracting responses to the capital gains provisions. In other words, there are laws that were specifically designed to defeat laws that were specifically designed to defeat other laws! The frustration becomes sociopathic after one discovers that the progressive rate structure itself is unnecessary. The same effect can be duplicated without the perverting effect of progressive marginal rates.

The fundamental purpose of a tax system is to raise revenue for the operation of the government. The questions then become what to tax and how to tax. There are many taxes. There are excise taxes on individual items such as tires and cigarettes. There are property taxes on real property, on personal property, both tangible and intangible, and on automobiles. There are sales taxes on most retail sales. There are import and export duties and tariffs. There are estate taxes and inheritance taxes. And, of course, there's the income tax.

Different principles justify the imposition of different taxes. The consideration that a tax should be readily determinable, simple to collect, and unobtrusive supports the levying of duties and tariffs, excise taxes, and sales taxes. These taxes tend to be collected in marginal increments on a daily basis, rendering them virtually invisible. The policy that economic externalities should be internalized--in other words, that an activity should pay for the services it requires--promotes the imposition of property taxes. Homes and businesses require police and fire protection. Automobiles need road service and construction. Finally, the precept that contributions to the maintenance of the public welfare should be based on one's ability to pay advocates the reliance upon estate, inheritance, and income taxes. Few individuals are in a better position to spare a portion of their wealth than are the deceased. Alternatively, those who inherit wealth inherit the means to pay an inheritance tax. Similarly, those who earn income earn the means to pay an income tax.

It is this notion of ability to pay that engenders the progressive rate structure. A person who earns very little must consume virtually the entirety of the meager compensation received. A tax would be a great burden to such an individual. On the other hand, a highly compensated individual can afford many things, including a tax, without fear of physical impairment. For instance, someone who made $10,000 a year maý be able to spare $1,000 for a tax. That would constitute a 10 percent tax on that person's income. However, someone who earned $100,000 a year could probably fend off starvation—even in Los Angeles— with less than $30,000. That would leave an ability to pay (although not necessarily a willingness) of $70,000, or 70 percent. Not only did the amount of tax paid increase from $1,000 to $70,000, but the proportion of income paid in tax increased from 10 percent to 70 percent. It is increases in proportions, not merely amounts, that determines whether a tax is progressive. A tax is progressive if the proportion of income paid in tax increases as income increases.

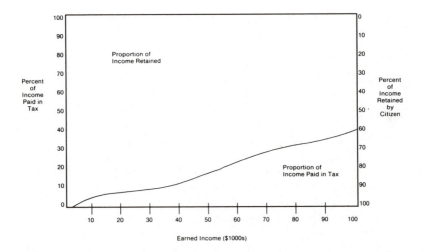

Figure 3.1   Progressivity of U.S. Income Tax

The present income tax law reflects this ability-to-pay principle in the progressive marginal rate structure. The tax rates for an unmarried individual in 1984 are shown in Table 3.1. In the progressive rate structure, each segment of income is taxed at progressively higher rates. As income rises, the marginal tax rate increases. It is important to remember that each higher tax rate applies only to the corresponding bracket of income. If someone makes $25,000, only the income segment from $23,500 to $25,000 (that is, $1,500) is taxed at 26 percent. The balance of the income below $23,500 is taxed at lower rates. Because the higher rate applies only to the last segment of income, and not retrospectively to the entire sum of income, it is not possible to lose income by earning more money from being "pushed into a higher tax bracket." On each dollar earned, the earner keeps part and the government gets part (Figure 3.2). The government's part of each successive dollar just gets larger.

Table 3.1

U.S. Progressive Marginal Income Tax Rates

unmarried individual

Income Segment ($)	Segment Tax (percent)
Under 2,300	0
2,300 to 3,400	11
3,400 to 4,400	12
4,400 to 6,500	14
6,500 to 8,500	15
8,500 to 10,800	16
10,899 to 12,900	18
12,900 to 15,000	20
15,000 to 18,200	23
18,200 to 23,500	26
23,500 to 28,800	30
28,000 to 34,100	34
34,100 to 41,500	38
41,500 to 55,300	42
55,300 to 81,800	48
Over 81,800	50

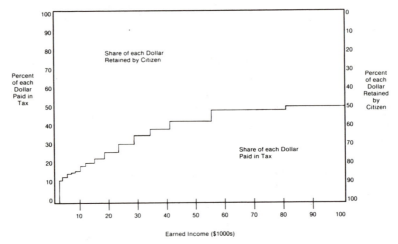

Figure 3.2   Division of Each Successive Dollar Earned--
Individual

   Although no one likes the idea of giving more money
to the government, it is a fair system.   John Rawls explores
this idea of social fairness in A Theory of Justice.   A system is fair if it is designed in a manner that a participant
wouldn't object to the design before knowing where in the
system the participant would be placed.   In other words,
if one didn't know if one would be poor or rich, one would
agree that poor people should keep most of their money,
and rich people should contribute more to the government.
That way, if no one ended up impoverished, one's position
wouldn't be made significantly worse from taxation.   And
if one ended up wealthy, the contributions could be made
painlessly from discretionary income.
   Although the idea of the progressive rate structure
is sound social and fiscal policy, the implementation is a
nightmare.   Because income is taxed at successively higher
rates, a taxpayer can save significant amounts of money if
the income can be split between recipients.   For instance,
if one person earns $163,600, that individual will pay
$69,355 in tax.   But if that income were divided between
two people at $81,800 each, their combined tax liability
would be $57,670.   They saved $11,665 in taxes.   If four
people were to split the money four ways, each earning
$40,900, their combined tax payments would amount to
$33,156, a savings of $36,179.   Consequently, there is a
great incentive to split income up among as many recipients
as possible.

The government may not be very creative, but it is not completely without foresight. The IRS knows that taxpayers are going to try to split income. Accordingly, a myriad of laws have been passed to attempt to prevent these efforts. One of the great devices to split income is community property. The Supreme Court held in Poe v. Seaborn, 282 U.S. 101 (1930), that in a community property state, both partners have an equal legal right upon the earning of the income by either partner. The Supreme Court did not characterize community property as the earning of income by one partner who then transferred half to the other partner. Accordingly, each partner was permitted to report one-half of the total income, even though it was earned by only one person. As may be expected, a trend erupted among the states to convert to community property. The federal government responded by enacting the joint return laws and rates. Joint returns now have lower rates than individuals (Table 3.2). However, two working individuals with the same income pay more tax together on a joint return than if they were single. This "marriage tax" penalty is yet another insidious consequence of the progressive rate structure.

Table 3.2

Comparison of Tax Based on Marital Status

Taxpayer	Tax
Two people each reporting $20,000 as individuals	$6,410
Married couple reporting $40,000 income jointly	7,858
One person reporting $40,000 as individual	10,737

The next favorite tax dodge was to assign income to other persons. The idea was to take income earned by a rich person and assign it to a low-income relative, such as a minor dependent. Of course, that income could then be used to pay for the dependent's food, clothing, recreation, and education, or saved for future needs. The real benefit came from having the income taxed at low rates rather than high rates. The courts, however, characterized this chain of events as income earned by the person who earned it, and therefore taxable to that person, with a subsequent "gift" transfer to another person.

That didn't stop many people--only wage earners. Property owners could transfer property to their children. The child would then earn the rent, interest, or dividends. Small family-owned businesses are exactly that--family-owned. The children are made "partners" and a share of the business profit is diverted to them. Finally, provisions were developed to permit people to place property in trust for ten years (or more, not less), with the income taxable to the beneficiary, and the corpus returnable to the grantor at the conclusion of the term. In other words, mother puts $100,000 in a savings account in trust for daughter. Daughter collects $10,000 per year for ten years and pays very little tax. Mother, a high-income person, avoids paying high taxes on the extra interest income for ten years. At the end of ten years, mother gets her $100,000 back. Mother has saved a lot of money in taxes. The $10,000 a year, of course, defrayed some expenses and established a college fund for daughter. It's all buried in the tax code.

Another tax trick inspired by the progressive rate structure that has required extensive legislative machinations to combat is the "loss sale" transaction. In this scenario, a high-income earning individual who owns a fluctuating property sells it at a low ebb to a low-income earning dependent. This generates a paper loss for the high-income earner. For example, father owns a volatile stock. He bought it for $100,000. It fluctuates between $110,000 and $80,000. When it reaches $80,000 he has his son "buy" it. Father gets to write off a $20,000 short-term (ordinary) loss. A more sophisticated version would be to permit different sons to sell to father during the peaks and father to sell back to different sons during the troughs. That way, father generates several $20,000 (high tax bracket) losses while various sons "earn" lower tax-bracket income. This can be done in any number of combinations of individuals, trusts, and corporations. Accordingly, the tax law prevents losses between related parties such as a taxpayer and the taxpayer's spouse, an entity controlled by the taxpayer, members of the taxpayer's family, and corporations in which the taxpayer owns over 50 percent of the stock. Also, two entities controlled by one taxpayer are considered related, as are a grantor and a fiduciary of a trust, two trusts with the same grantor, or many combinations of the aforementioned parties. All this regulation is needed just because there is more than one tax rate on income.

The progressive rate structure has necessitated a plethora of measures to prevent people from splitting income, and Congress has created a few measures to allow people to split income. However, the greatest accommodation to the progressive rate structure is the provision for capital gains. Income is measured in yearly increments. Each year the taxpayer takes another trip up the progressive rate structure, reusing the lower rates each trip. However, property owners do not report property gains each year. Property owners report income upon sale of the property. Accordingly, someone who sells a capital asset after ten years realizes ten years of gain in one year. But instead of making ten trips up the progressive rate structure, the property owner makes only one. All the income is bunched up at the higher tax brackets. The difference is significant. The tax on $100,000 is $37,935. However, the tax on $10,000 ten times is $10,750. The property owner, in this case, pays over three times as much tax because ten years of gain is realized in one year. Accordingly, under the capital gains provisions the property owner is permitted to exclude 60 percent of the gain. In the above case, only $40,000 would be reported, and only $9,749 would be paid in tax. Not only is less tax paid, but the compounding of interest due on the tax equivalent over the years is not even taken into account. As may be expected, there is a great incentive to convert ordinary income into capital gains.

A progressive rate structure makes a capital gains provision necessary. The capital gains provision makes a broad spectrum of regulations necessary to prevent people from taking an unfair advantage of this powerful tax-saving device. One method of converting ordinary income into capital gain is to retain current earnings in a corporation. (The double level of corporate taxes is avoided by the Subchapter S provisions.) Then, the corporation either redeems part of the stock for the accumulated earnings or the corporation is liquidated entirely. The assets are exchanged for stock, so the stock (if held sufficiently long) receives (long-term) capital gains treatment. To prevent this abuse, laws have been written that impose an additional tax on excess accumulated earnings held in a corporation. Language is carefully placed throughout the stock-transaction provisions to ferret out dividend income from capital gain.

A similar device applies to interest income from bonds. Rather than collect periodic interest payments, the bondholder arranges for the interest to accrue. Then prior to the repayment of the bond principal and interest, the bondholder sells the mature instrument. To prevent this transaction from being treated as the sale of a capital asset, a specific code section has been developed to separate the ordinary accrued interest income from the balance of the transaction.

Time and time again, the law is made increasingly complex by countermeasures to the economic incentives generated by the progressive rate structure. The law creates legitimate loopholes and battles any number of disfavored schemes. The loopholes that are created then in turn require more countermeasures to prevent further abuse. This expository discussion does not begin to illustrate not only how complicated, dense, and technical the language of the tax law is, but also how overwhelmingly interconnected its provisions are. Accordingly, the following excerpts are offered as a few examples of the skill of the drafters of the law on Capitol Hill.

Example 1. This excerpt is inspired by the capital gains provisions. Incidentally, this, please note, is one sentence.

Section 1101(c)(1)

DISTRIBUTIONS PURSUANT TO BANK HOLDING COMPANY ACT. PROPERTY ACQUIRED AFTER JULY 7, 1970.--

IN GENERAL.--Except as provided in paragraphs (2) and (3), subsection (a) or (b) shall not apply to--

(A) any property acquired by the distributing corporation after July 7, 1970 unless (i) gain to such corporation with respect to the receipt of such property was not recognized by reason of subsection (a) or (b), or (ii) such property was received by it in exchange for all of its stock in an exchange to which paragraph (2) or (3) applies, or (iii) such property was acquired by the distributing corporation in a transaction in which gain not recognized under section 305(a) or section 332, or under section 354 or 356 (but only with respect to property permitted by section 354 or 356 to be received without the recognition of gain or loss) with respect to a reorganization described in section 368(a)(1)(A),(B),(E), or (F), or

(B) any property which was acquired by the distributing corporation in a distribution with respect to stock acquired by such corporation after July 7, 1970, unless such stock was acquired by such corporation (i) in a distribution (with respect to stock held by it on July 7, 1970, or with respect to stock in respect of which all previous applications of this clause are satisfied) with respect to which gain to it was not recognized by reason of subsection (a) or (b), or (ii) in exchange for all of its stock in an exchange to which paragraph (2) or (3) applies, or (iii) in a transaction in which gain was not recognized under section 305(a) or section 332, or under section 354 or 356 (but only with respect to property permitted by section 354 or 356 to be received without the recognition of gain or loss) with respect to a reorganization described in section 368(a)(1)(A),(B),(E), or (F), or

(C) any property acquired by the distributing corporation in a transaction in which gain was not recognized under section 332, unless such property was acquired from a corporation which, if it had been a qualified bank holding corporation, could have distributed such property under subsection (a)(1) or (b)(1), or

(D) any property acquired by the distributing corporation in a transaction in which gain was not recognized under section 354 or 356 with respect to a reorganization described in section 368(a)(1)(A) or (B), unless such property was acquired by the distributing corporation in exchange for property which the distributing corporation could have distributed under subsection (a)(1) or (b)(1).

Example 2. This is part of an effort to prevent income manipulation through loss sales.

Section 302(c)(2)

DISTRIBUTIONS IN REDEMPTION OF STOCK CONSTRUCTIVE OWNERSHIP OF STOCK.-- FOR DETERMINING TERMINATION OF IN- TEREST.--

(A) In the case of a distribution described in subsection (b)(3), section 318(a)(1) shall not apply if--

(i) immediately after the distribution the distributee has no interest in the corporation (including an interest as officer, director, or employee), other than an interest as a creditor,

(ii) the distributee does not acquire any such interest (other than stock acquired by bequest or inheritance) within 10 years from the date of such distribution, and

(iii) the distributee, at such time and in such manner as the Secretary by regulations prescribes, files an agreement to notify the Secretary of any acquisition described in clause (ii) and to retain such records as may be necessary for the application of this paragraph.

If the distributee acquires such an interest
in the corporation (other than by bequest
or inheritance) within 10 years from the
date of the distribution, then the periods
of limitation provided in sections 6501 and
6502 on the making of an assessment and
the collection by levy or a proceeding in
court shall, with respect to any deficiency
(including interest and additions to the
tax) resulting from such acquisition, include one year immediately following the
date on which the distributee (in accor-
dance with regulations prescribed by the
Secretary) notifies the Secretary of such
acquisition; and such assessment and collection may be made notwithstanding any
provision of law or rule of law which
otherwise would prevent such assessment
and collection.

(B) Subparagraph (A) of this paragraph shall not apply if—

(i) any portion of the stock redeemed
was acquired, directly or indirectly,
within the 10-year period ending on
the date of the distribution by the
distributee from a person the ownership
of whose stock would (at the time of
distribution) be attributable to the
distributee under section 318(a), or

(ii) any person owns (at the time of
the distribution) stock the ownership
of which is attributable to the distributee under section 318(a) and such
person acquired any stock in the corporation, directly or indirectly, from
the distributee within the 10-year
period ending on the date of the distribution, unless such stock so acquired from the distributee is redeemed in the same transaction.

The preceding sentence shall not apply if
the acquisition (or in the case of clause
(ii), the disposition) by the distributee

did not have as one of its principal purposes the avoidance of Federal income tax.

Example 3. This is another effort to monitor corporate transactions.

Section 819(b)(2)

FOREIGN LIFE INSURANCE COMPANIES
DISTRIBUTIONS TO SHAREHOLDERS.--

DISTRIBUTIONS PURSUANT TO CERTAIN
MUTUALIZATIONS.--In applying section
815(e) with respect to a foreign corporation--

(A) the paid-in capital and paid-in
surplus referred to in section 815(e)(1)
(A) of a foreign corporation is the
portion of such capital and surplus determined by multiplying such capital and surplus by the percentage selected for the
taxable year under paragraph (1); and

(B) the excess referred to in section
815(e)(2)(A)(i) (without the adjustment
provided by section 815(e)(2)(B))is
whichever of the following is the
greater:

(i) the minimum figure for 1958 determined under subsection (a)(2)(A) computed by using a percentage of 9 percent in lieu of the percentage determined and proclaimed by the Secretary, or

(ii) the surplus described in subsection (a)(2)(B) (determined as of December 31, 1958).

These examples demonstrate the opaqueness of the
tax law and provide a hint at the extent of the endless
referring back and forth between sections of the law.
However, the interconnectedness of the tax law needs to be
illustrated more directly. Figure 3.3 is only a representa-
tion of explicit references made to the various sections
throughout the tax code. They include references out of

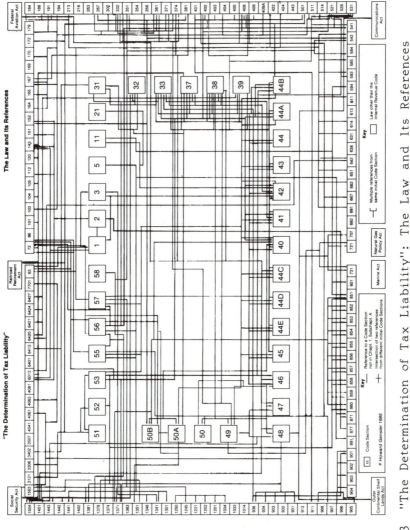

Figure 3.3 "The Determination of Tax Liability": The Law and Its References

the tax code, by the sections of the first subchapter (of 21 subchapters) of the first chapter (of 96 chapters) of the Internal Revenue Code.

The complexity of the law is indeed overwhelming. The complexity limits access by business and citizens to the genuinely salutary programs implemented through the tax law. The complexity permits wealthy industries to lobby for exclusions and windfalls, which go unnoticed in thousands of pages of technical verbiage. The complexity gives the government the power to destroy any business or any individual by aggressively auditing the victim and litigating each interpretation of each deduction in the most expensive discipline of an already frightfully inflated profession. The complexity allows some to gain advantage over others in virtually identical transactions. The bulk of this complexity arises from the initial unnecessary premise: progressive arithmetic marginal rates.

The idea that a greater proportion of income should be contributed to the public maintenance as income increases need not be implemented through direct, laborious arithmetic calculations. The same basic goal can be achieved by employing a proportional tax rate (one tax rate for all income) in conjunction with a transactions tax plus exclusions or credits. The advantage to employing a credit (a direct cash payment prorated over the course of the year) is that the requirement for income supplement programs is obviated. The welfare system can be replaced (and the overhead saved, and the humiliation and harassment eliminated) by employing a credit (or negative income tax notion). Table 3.3 compares the tax paid by an individual and a married couple under current law with the tax paid under a proportional (flat) tax of 40 percent when combined with a credit of $3,600 per year for an individual and $7,200 per year for a married couple. Of course, the current tax for zero income is not actually zero. Some amount would be paid under some income supplement program. The comparison, accordingly, is even closer than suggested here. The figures are rounded to the nearest $100 to facilitate comparisons.

An exact match of taxes paid is not necessary. Taxes change dramatically from period to period. The definition of income is also of central importance. The important consideration is that a progressive tax rate can be devised that closely approximates what is presently arrived at with current arithmetic progressive rates. Table

Table 3.3

Comparison of Present Progressive Tax System with a Flat Tax and Credit System

Income ($1,000s)	Individual Tax ($)		Married Joint Tax ($)	
	Current	$3,600 Credit and 40% Tax	Current	$7,200 Credit and 40% Tax
0	"0"	-3,600	"0"	-7,200
10	1,100	400	800	-3,200
20	3,200	4,400	2,500	800
30	6,100	8,400	4,800	4,800
40	9,700	12,400	7,900	8,800
50	13,900	16,400	11,400	12,800
60	18,400	20,400	15,200	16,800
70	23,000	24,400	19,400	20,800
80	28,000	28,400	23,600	24,800
90	33,000	32,400	27,900	28,800
100	38,000	36,400	32,400	32,800
110	42,900	40,400	36,900	36,800
120	48,000	44,400	41,800	40,800
130	52,900	48,400	46,700	44,800
140	57,900	52,400	51,600	48,800
150	62,900	56,400	56,500	52,800
160	67,900	60,400	61,400	56,800
170	72,900	64,400	66,400	60,800
180	77,900	68,400	71,400	64,800
190	82,900	72,400	76,400	68,800
200	87,900	76,400	81,400	72,800

3.4 compares the average (or overall) tax rate on income of the present law with the proposed credit and flat rate system just described. Again, the figures are rounded to the nearest percent to facilitate comparisons.

The relative similarity of the two systems is demonstrated by Figure 3.4. Again, it must be remembered that the various income supplement programs (welfare, social security, unemployment insurance, veterans' benefits, and so forth) would direct the line of the present tax system into the negative tax area, further promoting the similarity between the two systems.

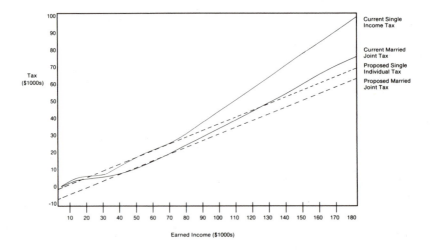

Figure 3.4   Current and Proposed Tax Levels

In conclusion, the advantage of the proportional (flat) rate tax system is that all income is taxed at the same rate, no matter who earns it. Moreover, since the tax rate does not increase, capital income accumulated over many years but realized in one year pays the same tax as if realized in each year. Therefore, a capital gains provision is not needed. By using a flat rate, all the incentive to divert and to split income is eliminated, and all the capital gains and counter-capital gains provisions are obviated. The complexity and bulk of the Internal Revenue Code would be greatly reduced and the federal income tax debacle would be alleviated.

Table 3.4

Comparison of Average Tax Rates under Current Law and Proposed Credit and Flat Rate Reform

Income ($1,000s)	Individual Average Tax Rate (%)		Married Joint Average Tax Rate (%)	
	Current	$3,600 Credit and 40% Tax	Current	$7,200 Credit and 40% Tax
10	11	4	8	-32
20	16	22	12	4
30	20	28	16	16
40	24	31	20	22
50	28	33	23	26
60	31	34	25	28
70	33	35	28	30
80	35	36	30	31
90	36	36	31	32
100	38	36	32	33
110	39	37	34	34
120	40	37	35	34
130	41	37	36	35
140	41	37	37	35
150	42	38	38	35
160	43	38	38	36
170	43	38	39	36
180	43	38	40	36
190	44	38	40	36
200	44	38	41	36

REFERENCES

Anderson, W. J. 1984. Statement before the Subcommittee of the Committee on Government Operations on Tax Evasion Through Use of False Foreign Addresses. February 28.

_____. 1983. Statement before the Subcommittee of the Committee on Government Operations on Tax Evasion Through the Netherlands Antilles and Other Tax Haven Countries. April 12.

_____. 1982. Statement before the Subcommittee of the Committee on Government Operations on Impact of Proposed Fiscal Year 1983 Budget on IRS Operations. March 17.

Archer, G. L., Jr. 1983. Statement before the Permanent Subcommittee on Investigations of the Committee on Governmental Affairs on Crime and Secrecy: The Use of Offshore Banks and Companies. March 15.

Barnard, D., Jr. 1984. Statement before the Subcommittee of the Committee on Government Operations on Tax Evasion Through Use of False Foreign Addresses. February 28.

_____. 1983. Statement before the Subcommittee of the Committee on Government Operations on Tax Evasion Through the Netherlands Antilles and Other Tax Haven Countries. April 12.

Bartlett, S., and G. D. Wallace et al. 1985. Money Laundering, Who's Involved, How It Works, and Where It's Spreading. Business Week, 18 March:74–82.

Bawly, D. 1982. The Subterranean Economy. New York: McGraw-Hill.

Blum, R. H. 1984. Offshore Haven Banks, Trusts, and Companies. New York: Praeger.

Chapoton, J. E. 1984. Statement before the Subcommittee of the Committee on Government Operations on Tax Evasion Through Use of False Foreign Addresses. February 28.

Chown, J. 1977. Who Uses Offshore Centres? Multinational Companies. The Banker. April:97–99.

Cohen, R. 1985. Laundry Service: How the Mob Is Using Financial Institutions to Disguise Its Gains. Wall Street Journal. 12 March, Western ed.:1,30.

Corporate Tax System Called "Seriously Deficient." 1985. Eugene Register Guard, 5 May.

Egger, R. L., Jr. 1984. Statement before the Subcommittee of the Committee on Government Operations on Tax Evasion Through Use of False Foreign Addresses. February 28.

_____. 1983. Statement before the Subcommittee of the Committee on Government Operations on Tax Evasion Through the Netherlands Antilles and Other Tax Haven Countries. April 13.

_____. 1982. Statement before the Subcommittee of the Committee on Government Operations on Impact of Proposed Fiscal Year 1983 Budget on IRS Operations. March 22.

Ernst & Whinney. 1985a. Summary of Major Tax Reform Proposals. Washington Tax Reporter. June.

_____. 1985b. 1984 Foreign and U.S. Corporate Income and Withholding Tax Rates. International Series.

Fedders, J. M. 1983. Statement before the Permanent Subcommittee on Investigations of the Committee on Governmental Affairs on Crime and Secrecy, the Use of Offshore Banks and Companies. March 24.

General Accounting Office. 1981. The Value Added Tax: What Else Should We Know About It? Washington, D.C.: Comptroller General of the United States.

_____. 1980. The Value-Added Tax in the European Economic Community. Washington, D.C.: Comptroller General of the United States.

Granwell, A. W. 1983. Statement before the Permanent Subcommittee on Investigations of the Committee on

Governmental Affairs on Crime and Secrecy: The Use
of Offshore Banks and Companies. March 15.

Grundy, M. 1984. The World of International Tax Planning.
Cambridge: Cambridge University Press.

Johns, R. A. 1983. Tax Havens and Offshore Finance.
New York: St. Martin's Press.

Kieschnick, M. 1981. Taxes and Growth Council of State
Planning Agencies. Washington, D.C.

Lindholm, R. W. 1984. A New Federal Tax System. New
York: Praeger.

_____. 1980. The Economics of VAT. Lexington, Mass.:
D. C. Heath.

Richupan, S. 1984. Income Tax Evasion: A Review of
the Measurement Techniques and Some Estimates for the
Developing Countries. Departmental Memoranda (DM)
Series, International Monetary Fund, Washington, D.C.,
June 15.

Rosenthal, B. S. 1982a. Statement before the Subcommittee
of the Committee on Government Operations on Improper
Use of Foreign Addresses to Evade U.S. Taxes. June 10.

_____. 1982b. Statement before the Subcommittee of the
Committee on Government Operations on Impact of Pro-
posed Fiscal Year 1983 Budget on IRS Operations.
March 17.

Roth, W. V., Jr. 1983. Statement before the Permanent
Subcommittee on Investigations of the Committee on
Governmental Affairs on Crime and Secrecy: The Use
of Offshore Banks and Companies. March 15.

Simon, C. P., and A. D. Witte. 1980. Executive Summary
of the Underground Economy: Estimates of Size, Trends
and Structure. Report to Permanent Subcommittee on
Investigations. October.

Starchild, A. 1979. Tax Havens for Corporations. Houston,
Texas: Gulf Publishing.

Tanzi, V. 1982. The Underground Economy in the United States: Annual Estimates for 1930–80. Departmental Memoranda (DM) Series. International Monetary Fund. Washington, D.C., December 21.

Tax Cheating Increases as Cynicism Takes Hold. 1985. Eugene Register Guard, 10 March:3ff.

U.S., Congress, House of Representatives. 1984. Tax Evasion Through Use of False Foreign Addresses. Subcommittee of the Committee on Government Operations. 98th Congress, 2nd session, February 28.

_____. 1983. Tax Evasion Through the Netherlands Antilles and Other Tax Haven Countries. Subcommittee of the Committee on Government Operations. 98th Congress, 1st session, April 12–13.

_____. 1982a. Improper Use of Foreign Addresses to Evade U.S. Taxes. Subcommittee of the Committee on Government Operations. 97th Congress, 2nd session, June 10.

_____. 1982b. Impact of Proposed Fiscal Year 1983 Budget on IRS Operations. Subcommittee of the Committee on Government Operations. 97th Congress, 2nd session, March 17.

U.S., Congress, Senate. 1983. Crime and Secrecy: The Use of Offshore Banks and Companies. Permanent Subcommittee on Investigations of the Committee on Governmental Affairs. 98th Congress, 1st session, March 15, 16, and May 24.

U.S., Internal Revenue Service. 1979. Estimates of Income Unreported on Individual Income Tax Returns. Publication 1101, Washington, D.C., September.

Wallace, G. D., and J. Templeman. 1985. The Long and Growing List of How-to-Money Havens. Business Week, 18 March:82.

4

The VAT Alternative

Leonard M. Greene and Bette K. Fishbein

INTRODUCTION

The tax structure in the United States encourages
the misallocation of resources. By providing wrong incentives, it encourages market participants to be inefficient.
Worse yet, most of these misallocations are popularly perceived as unfair. Serving neither the ends of efficiency
nor of equity, they represent pure waste. Indeed, serious
tax reform is in order, and the value-added tax (VAT) has
much to recommend it for inclusion in any reform package.
    If designed properly, the VAT would minimize eco-
nomic distortions by applying a uniform tax to a very broad
base. This would eliminate the disincentive to save that
is prevalent in our income and corporate taxation, and
could improve the competitive position of our export goods.
In addition, it would increase the private enforcement of
tax payments, minimizing underground economic activity.
These are the attributes that have led economists to give
serious consideration to the VAT as an alternative to existing components of the tax structure.
    A common criticism of the VAT relates to its supposed
regressivity. This chapter will demonstrate that any level
of progressivity can be incorporated solely at the discretion of public policymakers. The VAT can be combined
with an income transfer to produce the desired mix. This
can also be utilized as a funding mechanism to redistribute
income to the poor in the United States, thereby phasing
out the cumbersome welfare system.

DESCRIPTION OF THE VAT

At each stage in the production of a final good, the value of the good is enhanced by the producer and the additional inputs he uses.[1] For example, as the farmer buys seed, fertilizer, and so forth, and adds land, labor, capital, and his own knowledge, wheat is produced. The farmer's activity has enhanced the value of the component inputs. Further, when the mill owner purchases the wheat and adds labor, capital, and other intermediate goods, the flour produced represents another increase in the value of the component inputs. Proceeding one more step, as the baker buys flour, yeast, and the like, and adds labor and capital to produce bread, the value of the product is further increased. The VAT taxes the incremental value contributed by each producer in this chain; so that, by the time a good is in its final form, its entire value has been taxed a single time. In short, the VAT is one means of taxing national productivity, just as a national income tax is or as a national retail sales tax is. However, to say that all of these are national productivity taxes is not to suggest that they are identical in their effects or desirability. It is only to say that they are all broad-based taxes on production. An understanding of their differences requires further examination.

In general, three methods exist for the taxation of value-added. First, the subtraction method simply taxes the difference between the value of each producer's output and the value of the intermediate goods/inputs used. Second, the addition method taxes the sum of the payments to all inputs in a particular stage of production except for those inputs purchased from other firms. Third, the invoice credit method levies a tax on the gross value of a producer's output and allows tax credits to be given for the value-added taxes that have been paid previously by other firms at earlier stages of the production process.

In theory, these different methods imply exactly the same tax base; however, in practice the invoice credit method is preferred for its administrative ease and for the incentives it provides for the private enforcement of tax payments. To appreciate this, realize that the underground purchase of inputs imposes their tax obligation on the buyer/user of those inputs, since he cannot obtain a tax credit for the inputs unless he can show that the taxes on them have been paid previously. This invoice credit method, then, substantially improves the incentive to use legitimate markets and, therefore, for tax compliance.

The most important distinction among the alternative VATs, however, is the definition of the tax base, not the method of calculation. Their different treatments of capital goods is of particular note. The consumption–type VAT, the one that is of greatest interest in this chapter, allows a tax credit (using the invoice credit method) for all capital goods purchased in a time period. In other words, positive net investment (capital formation) is not taxed; and the VAT, therefore, constitutes a consumption tax. It has a base comparable to other consumption taxes, such as the consumption expenditures tax. As such, it does not provide the kind of bias against saving (capital formation) that is present in income taxation. Other types of the VAT treat capital differently and do result in this anticapital bias. Because of this, those VATs will not be considered here.

The last noteworthy distinction among the VATs is their use or nonuse of differential tax rates, including zero rates, on their bases. For purposes of achieving goals equity or for other motivations to influence resource allocation, policymakers can tax goods at differential rates and can exclude other goods from taxation altogether. As superficially appealing as these differential rates of taxation might be, they result in the creation of a bureaucratic morass. Without question, they induce people to misallocate their resources. They cause inefficiencies. And, though efficiency is not and should not be the only goal of policymakers, other goals, such as equity, should be pursued with as little loss of efficiency as possible. In most cases, there are superior ways to accomplish these goals than through the use of differential tax rates.

Consequently, this chapter will focus on the consumption–type VAT, calculated by the invoice credit method, and applied uniformly to all consumption goods except those few that are administratively impractical to include in the base. To examine an income–type VAT would serve little purpose in the United States since a desire for increased income taxation could be accomplished with minor changes in the present system of federal income tax. The major attraction of the VAT is its ability to move us away from this system of taxation and toward one that is more neutral economically.

HISTORY OF THE VAT

The VAT is a twentieth-century phenomenon, though the underpinning concepts are said to have their roots in American colonial times.[2] It was first proposed as a new tax policy by a German industrial executive in 1918; however, the idea did not catch on and lay dormant until mid-century. In 1940 the concept was revived by Senator Joseph O'Mahoney, who introduced a bill to implement such a tax in the Seventy-sixth Congress. The bill was not passed, but other initiatives were mounted within a little more than a decade. First, in 1950 Japan passed VAT legislation, revised the law in 1953, and repealed it in 1954 without its ever having been implemented. Second, the state of Michigan passed and enacted a modified version of the VAT in 1953. It was subsequently revised in 1967 and remains in place today.

In Europe, the continent where the use of the VAT is now most pervasive, the trend toward adoption was initiated by France in 1954. Some of the motivations that led more than a dozen European countries to adopt the VAT are unique to their experience. First, the VAT became a very attractive replacement for an extremely inefficient form of taxation used in several European countries, the cascade-type turnover tax. Like the VAT, it taxes the gross value at each stage rather than the value-added at those stages. The result is the multiple taxation of the same output. It led to distortions in the relative prices of final goods. By contrast, the VAT is neutral in this respect. Its substitution for the turnover tax represented a clear improvement in several European countries.

A second major motivation was a desire to pave the way for the economic union that would become known as the Common Market. The use of VATs, as replacements for most of their other indirect taxes, allowed these countries a means of insuring the common exclusion of export goods from major portions of their tax bases. It put these countries on a much more equal footing with respect to trade with each other. Consequently, the common adoption of the VAT provided a very important step toward the harmony required.

Since France adopted the VAT in 1954, all of the Common Market nations have followed suit, as have other European and Latin American countries. The list includes: Denmark (1967), Brazil (1967), West Germany (1968), Netherlands (1968), Sweden (1969), Luxembourg (1970), Norway (1970), Belgium (1971), Ireland (1972), United Kingdom (1973), Italy (1973), Argentina (1975), and Mexico (1980). In 1986 Greece is slated to become the next addition to the list.

In this country we neither have a turnover tax nor are we seeking to form an economic union with other countries that employ the VAT. However, as recently as 1979 Representative Al Ullman, then chairman of the House Ways and Means Committee, introduced a bill that would have substituted a VAT for portions of the individual and corporate income taxes and the Social Security payroll tax. Previous to that, in 1972 Richard Nixon's Presidential Task Force suggested the use of the VAT in the event that any additional revenues needed to be generated at the federal level. Nixon himself is known to have favored the use of a national VAT for the purpose of at least partially replacing the local property taxation that is used to finance educational expenditures.

With tax reform a major public priority, it is time to analyze the potential role of a VAT in our system. To do so, it is necessary to understand the principles of taxation and to apply these to an evaluation of the current mix of tax instruments in this country.

GENERAL PROBLEMS OF TAXATION:
A BRIEF REVIEW

Two broad categories of problems arise from an economy's use of taxes. One is with respect to the equity of the distribution of tax burdens across members of the population; the other concerns the efficiency of resource allocation within the economy.

Since taxes were first used, it has been recognized that their effects might be distributed unjustly. Though there exists no uniformly accepted, full-fledged criterion of justice, it is common to assess taxes on the basis of two simple notions: horizontal and vertical equity. In brief, the idea of a horizontally equitable tax is that it should have equal effects on people of equal means (that is, equal abilities-to-pay). The idea of vertical equity precludes the infliction of greater burdens on people of lesser means than on people of greater means; it allows for the possibility that people of greater means should bear greater bur-

dens.   Individual taxes or tax packages can be assessed
for their conformity to these two rules of equity.

The issue of efficiency, unlike that of equity, is
one about which it is possible to provide a much more
thorough analysis.   For resources to be allocated efficiently, market prices must correctly reflect the relative values
of the alternative uses of those resources, for these prices
are relied upon to convey the incentives and information
that influence market participants.   If the prices are distorted, as often happens with the use of taxes, individuals
are induced to make inefficient choices.   Consequently, tax
analysis must identify and judge the importance of any
tax-induced distortions.

The distortions in relative prices that result from
taxes may be of several types.   They may occur between
market and nonmarket goods, between taxed and untaxed
market goods, among the differentially taxed market goods,
and between current and future consumption goods (that is,
between current consumption and current saving).   For example, almost all forms of taxation reduce the rewards of
market activity relative to those of nonmarket activity.
Since taxes cannot in practice be levied against nonmarket
goods/activities, the imposition of taxes makes market activity relatively less remunerative.   That is, taxes may
make work in the marketplace less remunerative net of
taxes than, say, work for oneself in the household (or
even leisure).   Reduced work effort in the market may
manifest itself in a number of ways, some of which are not
readily recognized as such.   People may work short weeks,
choose different careers, undertake different amounts of
human capital accumulation (for example, education),
choose different ages for market entry, and choose different
retirement ages.   Likewise, decisionmakers within firms,
who face tax-induced distortions in relative input prices,
may choose different quantities of capital, labor, or raw
materials and express a different willingness to assume
risk.   With changed relative prices, consumers may demand
different mixes of final output and may choose a different
allocation of consumption/saving over their lifetimes.

In short, taxes may leave the population with a
different, less valued mix of final goods, and it may have
provided the incentives for these goods to be produced in
costlier ways than is technologically necessary.   However,
taxes are not identical in their effects on the efficiency of
resource allocation.   Some tax structures create far fewer

and less problematical price distortions than do others.
It is because of this that tax analysis is useful for efficiency purposes.

In general, price distortions can be minimized by
the use of taxes that define very broad bases, tax those
bases at uniform rates, do not tax savings, do not tax exported goods, and keep to a minimum the rewards from
underground economic activity. Broad bases mean that a
given volume of revenue can be raised with the use of
lower tax rates; and lower tax rates on market activities/
goods provide less incentive to substitute nonmarket activities. The uniform taxation of the base avoids the inducement for consumers to substitute among the goods they buy
as a result of the tax.

The exclusion of savings from the base leaves un-
disturbed the relative prices of current and future consumption goods. That is, it favors saving and current
capital formation. In turn, this allows for the production
of even greater volumes of output in future periods.

The exclusion of exported goods from the base improves the competitive position of domestically produced
goods on the world market.[3] A structure of incentives that
rewards the payment of taxes results in self-enforcement,
thereby minimizing underground economic activity. This
allows lower tax rates to be used to generate needed levels
of revenue. Therefore, with these principles in mind, we
can turn to an assessment of the system of taxes in this
country.

PROBLEMS OF THE PRESENT TAX SYSTEM
AND ADVANTAGES OF THE VAT

The current structure of taxes in the United States
violates all of the principles of efficient taxation in some
degree. The base is defined too narrowly and is taxed at
nonuniform rates. The structure penalizes savings, dis-
courages exports, and encourages underground economic activity. In contrast, the VAT can be structured to tax a
very broad base uniformly and to do so without extending
itself to the taxation of savings or exports. Furthermore,
the invoice credit method of calculating the VAT gives firms
the incentive to self-enforce tax compliance, reducing the
prospect of underground activity.

The problems of the current system begin with their definition and measurement of the base. Its narrowness, even when speaking of the "broad" federal income tax, is the product of a large and growing number of exclusions, exemptions, deductions, tax credits, and shelters. These have induced people to use their resources in ways they would have deemed to be of too little value had favored tax treatment not distorted their appeal.

The exclusions include such flows as fringe benefits, imputed returns from owner-occupied housing, interest income on state and local bonds, a portion of dividend income, and many governmental transfers. Certainly, it is no accident that employers and employees have both pounced on the opportunities provided by new legislation to channel compensation through untaxed fringes. A resulting inefficiency from the use of in-kind payments occurs when such forms of compensation are made relatively more attractive by their tax treatment, while, in fact, they are less valuable than a comparable amount of cash would be. In addition, the growth in untaxed fringes is often blamed for having contributed to other disruptions, such as the explosion of health care demand and costs in recent years. Even though these exclusions are often demanded in the name of equity, it is quite likely that the incidence of the benefits from the preferential treatment of fringes is distributed regressively over the population. The federal exclusion of interest income on state and local bonds means that, to attract resources, these governmental bodies do not have to bid nearly so high as their private competitors in the loanable funds markets. Therefore, the cost of debt-financed public expenditures takes on the appearance of being lower than it truly is. In short, this exclusion may lead decisionmakers to undertake projects that otherwise would not be judged worthy.

In a similar fashion, the deductions allowed by the federal income tax narrow its base. Again, state and local decisionmakers are influenced by the deductibility of state and local taxes on the federal returns of their constituents. The true costs of projects at these levels of government become understated. Some otherwise unworthy expenditures will be approved in a state or locality when a portion of the costs can be exported to taxpayers beyond their geographic and political boundaries.

Furthermore, the deductibility of the interest charges on home mortgage payments induces the flow of resources into residential capital rather than into other more valuable forms of capital. In short, we have a capital <u>mix</u> problem in this country in addition to our better known problem--that our overall capital stock has been growing very slowly. Most of this capital mix problem is directly attributable to our current tax structure.

Only those deductions that, in fact, represent the costs of doing business or of otherwise supplying resources are warranted on efficiency grounds; for they appear in the base already, in the prices of the final goods in which they are used. Deductions allowed for almost any other type of expenditures lead to allocative distortions.

On equity grounds, almost as strong a criticism can be made of deductible expenditures. The benefits of such preferential tax treatments are in direct proportion to the individual's marginal tax rate. Consequently, in a system of progressive marginal rates, those who have greater incomes will obtain greater benefits from any dollar's worth of a deductible expense. The person in the 50 percent bracket will be able to reduce his tax bill by 50 cents for every dollar of deductible expense, while the individual in the 20 percent bracket will get a tax reduction of only 20 cents for every dollar of deductible expense. Indeed, it would require a very peculiar criterion of fairness to justify such a distribution of benefits.

Not only do many exclusions and deductions lead directly to inefficient resource substitutions within the marketplace, they lead indirectly to another inefficiency: their narrowing effect on the tax base implies the use of higher tax rates on the remaining base to raise the needed revenues. As noted elsewhere, this provides labor the incentive to switch itself outside the marketplace. Less efficient, untaxed, nonmarket activities become more attractive than their more efficient but taxed counterparts inside the market.

The VAT can be designed to tax a very broad base; and a VAT/transfer sharply differentiates the functions of taxation and redistribution. If substituted for one or more of our current tax instruments, the VAT could avoid or minimize the kinds of problems produced by the narrow bases now in use. It would provide no incentive to substitute fringe benefit compensation, would do nothing to distort the cost and benefit perceptions of the electorate in decisions about state and local public expenditures, and would minimize the capital mix distortion. Further, it would lead to none of the secondary efficiency problems of preferential tax treatment. And, through the use of demogrants (transfers) it would avoid the horizontal and vertical inequities of a system that benefits taxpayers in inverse proportions to their marginal tax rates--that is, in inverse proportions to their incomes.

An issue that is at least as important as the breadth of the base is the uniformity with which it is taxed. Certain examples of differential taxation are well known, such as the placement of higher excises on luxury items. However, there exist other, far more pervasive forms of nonuniform taxation. One that is much discussed by economists but is largely unrecognized by others is the corporate profits tax. Since dividends are taxed once by this tax and again by the income tax, there is little question but that this influences the allocation of resources between the corporate and noncorporate sectors within the economy. It leads to a migration of capital out of many corporate uses and into such noncorporate uses as residential home building and agricultural enterprise. Though all of these noncorporate uses are valuable, an inducement to allocate the resources differently than they would be by well-functioning markets is an inducement to use those resources less valuably than they could be.

Furthermore, since most savings are taxed by the federal income tax system, existing loopholes that allow taxes on savings to be deferred become sites of further inefficiencies. For example, in catering to stockholder preferences, corporations have the incentive to retain more of their earnings (pay out fewer dividends) than they would otherwise, since this provides stockholders a means of deferring their taxes on savings. This alters the mix of financial instruments chosen by corporations and the level of accumulated wealth within them. In all likelihood, we save less and in different ways in this country than we would if savings were uniformly exempted from taxation.

Another among the ills of corporate taxation is the application of different depreciation schedules to different types of capital. Not only do these schedules fail to reflect the true diminution of the value of the capital to which they apply, they diverge differentially from reality. One type of capital may be fully depreciated in three-quarters of its lifetime while another is fully depreciated in one-half of its true life. The result is that the perceived relative values of different forms of capital diverge from their true relative values. Again, we have an instance in which an existing tax instrument alters the mix of capital formation.

With corporate taxation, then, we have an instrument that serves neither efficiency nor equity. The use of the corporate tax to heap greater tax burdens on the rich may miss the mark badly and, at the very least, is an extremely cumbersome way to produce the desired tax incidence within an economy. We have the capacity to control the tax incidence much more directly and with far more certainty than is possible with this type of taxation.

The use of a VAT, on the other hand, makes absolutely no distinction between economic activity that does or does not pass through corporations. If a consumption-type VAT were substituted for the U.S. corporate tax, we would notice immediate improvements in the mix of activity between the corporate and noncorporate sectors, in the form and level of savings within the country, and in the capital mix. No longer would the task of measuring depreciation be required for tax purposes. Gone would be its many problems of measurement error, its administrative cost, and its extreme vulnerability to political mishandling.

One last source of nonuniform taxation is worth mention. In several instances, the federal income tax has been and still is defined to tax nominal rather than real magnitudes. Capital gains taxation is an excellent example of this. If an asset, purchased and held for one year, were to appreciate by 10 percent in an environment of a 10 percent rate of inflation, no real gain would be realized upon the sale of the asset. However, under current law, this asset would be treated as if the owner had experienced a 10 percent gain on the sale. In this respect, not only are savings taxed, they may be taxed at higher rates than are other portions of the base. In fact, as shown here, the effective marginal tax rate applied to them can exceed 100 percent. The penalty on savings and capital formation is severe in times of high inflation.

In addition to this recognition of the problems that accompany the differential taxation of savings, many economists now agree that even a uniform taxation of savings invokes a penalty that our economy, with its sluggish growth in capital, can hardly afford.[4] Though recent years have witnessed the introduction of new vehicles for the deferment of taxes on savings, such as IRAs, these efforts leave us a long distance from having a true consumption tax. In many instances, the existing means of deferring taxes on savings constrain individual choice inefficiently. It would be far better to have a tax that uses only personal consumption expenditures as its base. The consumption-type VAT is particularly suited in this respect. Some forms of consumption taxes, such as the consumption expenditures tax, require the use of savings accounts or other special financial instruments in order to remove savings from the base. The VAT, however, can exempt savings without the use of any special means of monitoring savings activity. It is an extremely straightforward means of accomplishing this goal.

Apart from the major problems surrounding narrow and unevenly taxed bases, the effects of the U.S. tax system on exports is of significant interest. To the extent that our individual and corporate income taxes show up in the prices of goods, they make those goods less attractive to foreign demanders. They discourage exports, and they do this in ways that cannot be remedied administratively. Far better would be a system of taxation in which exports could be exempted at a reasonable administrative cost. In fact, the VAT provides such a system. The invoice credit method of calculating the VAT is well designed for the task. Under this method, the producer pays a tax on the gross value of his output and receives tax credits for invoices that demonstrate that value-added taxes have been paid at earlier stages of the production process by his input suppliers. To exempt exports, only one small alteration needs to be made. Producers may still receive tax credits upon the presentation of the invoices for their inputs; however, they are forgiven the gross tax on that portion of their output that is exported. In one simple step, the VATs are eliminated along the entire chain of production for exported goods. Few other tax instruments offer a means that is this simple; and it is clear that under the income and corporate taxes it would be difficult or impossible to exempt exports.[5] Furthermore, the VAT enjoys an institutional advantage that many other taxes do not. On the assumption that it is shifted forward into the prices of final goods, the VAT has been declared to be an indirect tax by the General Agreement on Tariffs and Trade (GATT). As such, GATT allows export goods to be exempted from the VAT, while it does not accord such exemptions for direct taxes. Consequently, nations that employ the VAT possess an advantage by virtue of an international accord.

One of the most distinctive advantages of the VAT is that its structure strongly encourages the self-enforcement of tax compliance. This was one of the features that made its adoption particularly attractive in Europe, where tax evasion existed in serious proportions. With estimates of growing underground economic activity in the United States, the advantages of the VAT in this country are growing similarly.

In order to illustrate the tax compliance incentives inherent in the VAT (using the invoice credit method of calculation), consider a numerical example. Assume that Producer A manufactures an intermediate good in an economy in which a 10 percent VAT is the only form of taxation. Producer A buys inputs on the legitimate market for $10 inputs on which $1 of value-added tax has already been paid. Now, Producer A adds $5 worth of value to the product. If he were to sell the intermediate good he has produced for $15 on the legitimate market, he would have to pay $1.50 in gross taxes but would receive $1 in tax credit for the taxes that had been paid already. In short, he would receive $4.50 net of taxes for his productive activity.

Contrast this with a decision by Producer A to sell his output, the intermediate good, underground. In this circumstance he would not be able to sell his output for more than $13.50, since anyone buying from him underground knows that this intermediate good will not earn him any tax credit. Therefore, Producer A will receive no more than $3.50 for his productive efforts. Producer A and those who buy from him have everything to gain by conducting their exchange in legitimate markets.

There is only one instance that stands as an exception to this conclusion. If Producer A were making and selling a final good rather than an intermediate one, he might realize a slight gain from going underground. For a final good, using the numbers from the foregoing example, the consumer might be willing to pay as much as $15. If Producer A were able to evade his gross tax, he might make as much as $5 for his productive efforts, despite the fact that when selling underground he would not be eligible for the tax credits on the inputs purchased.

What this allows us to conclude, then, is that the VAT provides incentives for tax compliance at all but the final stage in the production process; and at that stage the gains from going underground are limited to the VAT at that stage alone. Seldom do tax instruments provide such a strong mechanism for self-enforcement.

To summarize, the current U.S. tax system is laden with problems. The VAT offers an opportunity to substitute for some of the most problematical elements of this system. Seldom does one find a single tax to promote savings and exports, and to provide the incentives that lead to the self-enforcement of tax payments. The VAT can produce these results, while at the same time providing any of a wide variety of possible incidences. In short, the VAT meets head-on the major efficiency and equity problems in our tax system.

INCIDENCE: THEORETICAL BACKGROUND

The incidence of the VAT is a major concern of its critics.[6] Too often they discuss the VAT under the faulty presumption that it <u>must</u> be regressive. In contrast, it will be demonstrated here that the VAT, when combined with a transfer, can take on <u>any</u> incidence that is desired. It can be designed to be distributionally neutral or even quite progressive. The choice belongs to the policymakers.[7]

In order to understand the basis of the popular notion that VATs are regressive, it is important to make explicit the underlying assumptions.

1. It is assumed that the tax is shifted fully into consumer prices. Tacitly, this is usually taken to imply that there are no effects on the incomes of the productive factors.[8]
2. It is assumed that people who have low current incomes spend larger proportions of their incomes on consumption goods (save less) than do people with higher current incomes.
3. It is assumed that current income is the best measure of ability-to-pay that can be used in the calculation of a tax's incidence over the population.

Only the second of these three can go unchallenged. The other two warrant a closer examination.

The assumption that the full effect of the VAT will be on consumer prices can arise from any of at least three origins. It can derive from the mistaken use of partial equilibrium analysis on a problem that requires a general equilibrium approach. It can follow from an assumption that the VAT will be matched by a commensurate increase in the transactions velocity of the money supply. Or it can result from an assumption that the Federal Reserve will accommodate a new VAT with a commensurate increase in the money supply and that the transactions velocity of money will remain virtually unchanged.[9] Though the last of these possibilities is the most likely, at least brief attention should be paid to all three.

What becomes clear is that the effects on prices cannot be known with certainty in advance. Within the profession there exist theoretical disagreements about the expected effects of such a tax, and there is uncertainty about the institutional response to such a tax by the Federal Reserve. A full shift forward of the tax into consumer prices is at one end of the range of possible effects. However, there also exist the possibilities that there would be no shift forward, with the VAT affecting only factor incomes, or that there would be a partial shifting forward into consumer prices with the remaining effects falling on factor incomes. In short, we cannot be confident of the first of the conventional assumptions.

The second of the conventional assumptions is correct. People who have low current incomes spend larger proportions of their incomes on consumption goods than do people with higher incomes (see Table 4.1). It is easy to see how this evidence, combined with the assumption that a VAT would be shifted fully into consumer prices, has been the basis of the conclusion that VATs are regressive. However, unstated here is the third of the conventional assumptions: that current income is a satisfactory measure of ability-to-pay. In fact, it is far from ideal; and it biases calculations of incidence that are toward regressivity.

Table 4.1

Consumer Expenditures Survey

Income Quintiles	Mean Income	Mean Total Consump. Expend.	Average Propensity to Consume[10]
1st	$ 3,347	$ 7,852	2.26
2nd	9,791	11,570	1.18
3rd	16,809	15,736	.94
4th	25,128	20,714	.82
5th	44,616	30,563	.69

Source: Consumer Expenditures Survey, 1980-81.

To illustrate this, it should be pointed out that there is much greater uniformity in people's propensities to consume out of lifetime income than to consume out of current income. That is, over an entire lifetime, individuals spend similar proportions of their incomes on consumption goods, poor and nonpoor alike. Those proportions are thought to be between 95 and 100 percent.[11] The point is that if people had exactly uniform propensities to consume out of their lifetime incomes, the VAT would have a uniform or proportional incidence over this population.[12]

In summary, two of the conventional assumptions bias the calculations of the VAT's incidence toward regressivity. If it were assumed that the VAT is not fully shifted into consumer prices and/or that the incidence should be based on lifetime incomes, the VAT would exhibit little or no regressivity, even in the absence of any redistributive transfer.

CALCULATIONS OF INCIDENCE: PRELIMINARY ISSUES

In order to demonstrate the strength of the conclusion that the VAT need not be regressive, the case will be made under the least favorable assumptions. It will be assumed, as the critics do, that the VAT is fully shifted into consumer prices and that current family income is a satisfactory measure of ability-to-pay. A taxable transfer in the form of a demogrant will be joined with the VAT as the means of altering its incidence.

The second of the preliminary issues that must be settled concerns the definition of the tax base. The largest possible base for the VAT would equal the total personal consumption expenditures of the population. Any exclusions from this base would result in the distortion of the relative prices of the taxed and untaxed goods. Economic theory suggests that this price distortion would induce consumers to substitute from the purchase of more highly valued consumption goods into the purchase of less valued ones. Clearly, this would imply an inefficient allocation of resources. Nonetheless, there have been numerous suggestions that substantial exclusions be made from total consumption expenditures in defining the actual base. Usually, such exclusions are justified on grounds of equity or political feasibility. However, because of the inefficiencies that result from such exclusions and because there exist superior means of altering the incidence of the VAT, a very broad base will be defined for the purposes of this chapter.

Only two exclusions will be recognized here: one on the basis of theory, and the other primarily on the basis of administrative practicality. Specifically, personal expenditures on education and on housing will be excluded. The exclusion of educational expenditures is justified since, in large part, they represent the purchase of capital goods, albeit the capital is human. The inclusion of these expenditures would distort the relative rewards of this kind of capital formation.

By contrast, the exclusion of housing expenditures has mainly practicality to recommend it. The annual consumption flows to owner-occupied housing are very difficult to measure, since they constitute nonmarket services. To tax such housing at the time that it is first produced and passes through the market would be much easier administratively; however, it would amount to the taxation of a significant proportion of individual saving (and capital formation), something that the proponents of VAT and other consumption taxes attempt to avoid quite explicitly.

Though the rationale of administrative ease can be invoked to justify the exclusion of owner-occupied housing flows from the VAT base, the same cannot be said for the exclusion of tenant-occupied housing. In most instances, this kind of housing does pass through markets and has a value that can be measured with ease. Here, though, the argument for exclusion is on the basis of efficiency. The differential taxation of close substitutes causes far greater inefficient resource substitution than does the differential taxation of goods that are not close substitutes. Consequently, though the preferential tax treatment of all housing may cause some inefficient resource substitutions, such inefficiencies are likely to be smaller than those that would occur if preferential tax treatment were given only to owner-occupied housing.

Even with these two exclusions, educational and housing expenditures, the size of the VAT base used here is about 82 percent of total personal consumption expenditures. It is among the broadest of the bases used by tax analysts. Though other minor exclusions might be justified on practical grounds, their effects will not be examined here since their magnitudes are of little consequence. The purpose of this chapter is not to forecast the effects of VATs with absolute precision; it is to illustrate the importance of a number of major issues that surround this tax policy.

Finally, among the preliminary issues, is a designation of the size of the VATs and the character of the joint transfers that are to be examined. For purposes of this chapter, VATs will be considered that are similar in size to those that have existed historically and have been discussed for adoption at the federal level in this country. The transfer to be examined here will be taxable, but otherwise will not be contingent on any discretionary characteristic of the recipient population. It will be a transfer to the entire population, with the amount to be received by any individual dependent on that person's demographic attributes. Because this type of transfer has demographic determinants, it is often referred to as a "demogrant."

The strongest virtue of the demogrant is the fact that individuals have no discretion over the size of the gross transfer they receive. This characteristic serves well the end of equity; and, without question, it serves the goal of efficient resource allocation. The gross transfer, unlike many of those in the existing welfare system, does nothing to alter people's decisions about their use of resources. It is economically neutral.

The gross transfer itself, when added to a VAT, changes the incidence of the VAT. A transfer of any absolute size constitutes a larger proportion of a low income than it does of any higher income. Defining the transfer to be taxable income alters the incidence further, depending on the structure of the marginal tax rates over the income ranges. Assuming a progressive structure to the marginal tax rates, taxable transfers produce more progressivity than do untaxed transfers.

To summarize, calculations of incidence will be based on assumptions that: ability-to-pay will be measured by current family income; the VAT will be shifted fully into the prices of consumption goods; a broad base will be used; and taxable, demogrant-type transfers will be used as a device to alter the incidence of the VAT. As already noted, the first two of these assumptions are made not because they are ideal, but because they will produce the most regressive incidences. They allow a proof of our conclusions under the worst-case circumstances.

CALCULATIONS OF INCIDENCE

The results presented here, calculated for the worst-case assumptions, illustrate several points.[13] First, it is shown that a VAT that is unaccompanied by any transfer does have a regressive incidence. Second, it is demonstrated that a VAT that is accompanied by a transfer (of moderate size) can be distributionally neutral. Third, it is shown that a VAT accompanied by a somewhat larger transfer can have a progressive incidence. Fourth, the sensitivity of these calculations to our underlying assumptions is illustrated. Finally, as examples of the uses of the VAT, there are presented specific VAT-transfer combinations that could replace some of this country's most problematical current means of raising public revenues: the corporate profits tax and the terribly large annual federal deficits.

Table 4.2 illustrates the first point. It shows that a VAT unaccompanied by any redistributive transfer does have a regressive incidence under the worst-case assumptions. It is this scenario that underlies the critics' concern over the VAT. These numbers suggest that a 10 percent VAT tax bill (with no transfer) would constitute 17.97 percent of the pretax income of the average family in the lowest quintile, but would amount to only 5.57 percent of the pretax income of the average family in the highest quintile. This effect would be continuous over the intermediate income categories.

Table 4.2

Incidence: 10 Percent VAT with No Redistributive Transfer (percent)

1st Quin.	2nd Quin.	3rd Quin.	4th Quin.	5th Quin.
17.97	9.65	7.73	6.77	5.57

To reiterate, the use of more realistic assumptions would produce a much less regressive incidence, even without the use of a transfer. However, it is important to demonstrate that this incidence can be altered without making any changes in our assumptions. Tables 4.3 and 4.4 do just that.

Table 4.3

Incidence: 10 Percent VAT plus a Moderate Taxable Transfer
Demonstration of Distributional Neutrality (percent)

1st Quin.	2nd Quin.	3rd Quin.	4th Quin.	5th Quin.
4.46	4.84	4.82	4.70	4.62

Table 4.4

Incidence: 10 Percent VAT plus a Larger Taxable Transfer
Demonstration of Distributional Progressivity (percent)

1st Quin.	2nd Quin.	3rd Quin.	4th Quin.	5th Quin.
0.48	3.31	3.89	4.04	4.32

Distributional neutrality could be approximated for a 10 percent VAT by combining it with a taxable cash transfer (demogrant) that is structured to distribute: $140 to each child under 18 years of age; $240 to each adult from 18 to 65; and $380 to the elderly, those 65 and older. For the purpose of calculating incidences, the transfer to each individual is subject to the income tax at the marginal rate that applies to the average family in the individual's quintile. This incidence is about as close to distributional neutrality as could be hoped for in practice. Furthermore, the revenue cost of the net transfer would be 33 percent of the entire revenues generated by the VAT. This would leave fully two-thirds of the revenue for other uses.

All that would have to be done to alter the incidence further would be to change the size of the transfer. Consider, for instance, the same 10 percent VAT combined with a taxable transfer structured to distribute: $220 to each child; $300 to each adult; and $500 to each of the

elderly. The resulting incidence is illustrated in Table
4.3. Naturally, the use of larger transfers would diminish
the VAT revenues available for nondistributional purposes.
However, the transfer used here to produce a progressive
incidence would cost only about 44 percent of the VAT revenues. Over half would be free for other uses.

The mechanics that underlie these distributional effects are straightforward. Though transfers are given to
the entire population, any dollar given to families in the
lower quintiles constitutes a larger proportion of their incomes than does a dollar given to families in the higher
quintiles. Second, because the demographic structure of
the population is not identical over the income quintiles,
the demographic determinants of the transfer alter the incidence. For example, proceeding from the lowest to the
highest quintiles, we find increasing numbers of children
and decreasing numbers of elderly per family. Differential
transfers along lines of these characteristics can produce
greater progressivity than could the same volume of aggregate transfers that do not so differentiate. Finally, defining the transfer to be taxable income increases the progressivity to the extent that the structure of the marginal
tax rates is progressive.

Again, it is worth emphasizing the influence of the
underlying assumptions on the calculations of incidence.
Recall the distributional neutrality produced by the VAT-
transfer combination illustrated in Table 4.4. If the very
same policy combination were employed but the incidence
were calculated on the basis of per capita current family
income rather than total family income, the incidence illustrated in Table 4.5 would be obtained. What appear to be
distributionally neutral results under the set of worst-case
assumptions shown in Table 4.2 turn out to be highly progressive when just one of those assumptions is relaxed.

Table 4.5

Incidence: 10 Percent VAT plus a Moderate Transfer Demonstration—Calculations Are Highly Sensitive to Assumptions (percent)

1st Quin.	2nd Quin.	3rd Quin.	4th Quin.	5th Quin.
8.71	11.13	13.01	15.05	15.70

Similarly, any given VAT-transfer combination would produce a more progressive incidence if calculations were based on assumptions that: lifetime family income (or lifetime per capita family income) be used as the measure of ability-to-pay; and the effects of the VAT do not fall entirely on consumer prices but fall, at least in part, on incomes. Conversely, the proportion of the VAT revenues required to accomplish any given distributional goal (through transfers) would be much smaller than was true under the worst-case assumptions.

However, the most important points that have been demonstrated are that: any distributional goal can be achieved under the worst-case assumptions; and even under these assumptions, it requires only about a third of the VAT revenues to produce distributional neutrality and only about 44 percent of the revenues to produce substantial progressivity. Clearly, the critics' concerns over the distributional implications of the VAT are unwarranted.

Having laid to rest the distributional issues surrounding the VAT, it is important to recognize the ways in which the VAT might be used to replace other means of raising public revenues. Two revenue-generating instruments come to mind immediately, though they are presented here for illustration and should not limit our creative thinking about still other candidates for VAT substitution. I refer specifically to the use of the VAT to substitute for both the existing corporate profits tax and for a substantial portion of the extraordinarily large volume of deficit financing that is being conducted at the federal level.

The corporate profits tax enjoys popular support because of three misconceptions. First, it is thought that corporations owe some fair share of taxes. Second, the corporate tax is thought to be highly progressive. And third, this tax is not viewed to have any adverse economic consequences.

In fact, corporations do not ultimately pay taxes. Their owners do. Further, those who pay taxes are not necessarily the ones who bear the tax burden. To the extent that the taxes are passed on, the employees of corporations and the consumers who buy the goods produced by corporations bear the tax. If, indeed, the popular notion were correct, that corporate taxes are not borne by individuals, we should use nothing but corporate taxes to raise our revenues. This would be the best of all worlds, a means of obtaining resources for public use that would not reduce the resources in the possession of individuals. Unfortunately, neither the corporate profits tax nor any other human invention has been able to repeal the condition of scarcity in our world. Taking resources for public use inevitably reduces those available for private use.

The second misconception is that the corporate profits tax is a highly progressive tax. Since we are not absolutely sure of the incidence of this tax--whether it falls on corporate owners, corporate employees, purchasers of corporate goods and services, or even others in the population--it is not at all clear that this is a progressive tax. If the concern is about incidence, we should use tax instruments in which the distributional effects are better known. Furthermore, even if the entire burden of the corporate profits tax were to fall on corporate owners, the incidence would not have the progressivity it is commonly believed to have. A study by two economists has demonstrated that, under this assumption, the corporate tax is proportional over the first nine deciles of income in the United States.[14] Only between the ninth and tenth deciles does it take on any real progressivity. That is, for 90 percent of the population the corporate tax is distributionally neutral, under an assumption that the burden is proportional to families' income from corporate ownership. Abolishing this tax and replacing it with another tax that is distributionally neutral would have little net effect on the incidence of the overall tax structure. Further, replacing the corporate profits tax with, say, a VAT-transfer that is progressive, might very well increase the progressivity of the incidence of our overall taxes.

Finally, and most important, the corporate profits tax constitutes a double taxation of a portion of the tax base. Profits are taxed once as the company earns them, and again when they flow to individuals as dividend income. This double taxation creates an incentive to channel resources away from their more productive uses in the corporate sector and into less productive uses elsewhere. This inefficiency has motivated many economists to call for an end to the use of this tax instrument. The VAT offers much more efficient means of raising the same revenues.

To illustrate this point, consider the goal of replacing the corporate profits tax with a VAT-transfer that would leave the incidence of the overall tax structure virtually unchanged. If, as mentioned above, the incidence of the corporate profits tax is almost proportional across the income classes, the use of a VAT-transfer that has similar effects would accomplish the goal. Table 4.6 illustrates just this case.

Table 4.6

5.5 Percent VAT Transfer: Replacement of Corporate Profits Tax Unchanged Incidence in the Overall Tax Structure (percent)

1st Quin.	2nd Quin.	3rd Quin.	4th Quin.	5th Quin.
2.62	2.70	2.68	2.61	2.55

If we were to consider the use of a 10 percent VAT-transfer combination, having the incidence illustrated in Table 4.3, $128 billion in post-transfer revenue could have been generated in 1984. That would have been enough revenue to reduce the federal deficit in that year to $48 billion or about 1.3 percent of GNP. That would have returned the country's ratio of deficit to national product to the level that prevailed in the late 1970s, the period just prior to the large escalation of federal deficits. Within a fairly short period, it probably would have allowed real interest rates to return to ranges within historical precedent. That would have stimulated the demand for capital goods and would have eliminated our interest-rate-driven balance-of-trade problems.

These two cases of VAT substitution--for the corporate profits tax and for a large portion of the annual federal deficit--are quite important, but are only illustrations of the possible uses of the VAT. In short, in all instances in which there exist problematical revenue-raising instruments, the VAT is a strong candidate as a replacement. It approaches economic neutrality with respect to efficient resource allocation and, as we have shown, it can be structured to accomplish any distributional goal that is desired.

FINDINGS

My 1976 study, A Plan for a National Demogrant Financed by a Value-Added Tax, demonstrated that the VAT can be used as a vehicle for the purpose of income redistribution. When combined with a demogrant, it can produce a very progressive incidence and can serve as a far superior substitute for our current system. The incidence of a 5.5 percent VAT combined with a transfer which is structured to distribute: $75 to each child; $130 to each adult; and $210 to each of the elderly. This 5.5 percent VAT would finance the $71 billion required to replace the corporate profits tax revenues in 1984 and, additionally, would finance the net transfer.[15] It would replace a highly inefficient system of taxation in this country without changing the distribution of income. Instead of obtaining the revenue by placing a very high and uneven rate of taxation on a small portion of the base, as the corporate tax does, the VAT would obtain the revenue by the use of a much lower marginal rate spread over the entire base.

The illustration in Table 4.6, of course, would demonstrate the incidence for any $71 billion revenue use where the instrument to be replaced had, itself, a proportional incidence. Though the incidence of the United States' annual federal deficit is not known by economists, the above described VAT-transfer would be sufficient to replace a large portion of the deficit at its 1984 or 1985 level. For 1984 the federal deficit was about $176 billion; the 1985 deficit is likely to be at about the same level.

The system of welfare now in place is unworkable, inequitable, and ineffective. The individual redistributive programs that exist have taken on lives of their own, outgrowing the capacities of their administrative structures. Neither individually nor as a whole do they represent a consistent effort to redress the problem of poverty; by making individuals' benefit levels highly contingent on income, they have produced serious work disincentives. They have hampered economic growth, the best long-term promise for the elimination of poverty in this country.

These programs, in the name of equity, spend far too many resources on the administrative act of redistribution. They convey some of their benefits in-kind, a form that is less valued by recipients than would be an equal amount of cash. Through inconsistent practice and eligibility requirements, they treat equal individuals unequally. The same volume of resources could reduce much more poverty.

The VAT/demogrant study examined the poverty-reducing ability of a demogrant (treated as taxable income) that is financed by a 10 percent VAT. In contrast with the VAT/demogrant combinations discussed earlier in this chapter, in this instance the entire VAT revenues were devoted to the demogrant for redistributive purposes. The general conclusion was that this policy, examined for 1973 data, could then have reduced the size of the impoverished population in the United States by 31 percent; at the same time, 53 percent of the entire population would be net beneficiaries. Further, all of the poor would be aided—and in a consistent way. To the extent that income (before the demogrant) and family size are measures of need, this policy would remedy the severe inconsistencies of the existing system.

More important, the VAT/demogrant combination provides income redistribution without the usual work disincentives. The distinctive quality of a demogrant is that it does not penalize individuals who earn additional income. Under the present means-tested system, a poor person benefiting from several programs simultaneously can be subject to a marginal tax rate in excess of 100 percent. Additional income not only reduces benefits under the AFDC and food stamp programs, but can make the earner ineligible for in-kind programs such as Medicaid, school lunch, and public housing. Why take an entry-level job if it will make you "worse off"?

The poor find themselves locked into a position of dependency. Under a demogrant, additional earned income is subject only to the income tax, having a marginal rate for entry-level jobs of 14 percent or lower, depending on family size. Thus, the poor have an opportunity to improve their economic status substantially through additional earnings (Wall Street Journal, September 17, 1985, p. 1).

Table 4.7 summarizes the findings numerically. It reflects the 10 percent VAT already mentioned and a demogrant structured to distribute annually $522 to each adult and $232 to each child.

CONCLUSION

The structure of the U.S. tax system treats people unfairly and causes resources to be used inefficiently. Both popular misunderstandings and special interests have produced a narrow and unevenly taxed base in this country. Savings and exports are penalized, while nonmarket

Table 4.7

Families Made Nonpoor by VAT/Demogrant Plan

Family Size	1	2	3	4	5	6	7	Total
# of low-income families (000s)	4,674	1,697	863	741	620	368	539	9,502
Median income ($)	1,411	1,983	2,346	3,133	3,584	4,114	5,033	
Average demogrant ($)	522	957	1,178	1,465	1,732	1,999	2,373	
Census poverty line ($)	2,239	2,874	3,525	4,512	5,322	5,979	7,359	
Effective poverty income* ($)	1,908	2,130	2,607	3,386	3,989	4,422	5,540	
% of low-income families made nonpoor	20.5	41.9	40.7	42.0	39.4	41.5	38.4	30.9
# of low-income families made nonpoor (000s)	958	711	351	311	244	152	207	2,934
Gain for median low-income families ($)	381	759	943	1,152	1,374	1,588	1,870	

*Families whose income before the demogrant is above this level will receive a net gain from the program large enough to raise them above the census poverty line.
   Source: Author's estimates.

and underground activity are encouraged. The use of a value-added tax, in place of part or all of our current tax mix, would make real headway in solving these problems. The goal of efficiency would be well served; and, as the special contribution of this study, it has been demonstrated that a VAT/demogrant could fulfill any standard of equity. Indeed, a VAT/demogrant could achieve two large and separate policy purposes: tax reform and welfare reform.

If designed properly, the VAT would apply to a very broad base and would tax that base uniformly. It would do this without any bias against savings or exports, and in a way that would greatly reduce the incentives to engage in underground activity. Relative to the current system, it would drive far fewer resources out of their more productive market uses; and contrary to the conventional wisdom, the VAT/demogrant would be more compatible with common notions of equity. The choice of tax incidence would be in the hands of the policymakers; and their decisions would be more apparent to the electorate because of the simplicity of the VAT/demogrant structure. Furthermore, the use of this policy could eliminate the need for many layers of administrative bureaucracy, both in tax and welfare administration.

For a long while the economic neutrality of the VAT has been lauded by economists. This chapter has made it clear that the VAT can be fair and that the fairness can be produced at a lower cost than under extant policies. Having laid to rest any reservations about the equity of the VAT, the appeal of this policy instrument should be clear to all.

NOTES

1. Good bibliographies of the vast literature on the VAT are available in Richard W. Lindholm, "The Value-Added Tax: A Short Review of the Literature," Journal of Economic Literature 8 (December 1970):1178-79, and in Robert P. Crum, Research and Publication in Value-Added Taxation: A Comprehensive Background and Compilation (Monticello, Ill.: Vance Bibliographies, 1984). An excellent analysis of the VAT is available in Richard W. Lindholm, The Economics of VAT (Lexington, Mass.: D. C. Heath, 1980).

2. Robert P. Crum, "Value-Added Taxation: The Roots Run Deep into Colonial and Early America," Accounting Historians Journal 9 (Fall 1982):25-42.

3. To determine whether this favored treatment of exports is efficient requires a very involved examination of all of the other governmental influences of the prices of their goods. That kind of examination exceeds the scope of this chapter.

4. The question of whether it is efficient to exempt savings from the tax base is an empirical one. The exemption of savings narrows the base, which increases the marginal tax rate that must be applied to the remaining base if tax revenues are to remain constant. The preference for the exemption of savings is based on an assumption that tax-induced distortions of the savings decision lead to greater inefficiencies than do tax-induced distortions of the decision to conduct market activity, for example, through participation in the labor market.

5. It should be noted that the economic effects of the corporate and income taxes are not known with certainty. If these taxes do not get passed on to export goods, their replacement by a VAT would have little influence on the U.S. balance of trade.

6. The incidence of a tax on an individual is usually calculated as his or her tax bill (or tax effect) as a proportion of ability-to-pay.

7. The reader should be reminded that a preference for overall progressivity in the tax structure does not require each of a country's tax instruments to exhibit progressivity.

8. Productive factors are broadly classified by economists as land (standing for all natural resources), labor, capital intermediate inputs, and entrepreneurial ability.

9. The simple equation that summarizes these points is expressed: $MV = PT$, where M represents the size of the money supply; V represents the velocity or the rate at which the money supply is used to carry out the purchase and sale of newly produced final goods; P represents the prices of these final goods; and T represents the volume of the transactions (exchanges) of these newly produced final goods. It is, therefore, a simple matter to conclude that for P to rise there must be a compensating change in one or more of the other three variables.

10. An average propensity to consume is computed by dividing a family's consumption expenditures by its income. That is, it constitutes the proportion of a family's income that is devoted to spending on consumption goods. It should be noted that the family that has an average propensity that exceeds unity is either drawing down past savings or is borrowing against future savings.

11. The only exceptions to this are individuals at the high end of the range of lifetime incomes. They consume a somewhat smaller proportion of their lifetime incomes (save more on a lifetime basis) than do others.

12. One qualification of this statement is in order. Though individuals would bear the same nominal incidences over their lifetimes, the present values of these incidences might not be identical. They would differ if individuals proportioned their expenditures differently over their lifetimes. That is, one dollar spent now would have a greater present value than would one dollar spent in any future period, assuming positive interest rates prevail. Likewise, one dollar of a tax bill incurred now would have a greater burden than would one dollar of a tax bill incurred in any future time period.

13. All calculations of tax incidence that appear in the tables of this section are based on data obtained from the Consumer Expenditures Survey, 1980–81, recently published by the Bureau of Labor Statistics.

14. Edgar K. Browning and William R. Johnson, The Distribution of the Tax Burden (Washington, D.C.: American Enterprise Institute, 1979), Table 14.

15. If a more progressive incidence were desired, that could be accomplished with the use of a somewhat larger VAT and larger transfer.

REFERENCES

Aaron, Henry J., ed. 1981. The Value-Added Tax: Lessons from Europe. Washington, D.C.: Brookings.

Aaron, Henry J., and Joseph A. Pechman, eds. 1981. How Taxes Affect Economic Behavior. Washington, D.C.: Brookings.

Atkinson, A. B., and J. E. Stiglitz. 1972. The Design of Tax Structures: Direct Versus Indirect Taxation and Economic Efficiency. Journal of Public Economics 6 April:97-119.

Boskin, Michael J. 1978. Federal Tax Reform: Myths and Realities. San Francisco, Calif.: Institute for Contemporary Studies.

Bradford, David F., and the U.S. Treasury Tax Policy Staff. 1984. Blueprints for Basic Tax Reform. 2nd ed. Arlington, Va.: Tax Analysts.

Browning, Edgar K., and William R. Johnson. 1979. The Distribution of the Tax Burden. Washington, D.C.: American Enterprise Institute.

Crum, Robert P. 1982. Value-Added Taxation: The Roots Run Deep into Colonial and Early America. Accounting Historians Journal 9. Fall:25-42.

_____. 1984. Research and Publications in Value-Added Taxation: A Comprehensive Background and Compilation. Monticello, Ill.: Vance Bibliographies.

Due, John F. 1970. Proposals for a Federal Value-Added Tax. Illinois Business Review 27. February:6-8.

_____. 1965. Should the Corporation Income Tax Be Replaced by the Value-Added Tax? Proceedings of the Fifty-Seventh Annual Conference on Taxation, 1964. Harrisburg, Pa.: National Tax Association:431-39.

Greene, Leonard M. 1976. A Plan for a National Demogrant Financed by a Value-Added Tax. White Plains, N.Y.: Institute for Socioeconomic Studies.

Kaldor, Nicholas. 1964. A Memorandum on the Value-Added Tax. In Essays on Economic Policy, vol. 1. London: Duckworth, pp. 266-93.

Lindholm, Richard W. 1980. The Economics of VAT. Lexington, Mass.: D.C. Heath.

_____. 1970. The Value-Added Tax: A Short Review of the Literature. Journal of Economic Literature 8. December:1178-89.

McLure, Charles E., Jr., and Norman B. Ture. 1972. Value Added Tax: Two Views. Washington, D.C.: American Enterprise Institute.

O'Mahoney, J.C. 1940. Senate Bill 3560, 76th Congress, 2nd Session, March 11. Congressional Record 86 (Part 3), pp. 2648-53.

Pechman, Joseph A. 1983. Federal Tax Policy. Washington, D.C.: Brookings.

Pechman, Joseph A., ed. 1980. What Should Be Taxed: Income or Expenditure? Washington, D.C.: Brookings.

Schuyler, Michael. 1984. Consumption Taxes: Promises & Problems. Washington, D.C.: Institute for Research on the Economics of Taxation.

Shoup, Carl S. 1968. Consumption Tax and Wages Type and Consumption Type of Value-Added Tax. National Tax Journal 21. June:153-61.

_____. 1967. Fiscal Harmonization in Common Markets. New York: Columbia University Press.

True, Norman B. 1979. The Value-Added Tax: Facts and Fancies. Washington, D.C.: Heritage Foundation.

Ullman, A. 1980. Does America Need VAT? Yes. World 14. Winter:30-31.

United States Department of Labor, Bureau of Labor Statistics. 1985. Consumer Expenditure Survey: Interview Survey, 1980-81. Bulletin 2225. Washington, D.C.: U.S. Government Printing Office.

5

Withholding on All Incomes

Jim Bates and Dave Gerrie

INTRODUCTION

There is a growing realization on Capitol Hill that the nation faces an economic crisis that may well be far beyond the ability of the political system to handle. The deficit and debt continue to climb, and for all the rhetoric and ringing speeches by both parties there is little action that can be taken without damaging the political foundations that support the very politicians who must make the courageous decisions. There are few economic theorists in the Congress and even fewer theories that seem to address the underlying problems. The suspicion exists that outside the Floor, despair rather than a commitment to necessary change reigns.

During the great debate over savings and dividend income withholding, Senator Robert Dole's premonition that meaningful tax reform would be set back 20 years if the measure was defeated seemed to many like simple posturing. His words now haunt the halls of Congress as, one by one, the realities of reform slip past. Nonetheless, whether the theory advocated argues that it is a matter of growing out of the deficits or a matter of increased taxes and dramatic cuts, the fear is that no combination of tools exists that will curb the careening economy. There is a very real fear that we will drift into an uncontrollable chaos where draconian, emergency measures will chart the path.

It is not the intention of this chapter to rehash the debate over the deficits and the best means to reduce them.

The current state of our economy is, most would agree, perilous. It is the intention here to look closely at the opportunities to establish an expanded income tax withholding with an eye toward two goals: furthering the reform of the system and increasing revenues.

The system of revenue collection is responsive to neither the financial needs of the system nor to the political realities of Washington and the states. The failure of the tax system is, indeed, a debacle of monumental proportions.

There is a basic condition that must be met: whatever changes are made in the income tax system, they must, from a political perspective, be relatively gradual. It is unlikely that the Congress would be willing to undertake a major, untested overhaul of the system that provides the vast majority of the funds upon which the government operates. Revenue options that deal with the income tax system are, themselves, likely to be incremental. Even the massive reform packages that are seriously proposed on Capitol Hill are incremental in nature: closing loopholes, tightening compliance, insuring equity, and gaining unreported taxable income.

There is little debate that the U.S. income tax system meets most of the tests of a "debacle," a total failure or fiasco. No matter from which perspective you examine the system, there are cracks. From the perspective of the federal government, major problems begin with compliance--and the whole range of problems associated with taxpayers not paying their taxes either completely or on time. The ultimate end of taxation--raising essential revenues--is derailed with the inability of the Congress to legislate rational tax laws that raise adequate revenues to sustain consensus national goals without incurring excessive costs.

As lecturer and economist Alan Schick likes to say, "Congress is very good at distributing governmental largesse; it is not so good at distributing the pain that attends this distribution." In particular, he points to the changing nature of the federal legislative branch: through most of its recent history Congress, as an institution, spent much of its public time dispensing favors, dams, entitlements, and deductions. In recent years, however, the federal coffers have run low--for a whole host of reasons--and Congress now finds itself in the difficult position of dispensing program cuts. The process and programs for reductions are much different and much more difficult. The only alternative is to raise taxes . . . and thus the resultant partisan game of "chicken" on Capitol Hill.

From the perspective of those on the receiving end of tax reform--those who must do the collecting, make the plans, and carry out the private sector initiatives--the changes in the financial system are often catastrophic. The involvement of a variety of financial agents as lobbyists on the Hill illustrates the point, as they attempt to demonstrate the unfair burdens imposed upon one group or another by the latest wrinkle in the tax code. New information-reporting requirements, withholding practices, as well as new consumer services are all being eyed by the federal government. Resistance to these measures by the agents has itself intensified. As a result of some recent Washington battles, it is evident that changes in the tax law that would impose either restrictions or burdens upon these agents will be met with a spirited defense.

From the taxpayers' point of view, there is a consistent and widespread opinion that the income tax is unfair. Beyond that, the belief is common that this unfair system is also unfairly applied to the middle class while the poor and the wealthy escape. This sentiment is manifested in the decreasing compliance rates (even in areas where compliance is easily enforced) and in taxpayer participation in the underground and informal marketplaces, where income taxes are not collected.

For the system as a whole these are ominous signs. The tax system, even in its unreformed state, must continue to deliver a constant stream of revenue to the federal government. In the monumental tax compliance report of 1983, the IRS concluded that "The percentage of all income voluntarily reported declined from 91.2% in 1973 to 89.3% in 1981" (Department of Transportation, 1983). Obviously, there is no single, simple change that will resolve this debacle. Yet "tweaking the dial of tax reform" is a necessary beginning to reform the problems of overcomplexity, unfairness, and willful noncompliance. This section deals directly with one such change: the increase in the scope of tax withholding at the source, both in terms of types of income withheld and the methods of withholding.

The promises of such changes are that increased compliance will gain more revenue without increasing taxes, and gain those revenues in a far more timely fashion. A possible side benefit could be increased credibility in the tax system as well--something that is lacking in the current system.

Withholding appears from IRS statistics and from sources in other nations to be an effective means of gaining compliance and thereby increased revenues. Some of the revenue estimates, indeed, are substantial. The hypothesis is that "If some withholding is good, then more withholding would probably be better." We will test this hypothesis here.

We have examined the process of withholding--as currently practiced and as proposed--as a process that would increase tax compliance and credibility in the system. There are a number of components of withholding that make it more or less effective as a tax-collection tool. These components can be extrapolated onto various income types that are not now subject to withholding. This analysis can indicate (in the absence of other political factors) those incomes in which an incremental extension of withholding would be cost effective, manageable, and tolerated by the taxpaying public.

One final word about the political process itself that should be considered when dealing with avenues of tax reform: reality is malleable for the political world. Politics is seldom thoroughly footnoted and politicians are even less frequently taken to task for having had an incorrect theory. Expressed in the simplest form, the aphorism that "Outside the Beltway, people believe that if it works, it must be right: inside the Beltway, people believe that if it's right, it must work," is a telling comment on the political process. The individual politician has a difficult time weighing the material consequences of one policy against another. The political consequences-- again, whether or not they have any basis in reality--are far more easily weighed and acted upon. The lesson here is that political tradition and history are major factors in tax reform and withholding policy. These factors, whether right or wrong, form an economic reality that always must be taken into account.

INCOME TAX COMPLIANCE

A cornerstone of the U.S. income tax system is the voluntary compliance by taxpayers both to report their income and to pay their taxes. It is essential that the vast majority of Americans continue to comply voluntarily. There is no realistic means of enforcing compliance on an unwilling public; therefore, one of the great unspoken fears in government is a massive tax revolt. Noncompliance, as defined by the IRS, is up dramatically in recent years. It can be attributed to a number of factors, including willful tax evasion and accidental errors on the part of otherwise honest and willing taxpayers.

At the very top of those income groups that voluntarily comply are those who earn their income solely from wages and salaries. The stability of this compliance has been instrumental in keeping the overall compliance figures regularly stable over time. Without the wages and salaries factor, the overall figure would have declined far more than the actual drop from 1973 to 1981.

As Table 5.2 illustrates, compliance figures between different sources of income vary greatly and consistently over the years. This table also identifies the tools that the IRS uses to bolster withholding. These tools work to insure compliance by either negative or positive means:

1. Auditing and publication: a process where taxpayers' returns are inspected for accuracy, and the taxpayer is called to account.
2. Withholding at source of a percentage of the wage or salary against the total tax liability.
3. Fines and penalties: a stringent system of penalties for noncompliance.
4. Informational reporting: the reporting of transactions and income by transaction agents, brokers, and others.

Each of these compliance mechanisms has its inherent difficulties that sharply reduces its efficacy in practice. Auditing of returns has severe limitations from both a cost and a technical perspective. The blizzard of information reporting actually has clogged the IRS system. Simply matching the income reported with the tax return information has, at least to this point, overwhelmed the IRS and its ability to detect problems in any more than a small statistical sampling of taxpayers.

Enforcement measures such as auditing (either by category or return, sampling, or upon certain "trigger" categories of income) and the fines and penalties at the end of the taxpaying road, turned out to have severe limitations. Increased enforcement measures have only a very limited effect upon compliance and are usually viewed as little more than harassment by many taxpayers. In addition, enforcement has the problem of being wrong a substantial proportion of the time. The incidents of enforcement abuse are becoming more widely publicized:

> The number of innocent victims nabbed by
> the IRS is almost undoubtedly going to
> keep growing as the federal government in-
> tensifies its tax-collection efforts. . . .
> The consequences of the screwups, unless
> the agency takes extraordinary measures to
> rectify them, could be increasing tax eva-
> sion, even worse relations between the IRS
> and taxpayers and growing distrust of the
> government in general" (Swardson, 1985,
> p. 85).

A great deal of compliance rests upon the credibility of the system and the trust of taxpayers. In this situation, efforts by the IRS to increase compliance often damage this credibility and, if we are to believe the above author, further injure this essential credibility. The end result is more enforcement, more costs, and less compliance. The evidence suggests that the psychic side of compliance is, in the end, more important than any enforcement measures the IRS could bring to bear. "It is likely that the probability of detection is a more effective deterrent than civil penalties assessed and sustained in litigation" (Hoff, 1982, p. 444). From a policy point of view, then, we must choose compliance tools that do not damage the credibility and trust in the system.

The IRS has provided six primary reasons for increasing noncompliance in voluntary tax payments. They are as follows:

> 1. Changes in taxpayers' fundamental
> attitudes toward income tax compliance or
> their perceptions concerning the fairness
> of the tax laws.
> 2. Changes in the risks associated
> with noncompliance because of new provi-
> sions in the Internal Revenue Code or be-
> cause of changes in the levels of income
> tax enforcement activities.
> 3. Changes in the real marginal bur-
> den of income taxes.

4. Changes in the distribution of income among groups of taxpayers with different rates of compliance.

5. Shifts in the composition of income generally have better compliance to other types or vice versa, and

6. Improvements or deterioration in the quality of income tax compliance measurements and data (Department of Transportation, p. 7).

From what we have discussed previously, this listing is not complete without the addition of a seventh category. Listing obstacles placed before the taxpayer that would prevent, or at least make more difficult, voluntary compliance.

Obstacles to accurate and voluntary reporting of income are substantial, and for some income types are particularly significant. A discussion of these obstacles is relevant, especially when considering actual withholding compliance. In general, to complete an accurate and timely return, or to accurately withhold income for this return, the taxpayer or agent must have information on: gross annual income; the personal situation with the taxpayer's deductions and allowable costs of doing business; and a reasonable knowledge of tax preparation. For the actual process of withholding from income, substantial accounting and recordkeeping skills are essential. As we have noted, these requirements differ from one income to another depending upon the nature of the income and the presence or absence of an agent. We have summarized in Table 5.1, from the taxpayers' perspective, the potential obstacles to accurate and timely filing of withheld taxes.

From this table alone it can be seen that some income types are much harder than others to work with, as there are paperwork obstacles to filing adequate tax returns. It is probably not unreasonable to suspect that the harder the return to file, the lower the compliance rate.

One further problem comes from conflicting reports of income actually earned by a taxpayer (see Table 5.2). This is especially relevant in the case of income received from server tips. Other types of income may well be consistently underreported to escape tax liabilities; again, it is reasonable to suspect that this is the case with tip

income as well. Without a full accounting at any point in
the transaction, the tip income earner is free to provide
an estimate of income received. On the other hand, it is
to the benefit of employers in these cases consistently to
overestimate tip income, so as to compensate for the commonly low wages in the service sector.

Table 5.1

Filing Obstacles

	Record-keeping	Accounting	Gross Tax	Tax Forms	Knowledge Required
Wages and salaries	low	low	low	low	n/a
Dividends	high	high	low	high	mod.
Interest income	high	high	low	high	mod.
Capital gains	mod.	high	low	high	low
Self-employed	mod.	mod.	high	mod.	n/a
Informal supplier	mod.	mod.	low	mod.	mod.
Pensions and low annuities	low	low	high	mod.	n/a
Rents and royalties	mod.	high	low	high	low
Refunds	low	low	high	low	high
Tip income	mod.	low	high	low	high

Recordkeeping: The requirement that an employee or
agent maintain complete records of transactions.

Accounting: Does the employee or agent have to keep
separate accounts for tax purposes?

Gross tax: Is it required that the employee or agent
have a knowledge of what the gross annual income of the taxpayer will be?

Tax forms: How complete a knowledge is required of tax
forms and IRS regulations?

Knowledge of taxpayer: How complete a knowledge is required on the taxpayer's deductions, exemptions, etc.?

Table 5.2

Types of Income and Compliance

Income	Volun	Pub	Fin	In	W/h	Est. Tax
Wages and salaries	93.9	x	x	x	x	x
Dividends	93.7	x	x	x		
Interest	86.3	x	x	x		
Capital gains	59.4	x	x	x		x
Nonfarm prop.	50.3	x	x			x
Farm prop.						
Partnership	47.0	x	x			x
Informal supplier	20.7	x	x			x
Rents	37.2	x	x	x	x	x
Royalties	61.2	x	x	x		x
Estate	74.2	x	x	x	x	x
Tax refund	62.0	x	x	x		
Tip income		x	x	x	x	

From the point of view of this chapter, noncompliance is a serious problem. But more than the mere fact of foregone revenues to the federal government, if increased compliance can be gained without the appearance of taxpayer harassment, perhaps further and unexpected gains can be made that would be associated with the increased credibility. The "tax gap" of unreported income rose, for example, from $29.3 billion in 1973 to $87.2 billion in 1981. In addition, all available evidence points to the fact that this income is gained from sources outside the wage and salaries categories, and would probably be taxed at fairly high marginal rates. It is income that is gained, furthermore, in legitimate enterprise. As Table 5.3 notes, "income from legal sources, self-employment income and investment income, are the principal sources of income not reported" (Department of Transportation, 1983, p. 444).

In Table 5.3, the government has identified a sample of those who failed to comply with the tax code. In this sample, the IRS gained a record of 246 wins, 47 losses, and 66 draws out of the total of 359 cases that went to court. It is an enviable record for the IRS in terms of costs to the government and the actual collected amount. The conclusion of the study was that the "detection and estimate of income not reported on a false return is inefficient, and expensive in terms of man hours, and in addition the tax collection rate at the end of this process is unacceptably low" (Hoff, 1982, p. 450).

Table 5.3

Caught Protesters

Occupation	Percent
Proprietor	25.3
Shareholder	16.4
Professional	16.2
Waiter/waitress	8.6
Employee	9.2
Farmer	1.9
Landlord	1.1
Gambler	1.1
Housewife	0.6
Salesman	0.6
Cab driver	0.3
Gambler	6.7
Embezzler	1.9
Narcotics	0.8
Larceny/forgery	0.8
Other	4.2
Unknown	2.2
Total	100.0

The conclusion that has to be drawn is that increased enforcement, even down to the point of litigation and penalties, is probably not cost-effective. IRS Commissioner Sheldon Cohnen agreed: "1099s [information returns] and audits are not as effective as withholding." When we place all the compliance tools available to the IRS together, by far the competitive advantage is held by withholding at the source.

This is particularly accurate when we consider the category for noncompliance that was absent from the IRS listing of obstacles. For the average taxpayers who find themselves with income that is not subject to withholding, immediately obstacles appear in their path to accurate and timely compliance. The forms are cumbersome, complex, and, at times, difficult to procure. Estimated taxes require some lump-sum payment--sums that may not be available depending upon the cash flow of the operation and the net income of the enterprise. For incomes where the actual income is reported regularly to the taxpayer but where taxes may be paid only annually, the burden of lump-sum payment can be considerable.

These are obstacles that prevent even well-intentioned taxpayers from accurately reporting income and paying their taxes on time. All the compliance tools available to the IRS are, essentially, applied after the fact. They are irrelevant only to insuring voluntary compliance.

BACKGROUND

Withholding taxes from income has a long history in American tax law. The beginnings of withholding were relatively modest. From 1913 to 1916, a withholding requirement existed on certain interest payments to taxpayers. The Tariff Act of 1913 provided for withholding on this income in excess of $3,000. With the Revenue Act of 1917, a system of "informational reporting" for income over the personal exemption replaced the withholding provisions. This is the last the tax code saw of the withholding provisions on interest and dividends, although attempts were made to reintroduce it with the 1943 act, as part of a Revenue Act of 1950 (in this event a 10 percent flat rate was withheld), the Rate Extension Bill of 1960, the Revenue Act of 1962 (at a 20 percent flat rate), and in 1980 (15 percent), and finally in the 1982 tax measure (TEFRA, 10 percent).

The most common type of withholding began during World War I as a result of drastically increasing revenue requirements to keep the war economy supplied. After 1943 and to the present, this nation has had withholding on all wages and salaries in a graduated fashion, based upon estimated year-end gross income.

Up to World War II, income taxes had been primarily a matter for the wealthy. The Current Tax Payment Act of 1943 changed the income tax, and withholding on wages and salaries went well into the middle classes. It was recognized at the time of passage that this would work a hardship on many Americans who, after paying the prior year's full tax in a lump-sum payment, would then have current taxes withheld. As a result, the legislation provided for a six-month "forgiveness period" of the prior year's taxes.

The intent of the withholding provisions of the Current Tax Payment Act was twofold. On the one hand, it was recognized that the extension of income taxes to millions of Americans would require, under the then existing lump-sum payment system, considerable fiscal discipline for Americans to save for their tax payments. It was suspected that such savings would not be generally made, and that the result would be massive and immediate default. Withholding made these "savings" for the taxpayer, taking it relatively painlessly out of their pay envelopes.

A second and greater revenue consideration was that the government would get the use of the withheld funds far sooner under a current payment system than with a year-end lump-sum payment. Thus, withholding would result in increased revenues, as well as the use of these revenues far sooner.

As part of the Current Tax Payment Act, the estimated tax system was instituted for nonwage earners in which quarterly estimates of tax liability and payments of a portion of that liability were required.

If the original goals of withholding were to reduce the lump-sum burden upon taxpayers and to provide current payments of tax liabilities, then the current discussion of withholding focuses upon a far different intent. The goal of increased revenues remains stable, yet compliance with the tax laws has entered the equation as a major factor.

Withholding has evolved into probably the strongest compliance tool in the IRS arsenal. Much like "information reporting"--which, on the surface, is intended to provide information on types of transactions--the current system is now evolving into a compliance system of its own. That, however, was something different from what was originally intended, and marks a departure point for this chapter. The following sections of this chapter will look at the original concept and its evolution into a compliance tool, and then trace the characteristics of this tool, with the final goal of a means of identifying beforehand areas in which withholding could be profitably applied.

There are a number of ways in which we can examine withholding and the taxpayer's relation to paying taxes. Further still, the actual types of withholding common in tax practice can be closely scrutinized. The goal here is to examine, in a fairly rigorous fashion, the various styles and methods of withholding so that we can apply this knowledge to incomes and areas not covered by the current process.

As outlined previously, the practice of withholding rests upon two fundamental ideas: first, that taxpayer compliance is enhanced with withholding, and second, that the nonfinancial burden on the taxpayer will be minimized. As a practical matter, it is reasonable to assume that some component of compliance is, itself, the ease of payment. There are six basic factors that have to be considered when examining withholding: these factors, in sum, make for compliance and for simplicity of the system.

If a primary reason behind withholding by an agent is compliance, then the first factor we should consider is the presence or absence of an agent or third party to withholding. The role of the agent is to withhold a proportional sum from the gross payment. In addition, the third-party agent is essential, from a purely human perspective, in that the agent is far more likely to be consistently accurate about income amounts withheld. There is a disincentive to accurate reporting under current law for employers, but, by and large, the presence of third parties can insure high levels of compliance.

A second compliance-related factor involves the agent's knowledge of the taxpayer. Some schemes of withholding and types of income require a great deal of knowledge about the taxpayer. This information involves current financial and marital situation, number of dependents, possibly the gross family income, various identifying numbers, and the address of the taxpayer. On the other hand, some income agents require little knowledge about the taxpayer to calculate and return the required taxes. From our point of view, the higher the level of knowledge, the more accurate the withholding.

The type of payments by which the income is received is also an important factor. For certain types of income, withholding requires that the income be received in relatively regular, periodic, and proportional payments. A certain percentage of withholding can be calculated from this information. Other income may well arrive in one or two lump sums over the taxation period. To complicate matters, some of what might appear on a tranaction basis may well be a loss or cost of doing business, depending upon the peculiar circumstances of the taxpayer, which are also important. Given the relatively large numbers of inaccurate and incomplete returns, it is clear that not everyone is equally able to calculate income and tax liability. From a compliance point of view, the errors may be either to over- or underpay. From the individual's or agent's point of view, the level of expertise may require them to contract out for professional assistance, thereby considerably increasing the costs of paying taxes.

The type of tax payment is also important, from a taxpayer's point of view. It is generally recognized that lump-sum payments are much more difficult to make than graduated payments. In addition, the individual's discipline and financial circumstances during the tax year may well place self-withholding of funds in a different priority. Emergencies will, of course, occur. There is also a wide variation in the budgeting and discipline characteristics of individuals.

Considerable evidence supports this hypothesis of "ease to the taxpayer." As President Reagan summarized the sentiment in 1983, "Most wage earners already prefer to have tax withheld from their paychecks rather than having to come up with the whole bundle on that annual day of reckoning." He was not challenged on this assertion. The hypothesis is further supported by the experience of voluntary third-party withholding in France. While withholding from wages is not required in France, the option that taxpayers can bank deductions has gained nearly 30 percent of the wage earning public's support (Organization for Economic Co-operation and Development, 1983, p. 330).

GENERAL WITHHOLDING THEORY AND PRACTICE

Although the theory of withholding has not been well explored in the literature of taxation, we can identify a number of common threads that distinguish the range of withholding options and their strengths and weaknesses.

There are, in common use today, essentially two kinds of withholding and two other types of a system that we shall call, for lack of a better term, quasi-withholding practices or methods.

"Graduated withholding" is the most common system in the United States. It is, in effect, the process of estimating the employee's total annual tax liability, retaining part of this amount proportional to the amount of the year elapsed, and forwarding the money and the records to the IRS. Several distinguishing characteristics of this type of withholding should be carefully noted:

1. Withholding agent: This third party makes the tax liability estimates, withholds the appropriate amount, and is responsible for forwarding it to the IRS. Usually the agent, in the event of an employer, is required to withhold several types of taxes and to add a contribution to the employee's tax liability.

2. The relationship: The agent and the employee are required to have some relatively close, periodic relationship whereby the employee can modify the terms of withholding, depending upon the employee's situation.

3. Agent expertise: The agent is assumed to possess a relatively high level of knowledge about the tax structure and regulation. Without this, another professional must be retained to maintain these records. Although picking numbers off the tax tables commonly available to employers is simple, the whole process is more complex than what appears on the surface.

4. Ease of payment: From the employee's perspective, the graduated withholding is the easiest and simplest method of collecting, computing, and reporting income tax liability. At the beginning of employment and at changes of individual circumstances, the employee reports his or her tax status to the employer. From that point on the withholding tax is automatically removed from the gross pay, without the employee's intervention. However, some minimal recordkeeping on the part of the wage earner is required.

5. Lump-sum problems: Again, the graduated withholding tax provides relief from the problem of
   lump-sum tax liability that can plague other
   taxpayers. Lump-sum payment (or even periodic
   payment) requires that certain maintenance
   operations be completed accurately and faithful-
   ly throughout the year. In addition, the lump-
   sum payment of taxes demands that the payor
   maintain a certain economic discipline.
6. Level of expertise: An important criterion for
   the calculation of taxes and tax liability is
   the level of expertise required. Often it is
   fairly low.
7. Level of expertise, agent: The withholding
   agent may well need a substantial body of information. The agent must withhold the correct
   amount and then forward it to the Treasury.
   In the situation with the graduated withholding,
   the level of expertise required is fairly low.

The withholding tax is a separate and unique tax
apart from the income tax. It is due and payable on the
basis of gross amounts actually paid to an employee. The
tax collected is then credited against the year-end income
tax liability. This device makes the collected funds, or
deductions, in effect not the employee's money retained for
use by the federal government, but the government's money,
collected in a timely fashion, and credited against the employee's income tax.

It is a very useful device in that it immediately
transfers to the Treasury the collected amount, and no dispute can be raised over the interest gained from the tax
during the year. The device also proves useful as an enforcement means against both the employee and the employer, since the moment the wage is credited the tax becomes the property, now due and payable, of the Treasury.

FLAT RATE WITHHOLDING

In the process of flat rate withholding, an agent
for the taxpayer will withhold a certain flat percentage of
a transaction or gain as the withholding tax due the federal government. This is, again as in the case with the
graduated tax, credited against a year-end tax liability.

The flat rate withholding system is imposed where the situation between the agent and payor is substantially different than that of the graduated withholding system. The peculiar characteristics that differentiate it from graduated withholding include:

1. The agent and payor may well have a distant relationship. The agent of withholding can retain a certain percentage of the transaction or payment without knowing much about the payor.

2. The intent behind flat rate is that, having recognized that a precise tax liability cannot be ascertained by the agent, a certain small percentage of the transaction can be calculated to represent a portion of the estimated tax liability. This calculation must, for the agent, rest upon the single transaction at hand.

3. Ease of payment. From the perspective of the taxpayer, the flat rate withholding process is simple, direct, and relatively painless. The year-end lump-sum payment problems may well cause other difficulties.

4. In the first instance, the flat rate may be calculated as a single, relatively massive transaction. Here an actual lump-sum payment problem might be a problem. The problem would be partially alleviated by the fact that the taxpayer will not be in the situation of actually paying out more than has been received in the single instance—such as might be the case with nonwithheld wages and a single year-end tax payment.

5. Level of expertise, taxpayer. As in graduated withholding taxes, the level of expertise required is very low.

6. Level of expertise, agent. At this point, however, we must consider the bookkeeping requirements of the agent to record and file what may well be a myriad of small transactions. While the agent's required expertise may be relatively low, the expertise required to establish and maintain the system may be very high. When dealing with a multiplicity of agents for a single taxpayer, as on interest-bearing accounts, the problem is multiplied accordingly.

It is usually recognized that the flat-rate withholding collected by the agent is inexact and does not take the particular circumstances of the payor into account. This is especially true when considering that the payor may encounter quite different circumstances during the annual cycle. These circumstances may dramatically affect the eventual tax liability. In order to minimize possible adverse side effects, the actual rate is given by the agent, and is therefore not essential and, under most circumstances, not necessary.

QUASI-WITHHOLDING

In addition to the graduated and flat-rate withholding discussed above, there are two common methods of gaining either funds or information on a periodic basis. Although neither is, technically, withholding, they are important precursors to the methodology by which withholding comes into play.

Beginning in 1943, a declaration and payment of a portion of the estimated annual tax liability was required of taxpayers making certain levels of income not derived from wages or salaries, or from taxpayers whose nonwage and salary income exceeded $500. No declaration and estimated tax payment was required if withholding taxes fell below $100 of the total tax due. The declarations are required to be filed on a quarterly basis, and fairly substantial penalties are assessed for failure to file on time or to make the estimated tax payment.

Under this scheme, the payor estimates, on a periodic basis, the eventual annual tax liability and pays this amount as a "withheld tax" to the Treasury as a credit against the annual liability. There are several important distinctions to the estimated tax payments that should be considered in comparison with the graduated or flat-rate withholding.

The estimated tax payments and declarations are not strictly a withholding system, since the characteristics of true withholding are not present. This is especially true when we consider the actual effect of estimated taxes as compared to wage and salary withholding. The effect is to spread out the tax payment, accelerate the income to the Treasury, and, to some extent, increase overall compliance. It does this by providing for regular payments of the total tax liability, which places it well within the range of withholding.

1. As there is no withholding agent, this relationship does not exist. The taxpayer may secure an agent for the calculation of the taxes, but the responsibility remains with the taxpayer.

2. Since the agent is, in effect, the taxpayer, the taxpayer's current situation is known. This "knowledge," however, breaks down somewhat when we consider that many individuals who are required to file estimated taxes in lieu of withholding are engaged in small businesses where the situation can change dramatically in a short period of time. Initial calculation of tax liability may differ greatly from the final liability.

3. Types of income involved. Income is from any source not already withheld, and may be in addition to withheld wages or salaries or other categories of income. The income, therefore, may be periodic, sporadic, or one time, and may or may not be representative of the year-end gross income.

4. Ease of payment. Since income may be regular or sporadic, the payment scheme for self-withholding of taxes can be onerous for the individual. Corrections can be made to insure that the actual amount of estimated tax paid is within the 10 percent margin of error allowed by the IRS. Substantial lump-sum payments could be required depending upon individual circumstances.

5. Level of expertise required. The level of knowledge of recordkeeping, accounting, estimation, and total income and tax liability is very high. The responsibility for this lies with the individual taxpayer and is, of course, often contracted out to professional preparers.

INFORMATIONAL REPORTING

Certain kinds of informational reports are required by the IRS to provide information relating to eventual tax liability based upon periodic payments. This information reporting is accomplished by both agents and the payor and has the following characteristics:

1. There may or may not be a withholding agent, that is, someone who acts as an agent for the Treasury to

prepare the informational return. The relationship between the agent and the taxpayer varies widely as well.

2. The information about the payor's circumstances will vary, depending upon the relationship and the existence of an agent.

3. The income involved may be of any type--sporadic, periodic, or a combination.

Obviously, information reporting is not tax withholding at the source in any real sense. It does, however, have some of the characteristics of withholding, and can be viewed as a precursor in those areas of income subject to test by the IRS. It is not, in the experience of the IRS, any substitute for withholding. The IRS has stated that increased informational reporting does not replace withholding in cost-effectiveness. At best, it identifies areas and individuals that should be investigated. In the paper glut that the IRS is currently experiencing, the additional information is of little use. Having the information in hand about a potential tax liability is no substitute for having the withholding tax in hand. The costs of compliance can equal or exceed the revenues.

EXTENSION OF WITHHOLDING

This chapter has examined withholding from the viewpoint that it is an integral part of the income tax compliance and collection system. We have attempted to show that a definite relationship exists between the type of income and the appropriate compliance tools.

As part of the overall process of reform, changes in the system of withholding can play a substantial role. These changes would be, essentially, a process of extension of withholding into new income types and reform of existing withholding. As was pointed out earlier, considerable resistance has been generated when such an extension has been proposed for one particular source of income: dividends and savings interest. In this section, we will look at the downside of withholding, the general problems with withholding on particular incomes.

OBJECTIONS

Underlying most objections to an expansion or extension of withholding are two almost philosophical questions. The first one deals with the idea we have touched on previously of whose money is actually withheld.   Since acquiescence in an expansion program is politically essential, the answer to the question is central as well.   One's yearly tax liability is due and payable on April 15 of each year for the previous calendar year. If the government has taken, in a graduated and "current" fashion, the tax out of regular salary checks or interest payments, then the question arises: Hasn't the government diverted your funds to its uses prior to their being due?   The problem has been avoided by the withholding tax, in which the IRS defines that portion of your income withheld as the now due and payable tax, to be credited against another tax at the end of the year.

It is a finessing of the tax law that has worked for the most part on wages and salaries since the tax's inception. It does not work so well, however, when the income taxed and the tax both form part of the principal from which further income is derived, such as with interest income that is regularly compounded.   Undeniably, taxes withheld from interest income are not there to be further compounded, reducing the gross income.   The same argument appears to be appropriate for withholding on wages and salaries, where the withheld amount will not diminish the eventual income.   The argument has, in practice, usually been countered with the fact that such withholding would only reduce the year-end income by minuscule amounts.   It is probably an insufficient argument to make if major changes were proposed.   It would be, therefore, essential to make clear to taxpayers that withholding taxes on any income will reduce the gross income--whether the income is wages, interest, or dividends.   What is fair, therefore, for wage earners is fair for all taxpayers.

Another argument occasionally raised is: If it is so easy, and relatively painless, to pay taxes through the withholding system, are the American people really in touch with what the actual tax burden is?   This is perhaps more of a philosophical question than even political, but it does raise the point again of whose money it is. Although surveys of this sort are rare, one wonders just how much most Americans perceive that portion of their wage withheld by their employer for the government.   The suspicion exists that they do not consider the "deductions" part of their income at all; they have made the mental calculation to consider income as net, after-tax income rather than the gross income figure that they will have very little contact with, except for calculations at the end of the tax year.

If there is no pain with taxation, then the true costs of government and the willingness of Americans to become involved with that government are diminished, at least so the argument goes.

KNOWLEDGE

A major stumbling block to all forms of withholding is the actual information on the income itself. If the agent incorrectly estimates the annual income, obviously the amount withheld will not reflect the total tax liability. Lack of knowledge of the income is not just a characteristic of the informal economy--where such knowledge is avoided. The actual gain may well imply recovering the costs of original purchase or even mean a long-term loss. In the following example, a single transaction is examined. On the basis of that transaction, various extrapolations of total gross income and tax liability are made. The transaction on January 15, involves $100. The transaction may represent any one of the following:

1. A one transaction gain of $100, and a yearly gain of $100.
2. The recovery of part of a cost of a $300 item for a net loss of $100.
3. A regular payment and gain, every 15 days, of $100.

Thus, with information on only one transaction, we could variously estimate the net income of the transaction alone to be from a loss to a gain of $100, for a yearly income of $1,200. A taxpayer in this same example may or may not be required to file a return on the income. Obviously, without some further knowledge of the taxpayer and the long-term situation with the transaction, withholding is quite possibly inaccurate for a significant number of taxpayers.

POTENTIAL UNFAIRNESS

Since withholding is based upon either the transaction at hand or an estimation of the total year-end income, it is reasonable to assume that significant inequities could occur. This is especially possible where income payments are not representative of the entire income. The tax withheld from a business could be damaging to the business. The means of addressing this problem is usually to assign a small, flat-rate withholding to this type of income; yet, it is evident that this could not be sufficient amelioration on all occasions.

A second fairness-based critique of withholding is posited upon the system's actual effectiveness. Withholding from wages and salary is certain and swift under current law. The employee has only a very limited control over the amount of withholding—to the extent the employee can determine the number of deductions to the income. Certain other relatively minor modifications are possible. With other types of income, however, the potential for modifying the amount withheld would be considerable. Since it is generally accepted that the self-employed, for instance, pay a lower rate of taxes on income equal to that of pure wage earners, withholding would simply institutionalize this difference. On the other hand, the withholding process, when it is asserted by others, would equalize the taxes paid by wage and nonwage earners.

To summarize, the general objections to an expanded withholding are: it is potentially unfair to some income groups; and it is simple and unobtrusive enough to lull taxpayers into thinking the government is really taking their money, when, in fact, the government does have use of private funds well before they are actually due.

PROBLEMS WITH SPECIFIC INCOMES

The following section examines the taxation system of personal incomes as related to withholding or potential withholding. The current means of withholding is discussed, along with problems in withholding unique to that income type.

Wages and Salaries

An estimated 93.9 percent voluntary compliance rate is attained through withholding by the employer prior to the wage payment to the employee. In this case, the employer acts as an agent for the Treasury. In addition, the agent is required to withhold state and local taxes, Social Security taxes (FICA), and provide a 50 percent match to the FICA payroll tax. The interlocking network of agent and tax liability probably insures that the income will be reported. Unreported or under-the-table income is paid without payroll deductions, which, at some level, may benefit the employee through slightly increased wages; yet a disincentive is offered the employee because of the lack of unemployment benefits and other benefits that accrue to reported income earners.

Interest and Dividend Income

The 86 percent and 83 percent compliance rates for interest and dividend income are attained through estimated reporting of taxes by the individual taxpayer and through informational (1099) reporting by the bank, credit union, broker, or other agent.

The firestorm of protest that occurs every time withholding at the source for interest and dividend income is proposed speaks eloquently to the well-organized and finely tuned lobby that is regularly mobilized to defeat the legislation. The arguments, which have some relevancy to withholding on other types of income, can be summarized as follows:

Equity. Does withholding place an inequitable burden upon a special group of taxpayers who are particularly dependent upon this income and who may not, as a class, have the ability to pay this tax? It was estimated that if withholding were instituted, a net $1.5 billion would be lost to savers annually from income. In practice, however, the 48 cents per $1,000 is a trifling loss.

It was argued that the elderly would be especially hard hit by withholding, since they were the income group most likely to depend solely upon interest or dividend income. As a result, several modifications were introduced. It is possible to discount policy objections since relatively simple tinkering with the legislation can easily target one group or another.

Transactions. Opponents of withholding on interest and dividend income point toward the vast number of transactions that would be subject to withholding under the law: $400 million yearly by bankers' estimates. To institute the system would—again by the banking community's estimates—require $3 to $6 billion in start-up costs, and $1 billion annually for maintenance. (Treasury Secretary Donald Regan, on the other hand, estimated start-up costs in the area of $600-$700 million.)

From a policy standpoint, this cost object can be discounted since the mechanism for making these transactions exists, especially with electronic means. The sheer numbers of transactions are not, in themselves, overwhelming. There would be costs, but they would be surmountable. There would undoubtedly be additional "paperwork" (probably of an electronic nature), but again, not an insurmountable obstacle. Paperwork problems would increase with exemption forms that would be required for certain groups—according to whatever policy is being followed. Nonetheless, the costs would probably be transferred to the consumer and would constitute a substantial burden upon the agent.

Savings incentives would be diminished under this plan. With one of the lowest savings rates in the industrialized world at 5.6 percent of gross income, the United States needs every incentive to encourage savings, or so goes the argument against interest and dividend withholding. Since the withholding provisions simply reduce a small margin of the compounding, the income from savings and dividends would remain essentially the same, with small net reductions. Again, one can take considerable issue with this particular piece of legislation, but the exception does not veto the entire concept. Obviously, withholding reduces substantially the income for wage earners, yet it does not reduce the incentive to work. Interest and return rates vary greatly over time, and it is reasonable to assume that the small withholding would simply appear as a slightly smaller return.

Diversion. Lastly, opponents of withholding on interest and dividend income claim that the substantial amounts removed from the use of private bankers and into the Treasury—estimated by the banking industry at $30 billion annually—would dramatically reduce the savings pool for use in lending, and damage the private commercial economy. Of course, the response is that the severe deficits now being run by the Treasury are at least as unhealthy as the diversion of funds would be.

The conclusion we have to draw from this debate is that while it would work a slight hardship on the economy, it is not likely to cause a disaster. It would, in fact, be a net gain to the national economy. The objections raised could be addressed either through the legislative process or by targeting one or another group. Allowing the withheld funds to "float" for the remainder of the quarter could, for instance, cover all the costs of withholding provisions.

What the withholding could accomplish would be to greatly enhance compliance with tax laws. Withholding makes the process of collecting taxes far simpler for both the taxpayer and the Treasury. Since the actual tax has already been paid, the incentives and the opportunity to spend the tax are removed.

The argument in support of compliance focuses upon the 11 percent of interest income and 15 percent of dividend income that annually go unreported and untaxed. Taxes on this income were estimated at $8 billion for 1981 alone. The compliance level for wage and salary income is far higher. It would be unthinkable to remove withholding from this income type and depend upon "strict enforcement" as the only other means available to ensure compliance for wages and salaries.

Tip Income

Tips and gratuities are provided directly to the employee rather than through an employer. As a result of TEFRA, however, a scheme of estimating and reporting tips as a certain percentage of income was instituted. In addition to the reporting, the employer is required to withhold from wages an estimated proportion of taxes based upon this percentage. The scheme has drawn considerable opposition from taxpayers earning tip income, who claim that reporting continually overstates the amount of tips received. Further criticism focuses upon the point that the traditionally low wages of tip income earners is offset by the, up to now, tax-free nature of tips.

Although it is too soon to make many conclusions about withholding from this type of income, preliminary information indicates that an estimate of tip income and withholding on that income can be accomplished through the regular payroll tax without serious problems. It is a reasonable assumption that the objections center around the increased compliance--and therefore a greater tax liability-- rather than with the structure of the withholding itself.

Recent legislation has all the appearance of having been created to give tax breaks to the wealthy and to fuel a massive defense build-up. Having created this consciousness of impending fiscal doom, both parties are helpless to do anything about it. Proposed solutions tend to have a hollow ring.

In a recent budget exercise, members of Congress found that even the most brutal course of cutting programs and expenditures still resulted in deficits well over $100 billion, and with increasing costs in the future. The problem is therefore compounded by the disturbing realization that even the most energetic belt-tightening, combined with highly unpalatable increased taxes, would still not solve the problem.

Tax measures such as increased or enhanced withholding therefore exist in a slightly different fiscal atmosphere. This may lead to a time when lobbies that have been successful in resisting the encroachment of withholding might have to bow to limited measures in order to do their share, and to sacrifice other, now exempt, income types even more readily. Thus, we find ourselves in a situation where withholding might become an element in the revenue-deficit solution. Obviously it won't be a major component, but nonetheless a component.

LOOKING AHEAD

Projecting ourselves into the legislative future, where any and all revenue measures are considered, each income type has to be examined with an eye toward withholding wherever the returns of the system are greater than the costs of administering it. A further factor of political resistance has to be considered. Here, of course, the savings and interest lobby stands out prominently. There is no need for any cynical political assessments either. Presented fairly and as much across-the-board as practically possible, withholding can be beneficial both to the Treasury and to a sizable number of taxpayers.

Facing the deficit problems, individual tax loopholes, including an exemption from withholding, become less convincing politically. The arguments for withholding are more easily carried among the voters than is the fairness argument. There is even a positive side to the process. Nearly 70 percent of taxpayers who file their taxes

are due a refund. Many more who do file would also receive a net refund. For them, the tax system is probably
a net benefit--and allows them an enforced savings program.

SELF-EMPLOYMENT

A survey of filers would probably reveal that obstacles to correct filing are a substantial reason for noncompliance. An aggressive simplification program for self-
withholding is essential to reduce these obstacles. While
complex forms and computations provide employment for in-
numerable tax consultants, there are many filers who do
not wish to compound the difficulty of filing with the in-
sult of having to pay a consultant.

If, indeed, one of the less recognized benefits of
withholding is ease of reporting (since the majority of
taxpayers subject to wage and salary withholding do no
regular reporting paperwork themselves), then there should
be a streamlined mechanism for self-employed persons.

Corrections might possibly be entered into the system to detect only capital gains--yet the problem continues
to exist that one transaction alone is usually insufficient
on which to base withholding. Income realized over the
full year is a far better measure, yet that determination
would, of course, avoid the withholding process. We should
probably conclude that market activities such as these are
probably impossible to equitably withhold and to gain a
reasonable estimate of year-end income.

BARTER

Income where the trail of currency, credit, and
checks is almost absent and where the gain is often un-
measurable presents serious problems for a withholding
system of tax collection. Missing from the tax equation
is an estimate of "income" from the barter exchange.
Valuation of the items or services exchanged may be only
in the eyes of the beholder and not subject to itemization
on a tax return.

Barter exchanges, on the other hand, are subject
to informational reporting as provided by brokers and
third-party recordkeepers. With formal barter exchanges

the object is, clearly, to provide profits for the participants. Some estimation of that profit has to be made by the brokers involved. The train of logic concludes that service-for-service exchanges exist merely as trading personal items of equal value--where the costs of doing business are equal to any return. In light of these difficulties and without a solid and centralized system of valuation, it is extremely difficult to affix a value, estimate the net income, and withhold at the source.

CURRENCY TRANSACTIONS

Similar difficulties are present in currency transactions, where the perception or reality is that no gain is being made by either party to the transaction and therefore no income is generated. Garage and yard sales provide little or no actual income gain to participants, and the costs for recordkeeping and compliance would probably far exceed the revenue gained. In other areas, however, such as the previously mentioned swap meets and in other organized events, sizable gains are a regular feature for some participants. State sales taxes are collected at many of these events, and it seems reasonable that for these limited areas withholding and recordkeeping would be overly difficult.

Transactions that take place between individuals, however, are difficult to place within the process of withholding because of the sporadic nature of the transactions, the oftentimes small amounts of the exchange, and the lack of relationship between the gain on a single transaction.

1. Little knowledge about the supplier (with, perhaps, the exception of regular household and nursing help).
2. Approximately one-fourth of the suppliers were also a part of the regular economy and had earnings where withholding was probable.
3. The transactions that comprised the informal transaction required little actual paperwork of their own; therefore there are significant disincentives to even beginning the process of reporting if it can be avoided.

4. Since many of these operations have been established solely for the purpose of avoiding record-keeping, paying taxes, and purchasing the required permits and licenses, the potential for increased tax collection via withholding is minimal.

Table 5.4

Estimated Gross Income of Vendors in the Informal Economy—by Occupational Status

Occupation	Gross Sales, (in bill. $)
Regular job	$11,732
Unemployed/laid off	675
On strike	99
Retired	1,496
On-the-side operator	1,126
Housewife	112
Part-time worker	99
Student	329
Student, regular job	29
Friend, relative	4,040
Nurse	77
Babysitter	477
Day-care worker	6
Friend, day-care worker	9
Other	646
Don't know	2,159
Inappropriate to ask	18,378
Total	41,793

Source: Congressional Action to Reduce Expenditures and Consider Tax Reforms, p. 104.

ANALYSIS

On the surface, withholding at the source appears to have all the advantages of a revenue measure without many of the attendant political and institutional costs. The expansion of withholding into other income types from those now subject to the process could add substantially to revenues generated by the income tax, quite possibly without distorting any further the whole tax structure.

Political reality is not favorable to the expansion of withholding, especially into the areas that appear most profitable: interest and dividend income. The recent battles have put too many legislators on record against withholding for them to change their minds in such a short time. There is no new evidence, as well, that bloodshed can be avoided.

What was compelling, from a financial perspective, in 1980 and 1983 remains so today. The reality, however, is that the practical arguments are not strong enough to overcome the opposition of the banking industry.

It is reasonable, therefore, to look at expanded withholding in areas other than interest and dividend income. The areas are not as productive as withholding for interest and dividends, but they do appear to offer substantial opportunities. Expanded withholding is likely to be categorized as increasingly invasive and intrusive. Although, objectively speaking, this is not the case, it is a charge that is relatively simple to make and nearly impossible to refute.

It is also more than likely that any new withholding would be criticized as a "new tax," just as was true of the previous battle's rhetoric. Again, the logic that the taxpayer having less income being a new tax is compelling. In referring to the flat-rate tax on interest and dividends, the Banking Committee chairman called withholding a "hidden tax." With the perception this high, the chances of gaining a fair hearing with individual voters would be difficult.

Nonetheless, while the political fate of expanded withholding is low--especially in relation to interest and dividends--the increasing clamor in Congress and in the private sector for reduced deficits may bring some unexpected allies into the withholding camp. Sold under a package legislation, tax reform incorporating increased withholding is quite possible. Woe betide the first legislator, however, who mentions the topic.

Table 5.5 illustrates the income that might be best subject to withholding. We have used the criteria of possible tax revenues and ease of application to the taxpayer as the basis for this illustration.

Table 5.5

Tax Procedures

Income Type	Recommended Withholding
Wages and salaries	Maintain current system
Interest and dividends	Flat-rate withholding
Capital gains	Information returns, possible flat rate
Self-employment	Estimated tax system, flat rate
Informal supplier	Informational returns, estimated taxes
Tip income	Graduated, flat-rate withholding
Pensions	Graduated, current system
Rents, royalties, commissions	20 percent flat-rate withholding
Barter exchanges	20 percent flat rate

Tax reform is, by itself, only a portion of the entire system. There is a growing awareness among the American public that deficits and "excessive" government spending will have severe consequences, even if those consequences are not immediately evident at the individual level. This awareness is almost totally a direct result of massive educational programs launched by both political parties in order to gain political advantage. The Republicans have pointed to the "historical deficit" and the legacy of previous administrations. The Democrats illustrate the need for more expenditures.

CAPITAL GAINS

The problem with withholding on capital gains is in estimating the total tax liability for the year and in making a tax payment on that rather than on what may be the gain on a transitory profit. There appear to be very few mitigating measures that can be taken that would iden-tify the year-end or tax liability and provide accurate withholding transactions to pay for it.

RENTS AND ROYALTIES

The relatively low compliance rates on these incomes, 37.2 percent and 61.2 percent, respectively, point to the difficulty in identifying these incomes and matching them with personal returns. These incomes are not always passed through brokers or agents, and as such make withholding difficult. Withholding on royalties is not in effect where agents do act to make the transaction.

INFORMAL INCOME

Most of these transactions are not handled through any agent and are subject to considerable underreporting. The underreporting is not always intentional: reporting of this income, especially on estimated tax statements, can be a difficult process.

Some informal income is reported through agents at barter exchanges, through state sales tax information, reporting at "swap meets" and similar gatherings, and through the reporting and withholding of domestic service income. Again, the problem here is the relatively small amounts that are involved, the difficulty in valuation, and the knowledge level of those involved in gaining this income.

REFUNDS AND OTHER ONE-TIME INCOME

These types of incomes suffer from potential withholding obstacles noted for other types in that it is difficult to estimate the total tax liability from one such transaction and to accurately withhold on this income. The flat-rate withholding process can be useful, yet for large transactions, the relatively small flat rate will probably not suffice. In the area of refunds, there is an agent involved (the state); yet without adequate communications with the IRS, withholding is sure to be inaccurate.

SALE OF STOCKS AND BONDS

Withholding on the sale of stocks and bonds at the source would appear to be a simple and relatively fair operation. Unfortunately, the vagaries of the market do not permit this approach.

REFERENCES

American Institute of Certified Public Accountants, Federal Taxation Division. "Underreported Taxable Income: The Problem and Possible Solutions." Washington, D.C.:, January 1983.

Bureau of National Affairs (BNA). "Hidden Tax." Daily Reporter System 177, September 10, 1980.

_____. Daily Reporter System, G-2, January 28, 1983, K#20.

_____. "Compliance Easy." Daily Reporter System 73, April 14, 1983, G-7.

_____. Daily Reporter System 95, May 16, 1984, G-1.

Cohen, Sheldon, IRS Commissioner. Tax Notes. May 5, 1980.

Commerce Clearing House, Inc. "New Interest and Dividend Withholding under 1982 Tax Law." Chicago, Ill. 1982.

Congressional Action to Reduce Expenditures and Consider Tax Reforms.

Congressional Research Service, Library of Congress. Deficit Reduction Act of 1984. Washington, D.C.

Democratic Study Group. "The Withholding Controversy," Special Report. April 15, 1983.

Feingold, Fred, and Peter A. Glicklich. "Onerous FIRPTA Reporting Requirements Replaced by New Broad Withholding Rules." Journal of Taxation 61 (November 1984): 296-303.

Hoff, Reka Potgieter. "Tax Withholding at Source Would Reduce Underreporting of Income on False Returns." Tax Notes, February 22, 1982, pp. 443-50.

IMF. "Underground Economy Building on Illicit Pursuits Is Growing Concern of Economic Policymakers." IMF Survey, February 4, 1980, p. 4.

Internal Revenue Service, Department of Transportation, Office of the Assistant Commissioner. "Income Tax Compliance Research." Washington, D.C., July 1983.

LeDuc, John Andre. Tax Notes. May 5, 1983, p. 2027.

MacNeil-Lehrer Report, transcript, "Politics of Withholding." March 11. 1983.

MacNeil-Lehrer Report, transcript, "Great Withholding Battle." April 15, 1983.

New York State Bar Association, Committee on Employee Benefits. "Report and Recommendations on the Treatment of Fringe Benefits." Tax Notes. January 3, 1983.

Organization for Economic Co-operation and Development (OECD). "Income Tax Collection Lags." Paris, 1983.

Reagan Ronald. Transcript, radio address to the nation. April 16, 1983.

Regan, Donald, Treasury Secretary to Senate Finance Chairman, Robert Dole. March 1, 1984.

Schick, Allen, and Robert Keith. Manual on the Federal Budget Process. Washington, D.C.: Congressional Research Service, 1982.

Severt, James W., II. "The Battle over Interest and Dividend Withholding: Beyond the Hysteria." Tax Notes, May 23, 1983, pp. 683-91.

Swardson, Anne. Washington Post. April 14, 1985, p. 85.

Swenson, David. "Repeal of the Withholding Tax on Interest: Pros and Cons on Denying the Exemption Paid to CFCs." Practitioner's Viewpoint, September 1984, pp. 217-21.

U.S. Congress. Congressional Budget Office. "Reducing the Deficit." 1985 Annual Report, Part II. Washington, D.C.: Government Printing Office.

_____. Joint Committee on Taxation. "Description of Proposals Relating to Withholding of Interest and Dividends." Washington, D.C.: Government Printing Office, April 29, 1980.

_____. Joint Committee on Taxation. "Description of Possible Options to Increase Revenues." Washington, D.C.: Government Printing Office, May 15, 1982.

U.S. Government. Department of Treasury. "Tax Reform for Fairness, Simplicity and Economic Growth." Vol. 1. November 1984.

Vettel, Tom. "Compromise on Withholding." Tax Notes, April 25, 1983, p. 369.

6

Federal Income Tax Evasion

Steven E. Crane and Farrokh Nourzad

INTRODUCTION

The present U.S. Individual Income Tax Code has been attacked on a number of grounds. Many critics cite the unintended distortions in the allocation of resources and the redistribution of income caused by the tax code. Others fear it has significant adverse effects on individual incentives to engage in productive activity. Still others express concern that the complexity of the tax system makes both administration and compliance exceptionally difficult. In this chapter, we examine the issue of noncompliance with the tax code, or what is commonly referred to as tax evasion.

In recent years there has been growing interest among students of taxation about the issue of evasion. This has come about partly because of the rapid growth of this activity and the effect it has on government revenues.[1] But there is a more fundamental reason for the study of evasion. The U.S. personal income tax system is based on the concept of voluntary compliance. Increasing evasion represents a crumbling of the very foundation of the system. Thus, in many ways the rapid growth of evasion is the ultimate indicator of the untenable nature of the present system.

In order to appreciate the importance of economic analysis of income tax evasion, it is necessary to have some idea of the extent of the problem. Unfortunately, because tax evasion is, for the most part, an unobserved phenomenon, defining and measuring it is difficult. Loosely speaking, evasion is often associated with the so-called underground economy, which includes illegal activity, moonlighting, and other off-the-record transactions. Estimates of the magnitude of the underground economy are sometimes cited as evidence of the extent of the evasion problem. Representative of these estimates are Tanzi's figures, generated by following the traces left by undergound activity in monetary aggregates.

However, using these measures can be somewhat misleading. While it is true that the underground economy and tax evasion are related, the two are by no means the same. First, most illegal activity exists for reasons not directly linked to the tax system, and not all income from illegal activity goes unreported. Second, substantial amounts of income earned in the activity goes unreported. Second, substantial amounts of income earned in the "aboveground" economy can go unreported. Thus, the link between evasion and the popular concept of the underground economy should be quite loose.

More appropriate as indicators of noncompliance are the estimates that focus specifically on the amount of reportable income that is concealed from the tax authorities, regardless of whether this income is generated in the underground economy. Perhaps the most reliable estimate is that provided by the Internal Revenue Service (IRS), based on audits conducted within the Tax Compliance Measurement Program (TCMP).

An alternate estimate of unreported income is provided by the Bureau of Economic Analysis (BEA). This measure, known as the Adjusted Gross Income (AGI) Gap, is calculated by comparing the level of AGI estimated from the national income accounts with the AGI reported on tax returns. Since the former is a proxy for reportable income and the latter is income actually reported to the IRS, the Gap is an approximation of aggregate unreported income, and consequently an indicator of the extent of evasion. While not quite as accurate as the IRS figures, these estimates are generally in line with those of the IRS, and suggest that nonreporting is indeed a large and growing problem.

To provide an indication of the extent of the evasion problem, all three of the estimates of unreported income just discussed are reported in Table 6.1. Note that for any given year the amount of unreported income varies considerably across estimates. However, over time all three estimates indicate that evasion is a growing problem that can be considered a threat to the tax system. Therefore, it is important that this phenomenon be understood so that policies to counteract it can be developed. Toward this end, we review the potential causes of evasion as found in the economics literature, and discuss the implications for both compliance and stabilization policies. In addition, empirical evidence regarding the causes of evasion is presented, along with some analysis of the sensitivity of evasion to various policy moves.

Table 6.1

Alternative Estimates of Unreported Income in the United States, 1970–81 (billions)

	Tanzi (Monetary Aggregates)	IRS (TCMP)	BEA (AGI Gap)
1970	$45.0	n/a	$54.4
1971	50.2	n/a	56.9
1972	55.4	n/a	59.4
1973	58.9	93.9	74.3
1974	70.7	n/a	73.1
1975	76.9	n/a	71.8
1976	94.3	131.5	78.2
1977	99.6	n/a	92.2
1978	113.6	n/a	103.5
1979	130.3	194.5	134.4
1980	159.3	n/a	151.3
1981	n/a	249.7	173.7

Sources: Tanzi, 1983; IRS, 1983; and Park, 1981.

THE PROFESSIONAL ECONOMIC LITERATURE ON EVASION

There now exists a fairly extensive body of theoretical and empirical literature analyzing various aspects of income tax evasion. We review each of these in turn.

The Theoretical Literature

In order to understand what causes tax evasion, it is important to recognize the nature of the decision to evade. The first thing to note is that the evasion decision is an individual decision, and thus must, at least initially, be analyzed within a microeconomic framework. Second, since the individual evader may or may not be detected and punished, the decision is one made under uncertainty. As a result, the taxpayer's attitude toward risk taking has a bearing on the outcome of the decision.

Because of these aspects of the evasion decision, the theoretical analysis has drawn heavily on the microeconomic models of uncertainty and of criminal activity. Within this framework, analysts have attempted to identify and study the factors that affect a risk-neutral or a risk-averse individual's decision to evade. Several factors have been recognized. First, in an uncertain environment, the probability of detection and the penalty rate to which detected violators are subjected influence the evasion decision because these partially determine the expected gain or loss from evasion. Second, both because it is the base of the tax and because risk attitudes play a crucial role, the level of true income must be considered a determinant of evasion. Finally, the tax rate itself must be included, since with no tax rates there are no tax payments to be made, and hence no reason to consider evasion.

These four determinants of evasion have been examined under a wide variety of assumptions regarding the specific details of the evasion decision and the setting in which it is made. For example, evasion has been specified either in terms of the absolute amount of income not reported, or the share of true income that is not reported. In addition, analysis has been undertaken with the assumption that the tax structure is income progressive. Further, various penalty schemes have been postulated, including penalties based on either evaded income or evaded taxes, which are either proportional or progressive.

In most cases, negative relationships have been established between the two measures of underreporting and both the penalty rate and the probability of detection. This is because increasing either of these compliance policy tools reduces expected income for a risk-neutral individual, or expected utility of income for a risk-averse individual. As a result, it has been argued that these two policy instruments are substitutes. In fact, the possible trade-offs have been examined by exploring how these instruments could be varied while holding tax revenues constant. The so-called optimal penalty and probability rates that totally eliminate evasion have also been derived.

In contrast, ambiguous results have been obtained with respect to the effect of only true income on evasion. This is because the response to changes in income depends on an individual's risk attitude. Further, this response depends upon whether evasion is specified in absolute or relative terms. However, some general tendencies have been identified. Under a variety of circumstances, increases in true income lead to reductions in the proportion of income that a risk-averse individual underreports. On the other hand, given plausible assumptions, a positive relationship between true income and the level of unreported income has been established. This, coupled with the above finding regarding the proportion of income underreported, indicates that increases in true income lead to less than proportionate increases in the level of underreporting.

The effect of changes in the tax rate on evasion also cannot be unambiguously determined, a priori. Comparative static analysis reveals that a positive or a negative response may be expected, depending on the assumptions made regarding the individual's risk attitude or the nature of the tax system. This is because a change in the tax rate can affect the taxpayer in two ways. To illustrate, consider an increase in the tax rate. Since the higher tax rate makes evasion more profitable on the margin, there is a tendency to evade more. This is the substitution effect. But a rising tax rate also reduces the taxpayer's disposable income, which leads to the ambiguous response discussed above. The direction of this income effect depends on whether risk aversion increases or decreases as income decreases. Thus, it is at least possible that the income and substitution effects oppose each other, and therefore the total effect of a tax rate increase is, a priori, uncertain. Nevertheless, most scenarios lead to an increase in evasion in response to a rise in the tax rate.

The four factors just discussed are the most extensively analyzed determinants of evasion. However, other factors have been examined within the standard framework described above, and the analytical framework itself has been modified as well. For example, the effects of changes in the price level and interest rates have been analyzed. On the other hand, the analytic framework has been modified by assuming that the labor supply and evasion decisions are jointly determined, thereby making the level of true income endogenous. Distinguishing between tax evasion and tax avoidance has led to only limited additional insights, which we now briefly summarize.

Price level changes can affect the decision to evade in a number of ways. First, they can erode the real value of a given level of nominal disposable income, thereby providing an incentive for the taxpayer to preserve purchasing power through evasion. Second, if the tax system is progressive, the incentive to evade in the face of price increases may be reinforced by the bracket creep effect. Thus far, only the former channel of influence has been analyzed, and the results are ambiguous. A risk-neutral individual's evasion decision is independent of a change in the price level. On the other hand, the observed proportion of true income that is underreported by a risk-averse individual increases with the price level, provided relative risk-aversion increases with income.

In a dynamic context, interest rates should play a role in the evasion decision because they affect the individual's assessment of the expected costs and benefits of evasion. The expected benefits are altered because income that is successfully unreported can be invested in order to generate additional future income. Other things equal, this increases the return to successful underreporting, which should cause evasion to increase. On the other hand, the expected cost is affected because unsuccessful evasion results not only in additional taxes and penalties, but also in interest charges. Other things equal, higher interest rates increase the cost of unsuccessful evasion, and should cause evasion to decrease. The individual's actual response should depend, in part, on which of these two effects dominates. The few formal models that explicitly contain an interest rate variable tend to confirm this.

When the level of true income is made endogenous, the findings for the major determinants of evasion are similar to those already discussed, in that they depend on the risk attitude and the shape of the tax and penalty plus the speed and completeness of enforcement functions. However, allowing for this additional complexity tends to increase the ambiguity regarding the expected response of evaders to changes in these determinants. For example, it has been shown that, for a decreasingly risk-averse individual faced with a progressive tax system, it is not possible to determine, a priori, the nature of the relationship between evasion and almost all of the standard variables normally included in the evasion decision.

It has been suggested that the possibility of legal tax avoidance should be recognized when analyzing tax evasion. It is argued that tax avoidance and tax evasion are complements, in that collecting information about what options are available involves joint costs. But at the same time, avoidance and evasion are also potential substitutes. It turns out that, in general, the tax-avoidance response to changes in tax-detection probability and penalty rates is similar to the tax-evasion response, which depends upon the exact specification of the model.

In summary, the formal theoretical analyses have contributed much to our general understanding of the factors affecting the decision to evade. We now have a fairly solid grasp of the arguments that should be included in an evasion function. In a few cases, this theoretical work has also offered insights into the direction of the relationship between evasion and these arguments. However, the direction of influence of many of the arguments has remained uncertain. This has prompted a series of empirical efforts aimed at resolving these ambiguities.

The Empirical Literature

A major stumbling block for all empirical analysis of income tax evasion is the aforementioned measurement problem. To get around this, several analysts have generated their data either by using questionnaires or by conducting experiments (game simulations). The resulting data have been used to perform statistical tests of significance for some of the standard arguments found in the theoretical literature, and to examine the responsiveness of evasion to changes in these arguments. Also examined has been the effect of several demographic factors.

To date, these studies have met with only limited success in clearing up the ambiguities of the theoretical literature. However, some theoretical predictions have been confirmed, and other interesting results with respect to demographic characteristics have been generated. For example, tax rates have been consistently found to be positively related to evasion, while the penalty and detection probability rates have been shown to be negatively related. Further, women and younger taxpayers tend to underreport more frequently, but the former by smaller amounts.

Recently, empirical analyses of data taken from the IRS TCMP have been conducted. These studies examined the problem from a slightly different perspective and produced some interesting results. For example, significant positive relationships were found between both tax rates and true income and the level of unreported income, but the penalty or detection probability rates were not considered. Another study found the detection probability and the penalty rate to be negatively related to evasion. Demographic characteristics were also found to play a role.

In light of these empirical studies, our understanding of tax evasion is much improved. It now appears that individuals evade less as the detection probability and penalty rates are increased, and, in general, tend to evade more as their income and tax rates rise. This information provides some clues for those who are responsible for designing policies to combat evasion, and also offers some insight for those interested in redesigning the tax system. However, additional empirical work is clearly needed.

All of the empirical analysis has been undertaken at the microeconomic level using cross-sectional data. This, of course, makes sense given the nature of the evasion decision. But there are also some important macroeconomic issues that need to be addressed. For example, it is essential to know the marginal impact of the determinants of tax evasion on aggregate tax revenue. Moreover, there may be significant interactions between tax evasion and stabilization policies. These interactions may arise from the fact that some of the determinants of evasion--such as the inflation, tax, and interest rates--affect and are affected by stabilization policies. Therefore, empirical analysis of evasion at the macroeconomic level is warranted. In the next section, we contribute to the empirical literature by conducting an aggregate time-series analysis of evasion in the United States.

AN AGGREGATE EMPIRICAL MODEL
OF INCOME TAX EVASION

Several problems are encountered when conducting an aggregate empirical analysis of the effect of various factors on income tax evasion. First, as mentioned above, it is difficult to obtain accurate measures of evasion since it is an unobserved phenomenon. Second, our desire to include interest rates and the inflation rate requires us to use time-series data, thereby limiting our choice of an evasion measure even further. Third, our interest in aggregate analysis poses not only the usual aggregation problems, but also the additional difficulty of aggregating risk aversion.

Fortunately, these problems are not insurmountable. As indicated by the representative sample of estimates in Table 6.1, a number of attempts have been made to determine the extent of tax evasion in the United States. Of the available measures, the AGI Gap is most suitable for our purposes because it is both a reasonable approximation of what we wish to measure, and because it is in the form of a time series spanning a period of sufficient length. Moreover, both aggregation problems can be overcome. First, aggregate counterparts of all of the arguments in the tax-evasion function can be developed. Second, recent work provides a theoretical justification for the aggregation of risk aversion. Therefore, a link can be established between the microfoundations laid out in the previous section and the aggregate analysis we wish to undertake.

Using the microtheoretic literature as a guide, we postulate that aggregate tax evasion is a function of the probability of detection, the penalty or fine rate, the level of real true income, the tax rate, the rate of inflation, and the real interest rate. However, there are several additional considerations that must be taken into account. First, the U.S. tax code specifies that taxes on some types of income (such as wages and salaries) are to be withheld at the source. This makes these income flows much more difficult to conceal from the tax authorities than others. Therefore, a separate variable should be included in the estimated equation to control for the effect of this institutional arrangement. Second, since we are undertaking a time-series analysis, there is likely to be a common trend in many of the data series. Therefore, a time trend should

be included in our empirical evasion function. Failure to
do so would increase the chances of obtaining biased results.

We therefore posit the following aggregate empirical
income tax evasion function,

$$(1) \quad \underline{E}_{\underline{t}} = \underline{a}_0 + \underline{a}_1 \, \underline{\frac{D}{\underline{t}}} + \underline{a}_2 \, \underline{F} + \underline{a}_3 \, \underline{Y}_{\underline{t}} + \underline{a}_4 \underline{TR}_{\underline{t}}$$

$$+ \, \underline{a}_5 \, \underline{\frac{I}{\underline{t}}} + \underline{a}_6 \, \underline{R}_{\underline{t}} + \underline{a}_7 \, \underline{W}_{\underline{t}} + \underline{a}_8 \, \underline{\frac{t}{}} + \underline{e}_{\underline{t}}$$

where $\underline{E}$ is a measure of tax evasion, $\underline{D}$ is the probability
of detection, $\underline{F}$ is the fine rate, $\underline{Y}$ is real true income, TR
is the tax rate, $\underline{I}$ is the inflation rate, $\underline{R}$ is the real rate
of interest, $\underline{W}$ is the institutional variable identified below,
$\underline{t}$ is an annual time index, and $\underline{e}$ is the error term. The
variable definitions and expected signs are as follows.

As mentioned above, our measure of evasion is based
on the AGI Gap, which is the difference between AGI derived from the national income accounts and AGI reported
on tax returns. However, there is a major problem with
using the Gap. By construction, it treats the income of
those not legally required to file tax returns as unreported
income. This tends to cause the AGI Gap to overstate the
magnitude of the problem. Therefore, prior to estimation
we adjust the Gap by removing from it an imputed value
of the AGI of those not required to file tax returns.

To quantify the probability of detection, we use the
one-year lagged value of the percentage of total tax returns audited each year by the IRS. Our reasoning is
that an individual's subjective evaluation of the probability of being detected will in part depend on whether he or
she knows someone who has been audited, and that this
will be a positive function of the percentage of last year's
returns that were audited. Both the theoretical and empirical literature suggest that the coefficient of $\underline{D}$ should
be negative.

Obtaining a single measure that reflects the penalty
rate for noncompliance with the U.S. tax code is quite difficult because there are different fines for different offenses. To capture the overall effect of these different
charges, we construct an aggregate effective fine rate by
expressing the additional taxes, penalties, and interest
assessed by the IRS during the year in question as a
percentage of the amount of taxes evaded. However, be-

cause there is a potential econometric problem with using this particular variable in our equation, we follow Durbin's approach for constructing an instrumental variable that can be used as a substitute for the fine rate. The coefficient of this variable should also be negative.

The proper measure of real true income is partially determined by our choice of the dependent variable. Since our measure of unreported income is an adjusted version of the AGI Gap, the appropriate measure of Y is BEA AGI, adjusted both to remove the income of those not required to file tax returns and for changes in prices. The former adjustment is discussed above and the latter is accomplished using the consumption expenditures component of the GNP deflator. However, including such a variable may produce a simultaneity bias. Therefore, an instrumental variable approach is used for this variable. Despite the fact that there is some ambiguity in the theoretical and empirical literature, we are inclined to expect a positive sign on the coefficient of the income variable. Note also that this variable is expressed in logarithmic form to allow for the possible nonlinearities arising from risk aversion.

The aggregate tax rate in our model is a weighted average marginal tax rate. It is constructed by using a scheme that calls for averaging the marginal rates in each year's tax schedule after weighting them by the percentage of total AGI in each of the corresponding tax brackets. From our previous discussion, it is clear that technically no sign expectation can be drawn from the theoretical literature because of the potential ambiguities with respect to the income and substitution effects. However, given that: the most common result in the theoretical literature is a direct relationship between the tax rate and evasion; in economics, usually the substitution effect is expected to be the dominant force; and some previous empirical work indicates a direct relationship; it seems reasonable to expect a positive sign for the coefficient of TR.

For our measure of the rate of inflation, we use the rate of change of the Consumer Price Index (CPI). The CPI is chosen because it is the most widely recognized measure of changes in the prices that are likely to affect taxpayers' cost of living. Since the inflation rate has not been incorporated into previous theoretical or empirical work, no formal sign expectation can be posited. However, based on the intuitive reasoning expressed above, we would not be surprised to obtain a positive sign of determination.

Our measure of the rate of interest is an average of the savings and time-deposit rate. However, this figure includes a premium for expected inflation, which is undesirable since the inflation rate enters our equation as a separate explanatory variable. Therefore, the savings and time-deposit rate is converted to real terms by removing it from the inflation rate as defined above. This allows us to capture the pure effect of interest rates on evasion. In light of our discussion, no sign expectation can be established for the coefficient of real interest rates.

The variable included to control for the effect of automatic tax withholding is calculated by expressing the level of wages and salaries in national income as a percent of that base. Other things equal, a larger wage and salary share of overall income should mean less underreporting, which means a negative sign should be expected on the coefficient of this variable.

Finally, as is standard practice in time-series analysis, a trend variable is added to control for the movements of the dependent variable along the trend. To avoid severe multicollinearity problems, we detrended all other independent variables prior to adding the time trend. Given the pattern of the figures in Table 6.1, the coefficient on this variable should be positive.

The aggregate evasion function was estimated using the Cochrane-Orcutt autoregressive procedure with first- and second-order coefficients of autocorrelation of 0.65 and .17, respectively. The following results were obtained, with the $\underline{t}$-statistics in parentheses.

$$(2) \quad \underline{E}_t + -403.48 - 3.335 \, \underline{D}_t - 1.486 \, \underline{F}_t + 2.533 \, \underline{TR}_t + 126.240 \, \ln\underline{Y}_t + 9.308 \, \underline{I}_t$$
$$\phantom{(2) \quad \underline{E}_t +} (-1.61) \quad (-2.59) \qquad (-1.90) \qquad (4.18) \qquad (2.81) \qquad (4.60)$$

$$+ \; 9.922 \, \underline{R}_t - 4.899 \, \underline{W}_t + 20.668\underline{t}$$
$$ (4.42) \qquad (-3.19) \qquad (2.01)$$

$$\bar{R}^2 + 0.95 \qquad \underline{DW} = 1.76$$

From these results, it is clear that our effort to estimate empirically our aggregate evasion relationship has been successful. The adjusted $\underline{R}^2$ indicates that 95 percent of the overall variation in unreported income has been explained by the model. In addition, all relevant parameter estimates are statistically significant at the 0.05 level or better, and there are no unexpected signs.

Further, the parameter estimates are of reasonable magnitudes. Given this success in estimation, it seems appropriate to discuss some of the policy implications suggested by these results.

Policy Discussion

There are two major types of public policies for which our results are relevant. First, our estimated coefficients for the probability of detection and fine rates—and to some extent the wage and salary share—provide some evidence regarding the effectiveness of various compliance policy tools. Second, the coefficients for the income and the tax, inflation, and interest rates offer some new insights into the interaction between tax evasion and stabilization policy. We consider the policy implications of our results in that order.

Compliance Policy Implications

From a compliance policy perspective, the primary concerns are whether the available tools have a deterrent effect on underreporting; how sensitive the level of underreporting is to changes in these tools; and what, if any, trade-offs exist between the different tools. Our results indicate that aggregate evasion decreases with increases in the penalty rate, the probability of detection, and the wage and salary share of income. Thus, both of the major compliance policy tools, as well as withholding requirements, do have the expected deterrent effects.

Based on our results, it appears that the detection probability and the fine rate are substitutes for one another. However, given that the estimated coefficient of the detection probability is nearly 2.25 times that of the penalty rate, these two policy tools are far from perfect substitutes. A one percentage point increase in the average annual audit rate would have resulted in an additional $3.3 billion in annual reported income over the sample period. Based on the period's mean tax rate of 29.9 percent, this would have generated $987 million more tax revenue annually. In contrast, a one percentage point increase in the effective penalty rate would have produced $1.5 billion and $449 million of additional reported income and tax revenue, respectively.

The finding that changes in the audit rate are more effective in deterring evasion can be explained in part by the fact that over the period of study, the mean value of the audit rate was relatively low, slightly more than 3 percent. Starting with a low rate, a one percentage point increase in the audit rate will have a larger marginal impact on unreported income than when this rate is already relatively high. Moreover, it is sensible that high penalties coupled with low probabilities of detection are not strong enough deterrents. As Kolm puts it, this is like "hang[ing] tax evaders with probability zero." On the other hand, a high probability of detection together with low monetary costs may be a more effective deterrent, partly due to non-pecuniary costs associated with prosecution.

Although plausible, the above discussion ignores an important consideration. Increasing the penalty rate would require nothing more than a stroke of the pen, since it is virtually free of cost. But raising the probability of detection would mean increasing the number of audits, which would involve costs. Therefore, an appropriate comparison of the effectiveness of the two policies would require consideration of the net additional revenues they would have produced.

Unfortunately, such a comparison cannot be done for the entire sample period because the relevant audit cost data are not available. However, to obtain a first approximation of the relative effectiveness of these two policy instruments, we proceed as follows. Using the available audit cost data for the period 1955–81, we find that on average the per audit cost was $120. Assuming this to be representative of the entire sample period, the average annual additional cost needed to raise the audit rate by one percentage point was determined to be $111 million. This was subtracted from the additional annual gross tax revenue ($987 million), resulting in $876 million of net additional revenue. This is nearly twice the revenue associated with increasing the penalty rate by one percentage point. Therefore, even after adjusting for the additional resource cost, on the margin, raising the probability of detection through more audits appears to be a more effective policy for discouraging tax evasion than raising the penalty rate.

It should be emphasized that this result is based on, among other things, the assumptions that fines were proportional to the amount of taxes evaded, that average audit cost for the 1947–81 period was not substantially different from the 1955-81 period, and that there were no costs associated with raising the penalty rate. If any of these assumptions were changed (for example, penalties could be made progressive), the relative effectiveness of the two compliance policies could be different.

Another approach to analyzing tax compliance policy is to determine the <u>optimal</u> level of the probability of detection and the penalty rate. This is that value of each rate that would completely eliminate underreporting, holding everything else constant. Clearly, these optimal values depend on the values of the other explanatory variables of the model. In a dynamic framework, where these variables take on different values in different time periods, it is highly unlikely that the optimal rates would remain constant over time. Nevertheless, to shed some light on this issue, we set the estimated aggregate evasion equation equal to zero, and substitute the mean values of the other variables in the model in order to solve for the average annual values of the probability of detection and the penalty rate over the period of study. This yields 15 percent and 51 percent for these two policy tools, respectively. Thus, the penalty rate must be increased by a much larger percentage than the probability of detection if the income gap is to be closed. This is consistent with our earlier finding that, on the margin, increasing the probability of detection is a more effective compliance policy. However, neither of these figures is likely to be administratively or politically feasible to implement. As a result, some other approach to controlling evasion is needed. This should be taken into consideration by those interested in tax reform.

Stabilization Policy Implications

The question of tax evasion has not generally been associated with macroeconomic stabilization policy. For the most part, the discussion has been limited to general statements by advocates of supply-side economics that cutting the marginal tax rate might not cause total tax revenues to decline. The argument is that lower rates would lead to, among other things, a larger tax base as taxpayers reduce their efforts at sheltering income from taxation. Our results have a bearing on this issue, as well as for several other aspects of stabilization policy.

Before we can carefully discuss the interrelationship between income tax evasion and stabilization policies, we must have some idea of the pattern in tax evasion over a business cycle. Therefore, let us begin our discussion by considering our results with respect to real income. In general, the empirical results for the real income variable suggest that increased tax evasion has gone hand-in-hand with economic growth. That is, income underreporting is a procyclical phenomenon, rising during economic expansions and falling in recessions.

Using the coefficient of the income variable and the sample period's mean tax rate, we find that a one percentage point increase in the growth of real income generates an additional average annual loss of $37.7 billion in tax revenue. This is an interesting counterpoint to those who argue that we can simply grow our way out of the current deficit problems. Of course, the issue is more complex than that. The loss in tax revenue from the additional evasion that results from growth in real income may be far outweighed by the growth in revenues and the reduction in expenditures that typically occur during expansions. Therefore, additional analysis of the income elasticities of government revenues and expenditures is needed before any firm conclusions can be reached on this matter.

Now that the procyclical nature of income tax evasion has been established, let us return to the supply-side argument that cutting tax rates need not lead to reduced revenues. Our estimates indicate that there is indeed a direct relationship between the tax rate and the level of underreporting, which is in line with both our expectations and the empirical finding of others. From a theoretical perspective, this suggests that the substitution effect of a tax rate change either dominates or is reinforced by the income effect. But as a practical matter, these results provide some support for the supply-sider's tax-cut proposition. We find that, other things equal, a one percentage point reduction in the tax rate would have caused, on an average annual basis, the tax base to increase by $2.5 billion due to reduced underreporting.

In view of the relatively modest reduction in underreporting, it is questionable whether the resulting increase in tax revenue would have been sufficient to offset the loss of tax revenue due to the lower tax rate. Furthermore, to the extent that tax cuts would have stimulated the economy and generated more rapid growth, they would have increased evasion as discussed above. Thus, the support our analysis provides for the self-financing tax-cut hypothesis is somewhat limited. Additional research using an evasion-adjusted tax multiplier is needed before a firm conclusion can be reached regarding this issue.

Turning to the effect of changes in the inflation rate on underreporting, our results indicate a positive impact. A one percentage point increase in the inflation rate generates nearly $9.3 billion of additional unreported income on an average annual basis. This, too, has an interesting implication. It is often argued that because of the bracket-creep effect, inflation enhances tax revenue. However, in view of the positive relationship found here, the net effect of inflation on tax revenues may not be as significant as is generally believed. Evidently, many taxpayers respond to the nonlegislated tax increase caused by inflation by instituting their own nonlegislated tax cut through evasion. While this is a perfectly rational response, it tends to undermine the voluntary compliance aspect of the tax code. This underscores the need for fully indexing the tax system.

Finally, let us consider our results with respect to the effect of the interest rate. From our estimated equation we see that the interest rate is positively related to unreported income. Based on the coefficient of the inflation-adjusted (real) rate of interest, a one percentage point increase in this rate results in a $9.9 billion increase in underreporting. This suggests that, other things equal, U.S. taxpayers have found, on average, that the expected gain from investing unreported income to be greater than the expected interest cost associated with unsuccessful evasion. This may be explained, at least in part, by the fact that penalties imposed on detected evaders are not fully retroactive.

The positive relationship between interest rates and underreporting also has an interesting implication for fiscal policy. It has long been argued that nonmonetized expansionary fiscal policy generates higher interest rates, which crowd out private spending. This makes fiscal policy less effective and adds to the deficit by increasing the interest cost of servicing the national debt. Our finding indicates that the deficit-induced higher interest rates lead, ceteris paribus, to more evasion, less tax revenue, and therefore a further increase in the deficit. In other words, tax evasion represents another channel through which the crowding-out effect adversely influences the budget.

To summarize, we have presented an empirical analysis of aggregate tax evasion in the United States over the period 1947-81. We have found that aggregate income tax evasion has increased with rising income, marginal tax rates, inflation, and interest rates, but has fallen with increases in the probability of detection, the penalty rate, and the wage share of income. A number of interesting implications for both compliance and stabilization policies have been drawn from these results. In particular, we have found that the marginal impact on evasion of changing the audit rate is larger than that of the penalty rate, even when implementation costs are considered. We have also found some support for the argument that tax cuts need not result in reduced revenues. On the other hand, we have found that, contrary to the popular belief, inflation may not generate a net increase in revenues. Finally, we have identified the sensitivity of tax evasion to the rate of interest as an additional channel through which crowding out can occur.

FINDINGS

The rapid growth of tax evasion represents a serious threat to the U.S. income tax system. For this and other reasons (discussed elsewhere in this book), it is clear that an overhaul of the system is needed. However, as the recent budget negotiations have demonstrated, achieving satisfactory reform while maintaining revenue neutrality is not a simple task. Reducing tax evasion would both complement and simplify this effort. First, by increasing voluntary compliance, it would shore up the foundation of the tax system. Second, by tapping a previously untouched source of taxable income, it would reduce the revenue constraint faced by reformers. The analysis presented in this chapter provides some insights that allow us to identify the following options for reducing tax evasion.
There are several possible policy actions that can be taken to attack tax evasion directly. The most obvious policy response to growing evasion is to increase compliance efforts through auditing a greater percentage of tax returns or imposing stiffer penalties. Our analysis suggests that the former action would be more effective than the latter, given the existing auditing procedures and penalty rate structures. However, in light of the relative insensi-

tivity of evasion to the audit rate, a significant increase in audits would be required in order to resolve the evasion problem. Unfortunately, it is not clear that such an increase would be politically feasible.

A related move is to align more closely the applicable interest charges with market rates. This would raise the expected cost of evasion and therefore bring it in line with the expected gains. A further step in this direction would be to make penalties fully retroactive by eliminating the existing statute of limitation. These changes might make penalties a more effective compliance policy tool.

An additional approach for increasing compliance is to expand automatic withholding and employer-reporting requirements to include other major sources of income besides wages and salaries. The recent legislation requiring financial institutions to withhold taxes on interest income is a step in the right direction. However, additional analysis of the propensities to evade out of different sources of income should be undertaken before further steps in this direction are taken.

In addition to the above approaches that affect evasion directly, there are also a number of indirect policy actions that can be incorporated into an overall tax reform package. One such action is to cut the marginal tax rates. We conclude from our findings that cutting the individual income tax rates would reduce evasion, thereby leading to more tax revenues. As a result, reforming the individual tax rate structure might be worth pursuing in that it need not be inconsistent with revenue neutrality. However, in the absence of a comparable analysis of the effects on evasion of changes in the corporate tax structure, no firm conclusions can be reached regarding this issue.

A more significant reform is to fully index the tax system. From our analysis it appears that eliminating the effect of inflation on the tax system would be very effective in combating evasion. This provides some support for the recently enacted indexation program. However, there is an ongoing debate over the proper extent of indexation. The standard argument in favor of it is that it is necessary for neutralizing the distortions caused by bracket creep. On the other hand, the usual argument against full indexation is that it will be too costly in terms of lost revenues. Both sides have ignored the significant effect of inflation on tax evasion. We believe that the reduction in evasion that will result from neutralizing the bracket-creep effect tips the scale in favor of full indexation.

REFERENCES

Allingham, M. G., and Sandmo, A. Income Tax Evasion: A Theoretical Analysis. Journal of Public Economics, 1972, pp. 323-38.

Andersen, P. Tax Evasion and Labor Supply. Scandinavian Journal of Economics, 1977, pp. 375-83.

Arrow, K. J. Theory of Risk Bearing. Markham, 1971.

Becker, G. S. Crime and Punishment: An Economic Approach. Journal of Political Economy, 1968, pp. 169-217.

Christiansen, V. Two Comments on Tax Evasion. Journal of Public Economics, 1980, pp. 389-93.

Clotfelter, C. T. Tax Evasion and Tax Rates: An Analysis of Individual Returns. Review of Economics and Statistics, 1983, pp. 363-73.

Cross, R., and Shaw, G. K. On the Economics of Tax Aversion. Public Finance, 1982, pp. 36-47.

_____. The Evasion-Avoidance Choice: A Suggested Approach. National Tax Journal, 1981, pp. 489-91.

Durbin, J. Errors in Variables. Review of the International Statistics Institute, 1954, pp. 23-32.

Fiege, E. L. How Big Is the Irregular Economy. Challenge, 1979, p. 513.

Fishburn, G. Tax Evasion and Inflation. Australian Economic Papers, 1981, pp. 325-32.

_____. On How to Keep Tax Payers Honest (or almost so). Economic Record, 1979, pp. 267-70.

Frey, B. S., and Pommerhene, W. W. Measuring the Hidden Economy. In The Underground Economy in the United States and Abroad, ed. V. Tanzi. Lexington, 1982, pp. 3-27.

Friedland, N., Maital, S., and Rutenberg, A. A Simulation Study of Income Tax Evasion. Journal of Public Economics, 1978, pp. 107–16.

Goode, R. The Individual Income Tax, rev. ed. Brookings, 1976.

Guttmann, P. M. The Subterranean Economy. Financial Analysts Journal, 1977, pp. 24–27.

Internal Revenue Service. Income Tax Compliance Research: Estimates for 1973–1981. U.S. Government Printing Office, 1983.

Kolm, S. C. A Note on Optimum Tax Evasion. Journal of Public Economics, 1973, pp. 265–70.

Koskela, E. On the Shape of Tax Schedule, the Probability of Detection, and the Penalty Schemes as Deterrents to Tax Evasion. Public Finance, 1983, pp. 70–80.

_____. A Note on Progression, Penalty Schemes and Tax Evasion. Journal of Public Economics, 1983, pp. 127–33.

Long, S. B. The Internal Revenue Service: Measuring Tax Offenses and Enforcement Response. U.S. Department of Justice, National Institute of Justice, September 1980.

Marchon, M. N. Tax Avoidance, Progressivity, and Work Effort. Public Finance, 1979, pp. 453–59.

McCaleb, T. S. Tax Evasion and the Differential Taxation of Labor and Capital Income. Public Finance, 1976, pp. 287–94.

Mork, K. A. Income Tax Evasion: Some Empirical Evidence. Public Finance, 1975, pp. 70–76.

Nayak, P. B. Optimal Income Tax Evasion and Regressive Taxes. Public Finance, 1978, pp. 358–66.

Park, T. S. Relationship between Personal Income and Adjusted Gross Income, 1947–78. Survey of Current Business, 1981, pp. 24–28.

Pencavel, John D. A Note on Income Tax Evasion, Labor Supply, and Nonlinear Tax Schedules. Journal of Public Economics, 1979, pp. 115–24.

Richard, J. A., Russell, A. M., and Howroyd, T. D. A Tax Evasion Model with Allowance for Retroactive Penalties. Economic Record, 1982, pp. 379–85.

Sandmo, A. Income Tax Evasion, Labor Supply, and the Equity-Efficiency Tradeoff. Journal of Public Economics, 1981, pp. 266–88.

Singh, B. Making Honesty the Best Policy. Journal of Public Economics, 1973, pp. 257–63.

Spicer, M. W., and Becker, L. A. Fiscal Inequity and Tax Evasion: An Experimental Approach. National Tax Journal, 1980, pp. 171–75.

Spicer, M. W., and Lundstedt, S. B. Understanding Tax Evasion. Public Finance, 1976, pp. 295–305.

Sproule, R., Komus, D., and Tsang, E. Optimal Tax Evasion: Risk-Neutral Behavior Under a Negative Income Tax. Public Finance, 1980, pp. 309–17.

Srinivasan, T. N. Tax Evasion: A Model. Journal of Public Economics, pp. 339–46.

Szpiro, G. G. The Aggregation of Risk Aversion. Mathematical Social Sciences, 1983, pp. 55–59.

Tanzi, V., ed. The Underground Economy in the United States and Abroad. Lexington, 1982.

_____. The Underground Economy in the United States: Annual Estimates, 1930–80. International Monetary Fund Staff Papers, 1983, pp. 283–305.

Witte, A. D., and Woodbury, D. F. The Effect of Tax Laws and Tax Administration on Tax Compliance: The Case of the U.S. Individual Income Tax. National Tax Journal, 1985, pp. 1–13.

Wright, C.   Saving and the Interest Rate.   In The Taxa-
    tion of Income from Capital, ed. A. C. Harberger and
    M. J. Bailey.   Brookings, 1969, pp. 275-300.

Yitzhaki, S.   A Note on Income Tax Evasion: A Theoretical
    Analysis.   Journal of Public Economics, 1974, pp.
    201-02.

7

The Adjustableness
of the Federal Income Tax System

John Tatom

The personal income tax has been the centerpiece of federal budget policy for several decades because of the ease with which it automatically adjusts to changing revenue requirements of the government, because it easily allows for fairness considerations in revenue collection, and because its automatic adjustableness is believed to efficiently promote macroeconomic stability.

But over the past two decades this inherent adjustability has become the source of adverse effects on the allocation of the nation's resources, on the achievement of fairness objectives of the tax system, and on the promotion of economic stability. The principal source of these adverse effects has been the pace of inflation, coupled with the fact that the personal income tax progressively taxes nominal income. This gave rise to the phenomenon called "bracket creep," which entailed the adverse effects noted above.

Over the same period, the changing composition of federal government activity led to changes in the composition of taxes that dramatically increased the importance of the Social Security taxes on labor income and raised marginal tax rates, impairing the ability of the personal income tax to promote the allocative, equity, and stabilization objectives of federal budget policy. The major development

*This chapter draws heavily upon two earlier articles by the author in 1984 and 1985.

has been the growth of the transfer function of the federal government and its principal funding mechanism, the Social Security tax.

This chapter discusses the adjustableness of the federal income tax, focusing on the objectives of tax policy, the general properties of the income tax, trends in federal revenues, and changes in tax rates and the tax base. What emerges is the increasing inability, over the past two decades, of the personal income tax to promote automatically the desirable objectives of the tax system. At the end of the chapter, the implementation of "indexation" is discussed. This new feature largely eliminates one culprit in the deterioration of the efficiency and fairness of the tax system.

GENERAL PRINCIPLES OF TAXATION

Before considering how the taxation of personal income has evolved over the past 20 years, a delineation of general considerations for and properties of an optimal tax system is in order to provide criteria for judging this evolution.[1]

Allocative Considerations of the Tax System

The tax system affects the allocation of the nation's resources. Generally speaking, a tax on anything yields fewer resources devoted to that thing's production and, hence, less of it for consumption. The tax can be avoided by using resources in nontaxed areas. In the case of the income tax, the allocation of labor resources to leisure or of capital resources to the production of nonpecuniary, or nontaxed, income (such as the services of consumer durables like housing, luxury cars, and so forth) lessens the tax burden by diverting resources to nontaxed uses. The lower are taxes, or the less available are options for such substitution, the smaller are these losses in tax receipts and efficiency. As a result, taxes that apply to broader tax bases and, hence, at lower tax rates in order to obtain a given flow of tax receipts, are more efficient.

Another desirable feature of a tax system is that the tax base be "elastic." As public demand for goods and services or income redistribution grows in an expanding economy, tax receipts will have to expand to pay for these increased expenditures. Such increased receipts require either higher tax rates or a tax base that grows in line with public demand for government services. In the latter case, the tax base is said to be elastic. Taxes applied to goods for which the demand is not responsive to economic growth are said to be inelastic because revenue from such taxes does not expand as fast as the economy generally, in the absence of tax rate increases. The personal income tax provides even more elastic revenues because it is "progressive." As income rises, taxes rise faster since the tax rate on additional dollars of income exceeds the average tax paid at any given level of income, so that as income rises, the average tax rate on income rises. This property is described in more detail below.

Equity Aspects of the Tax System

The federal tax system relies heavily on ability-to-pay considerations of fairness. This principle suggests two normative notions of fairness to some analysts. First, horizontal equity refers to taxing two individuals with equal abilities to pay, equally. Where ability to pay is judged by income, this means individuals with equal incomes should pay equal taxes. The second principle is referred to as vertical equity. According to this principle, it is fair for individuals with greater ability to pay (income) to pay more in taxes.

Macroecoonomic Aspects of the Tax System

Tax policy affects the economic performance of the nation, including its cyclical stability. This feature, referred to as built-in stability, is an important function of tax policy. Such policy-induced stability refers to the adjustableness of total tax liabilities to cyclical fluctuations in spending, output, and employment. When income and spending decline in the economy, taxes decline, absorbing part of the income loss so that private spending does not decline as much as it would if tax liabilities did not change. With progressive taxes (such as the personal income tax), taxes fall more than proportionately to income, further cushioning the decline in private spending that would otherwise occur. Thus, the adjustableness of the tax

system serves as a cushion that reduces the cyclical variability of national income and employment.

Of course, the level of tax rates has other important
effects on the overall macroeconomic objectives of the nation. For example, inefficiencies arising from relatively
high tax rates noted above reduce current output from
available resources, as well as reducing the resources
available. Tax incentives can also reduce the pace of accumulation of resources and, hence, the economic growth
rate of the nation's output. Thus, all three objectives--
allocative efficiency, equity, and macroeconomic goals--are
interrelated, but generally are promoted by broad-based
taxes with relatively low tax rates on relatively elastic
bases. The personal income tax (more than other taxes)
has historically been considered, in principle, to further
these objectives best.

THE CHANGING COMPOSITION OF FEDERAL REVENUES

The importance of the federal personal income tax as
a source of revenue has been relatively stable over the
past 25 years, but the composition of federal receipts has
changed markedly. Of particular importance has been the
rapid growth of taxes on labor income for "social insurance,"
largely Social Security. Table 7.1 provides data for personal income tax receipts, social insurance contributions,
corporate income taxes, and other sources of federal revenue
including indirect business taxes, estate, and gift taxes.
The data show taxes as a percent of gross national product
and as a percent of total federal receipts. All data are
on a national income and product account (NIPA) basis and
are for calendar years.

The data indicate that, from 1960 to 1984, receipts
have fluctuated between 18 and 20.6 percent of GNP. Personal income taxes, the largest share of receipts, have
fluctuated between 7.2 and 9.9 percent of GNP. As a
share of total receipts, the personal income tax has contributed 40 to 48.4 percent. Over the period, however,
social insurance contributions have risen steadily as a
share of GNP and as a share of total receipts, with each
share more than doubling since 1960. This rise has been
offset by declining corporate income tax receipts and "other"
receipts, both relative to GNP and as a share of total receipts. The declining shares of these taxes largely reflect
the relatively slow growth in their tax bases relative to GNP.

Table 7.1

The Changing Composition of Federal Revenues

			As Percent of GNP		
	All Receipts	Personal Income Tax	Social Insurance Contributions	Corporate Income Tax	Other
1960	19.0	8.3	3.5	4.2	3.0
1961	18.7	8.1	3.5	4.1	3.0
1962	18.8	8.2	3.6	4.0	3.0
1963	19.2	8.2	3.9	4.1	2.9
1964	18.0	7.2	3.8	4.1	2.9
1965	18.0	7.4	3.6	4.2	2.8
1966	18.8	7.8	4.4	4.2	2.5
1967	18.8	8.1	4.6	3.8	2.4
1968	20.0	8.8	4.7	4.1	2.4
1969	20.9	9.7	4.9	3.8	2.4
1970	19.3	8.9	5.0	3.1	2.3
1971	18.4	8.0	5.0	3.1	2.3
1972	19.2	8.7	5.3	3.1	2.2
1973	19.5	8.3	6.0	3.3	2.0
1974	20.1	8.8	6.3	3.1	1.9
1975	18.5	8.0	6.1	2.8	1.9
1976	19.3	8.2	6.2	3.2	1.7
1977	19.6	8.5	6.2	3.2	1.7
1978	19.9	8.8	6.3	3.3	1.6
1979	20.4	9.3	6.6	3.1	1.5
1980	20.6	9.5	6.6	2.7	1.7
1981	21.1	9.9	6.9	2.2	2.1
1982	20.1	9.7	7.0	1.5	1.8
1983	19.4	8.7	7.1	1.8	1.8
1984	19.2	8.4	7.2	1.9	1.7
			As Percent of Total Federal Receipts		
1960	100	43.5	18.3	22.3	15.9
1961	100	43.5	18.7	21.9	15.9
1962	100	43.8	19.3	21.2	15.7
1963	100	43.0	20.2	21.5	15.3
1964	100	40.0	20.9	22.7	16.4
1965	100	41.1	20.1	23.3	15.5
1966	100	41.3	23.3	22.1	13.2
1967	100	42.8	24.4	19.9	13.0
1968	100	43.9	23.3	20.7	12.1
1969	100	46.5	23.7	18.3	11.5
1970	100	46.3	25.7	15.9	12.1
1971	100	43.2	27.4	16.9	12.6
1972	100	45.1	27.6	16.1	11.2
1973	100	42.3	30.7	16.7	10.2
1974	100	43.9	31.2	15.7	9.2
1975	100	42.0	32.8	15.2	10.0
1976	100	42.7	32.1	16.5	8.8
1977	100	43.4	31.6	16.4	8.6
1978	100	43.9	31.8	16.5	7.8
1979	100	45.5	32.3	15.0	7.1
1980	100	46.4	32.2	13.0	8.5
1981	100	46.7	32.7	10.5	10.2
1982	100	48.4	34.9	7.6	9.1
1983	100	45.0	36.5	9.3	9.2
1984	100	43.8	37.4	10.0	8.8

Source: U.S. Treasury statistics.

The most noteworthy feature of Table 7.1 is the spectacular growth of taxes on labor income for social insurance contributions. Such taxes were only slightly larger than the "other" component in 1960, but have risen to exceed the combined total of corporate income taxes and other since 1972. Indeed, by 1984 these taxes were over 2.6 times as large as the combined total of corporate and other taxes. Moreover, by 1984, such taxes were closing in on the personal income tax as the major source of federal revenue, equaling 37.4 percent of federal revenue, while the personal income tax equaled only 43.8 percent. Thus, the federal government collected 85.3 cents from social insurance contributions for every dollar paid in personal income taxes. At the pace of expansion of social insurance contributions relative to GNP maintained since 1980, such taxes will exceed 10 percent of GNP by the year 2000, and will likely represent the biggest share of federal receipts.

Thus, in assessing the federal income tax burden, social insurance contributions must in some fashion be taken into account. Of course, such taxes, like the personal income tax, are imposed directly on an individual's wage and salary income, the principal base of the personal income tax as well, so there is little reason to differentiate the two taxes. In contrast, the corporate income tax falls on a relatively small part of national income and is not levied directly on individuals, although, like all taxes, it is paid by individuals.

The aggregate data in Table 7.1 provide a useful point of departure in that, while they show a nearly constant relative importance for the personal income tax, they mask the changing nature of that structure. In order to examine these changes in more detail, a look at the changing burden on representative taxpayers is required. Over the past 25 years, there have been important changes in the real incomes of typical families, in the distribution of individuals among filing categories for the income tax, the number of workers per household and in the size and age distribution of families. Representative families in this chapter are the 1980 median income family with four members and families with half and twice this income.

THE 1980 TAX BURDEN

The median family income in 1980 was about $21,000.[2] Table 7.2 shows the 1980 federal personal income tax and

Table 7.2

The 1980 Federal Tax Burden at Three Levels of Income

	One-half Median Income	Median Income	Twice Median Income	
			One Wage Earner	Two Wage Earners
1980 Income	$10,500	$21,000	$42,000	$42,000
Personal Income Tax	$454	$2,505	$9,366	$9,366
Average Tax Rate	4.3%	11.9%	22.3%	22.3%
Marginal Tax Rate	16.0%	24.0%	43.0%	43.0%
Employee-Paid Social Security Tax	$644	$1,287	$1,588	$2,575
Personal Tax Plus Employee-Paid Social Security Tax				
Average Tax Rate	10.5%	18.1%	26.1%	28.4%
Marginal Tax Rate	22.1%	30.1%	43.0%	49.1%
Total Tax Burden*				
Average Tax Rate	16.6%	24.2%	29.9%	34.6%
Marginal Tax Rate	28.3%	36.3%	43.0%	55.3%

*Includes personal income tax and employee- and employer-paid Social Security tax.

169

Social Security tax liabilities for this level of income and for one-half and twice this median income. In computing personal taxes, it is assumed that there are four people (exemptions) in each household, that a joint return is filed, that all income is adjusted gross income, and that there are no other deductions, credits, or income adjustments.

In 1980 the employee-paid Social Security tax equaled 6.13 percent of wages up to a maximum of $25,900, with an equal amount being collected from the employer. Since the cost of employment includes both payments, the tax burden borne by the recipients of the respective income levels are given both ways: including and excluding the employer-paid Social Security tax. It is the former that represents the total federal tax burden.[3] The analysis here concerns wage income; the overall tax burden, at the personal level, on such capital income as dividends or interest is limited to the personal income tax rates. The additional taxation of income from capital at the corporate level, however, is generally greater than the additional burden of Social Security taxes shown here.[4]

The tax burden is measured in two ways: by the average tax rate and the marginal tax rate. The average tax rate is simply the amount of taxes paid per dollar of total income. The marginal tax rate is the increase in federal tax liability per dollar of additional income; it is the relevant measure of the impact of the federal taxes on incentives to work, save, and invest. Both measures are shown in Table 7.2.

The tax calculations apply to a one- or two-wage-earner family at the $10,500 and $21,000 levels. At $42,000, however, the taxes are calculated for both one-wage-earner and two-wage-earner families. For the latter, it is assumed that each wage earner earns less than the Social Security maximum tax base of $25,900 in that year.

If one worker's earnings exceed this base in 1980, then the relevant marginal tax rate applicable for the high-wage earner is that indicated in the one-worker calculation, while the rate applicable for the low-wage earner is that indicated for the two-worker calculation. The average tax rates for such a family are in the range bounded by the average tax rates for the one- or two-wage-earner families. For example, if one worker earns $26,000 and the other earns $16,000, the former faces an overall marginal tax rate of 43 percent, while the latter faces a marginal tax rate of 55.3 percent. Such a household had an average tax rate of 34.5 percent, based on the $9,366 paid in personal income taxes, the maximum Social Security payment of $3,175 by the high-wage earner, and $1,962 paid in Social Security for the low-wage worker for a total of $14,503 on $42,000 of income. More work on Social Security taxes is needed.

Some General Properties of the Federal Tax System

The data in Table 7.2 provide an illustration of the progressivity of personal taxes and of the relative importance of the regressive Social Security tax. Moving from left to right in the table, one observes how average tax rates rise as income rises, because at each income level the marginal tax rate exceeds the average tax rate. In addition, one can observe the relative importance of Social Security taxation for both average and marginal tax rates.

At the low income, the employee-paid Social Security tax (one-half the total) exceeds the personal income tax liability. Even at the 1980 median income, the total Social Security tax liability $[(.1226)(\$21,000) = \$2,575]$ exceeds the personal income tax liability ($2,505). Moreover, the Social Security tax is regressive since, at wage-income levels above $25,900 in 1980, the marginal Social Security tax rate is zero. Thus, the gap between the average or marginal personal income tax rates and the average or marginal tax rate measures of the total burden narrows as income moves above $25,900. For example, at the $42,000 income (one worker), the difference between the overall tax burden and personal income tax average rates is only 7.6 percentage points (29.9 - 22.3); for the marginal tax rates, the difference is zero. At the lower two-income levels, these differences are 12.3 percentage points.

Assessing the Trend in the Personal Income Tax Burden: The 1965 Tax Structure

Before 1981 marginal tax rates under the personal income tax had not been altered since 1965. From 1965 to 1981 many changes did occur. These changes included alterations in standard deductions, personal exemptions, and changes in the incomes associated with brackets. The number of brackets and bracket rates, however, did not change.

Table 7.3 shows the three representative 1980 families' tax position (from Table 7.2) based on 1965 taxes and prices for one-wage-earner families. In 1965 the Social Security tax was only 3.625 percent on wages up to $4,800 for both the employee- and the employer-paid amount. In 1965 prices, the 1980 income levels are considerably smaller, but purchasing power has been held constant. At the smaller 1965 nominal earnings, the 1980 median real income exceeded the maximum Social Security tax.

It should be noted that, at the income levels given for 1965, the 1980 families had considerably more real income than similarly placed families in 1965; the 1965 median-family income was only $6,957. The examples in Table 7.3 are for families that were comparatively better off than their 1965 counterparts; their real incomes were about 15.6 percent above the respective multiples of median income in 1965. Thus, their tax treatment represents higher tax rates for income than their 1965 counterparts, so that taxes on their actual counterparts in 1965 actually rose more than indicated by comparing Tables 7.2 and 7.3.

The average personal income tax at each income rose substantially from 1965 to 1980. For the 1980 median income, the increase is 22.7 percent of the 1965 tax burden of 9.7 percent. Even at the low income, the average tax burden rose sharply (19.4 percent). At twice the 1980 median income, the average personal income tax rate rose from 15.1 percent in 1965 to 22.3 percent in 1980, a 48 percent increase in taxes per dollar of income, despite no change in real income. The marginal personal income tax rates rose sharply as well, increasing 6.66 percent at the low income, 26.3 percent at the 1980 median, and 72 percent at the high income.

The overall tax burden on these unchanged real incomes ballooned much more. The overall marginal tax rate on the 1980 median income almost doubled, rising from 19 percent to 36.3 percent. The total marginal tax rate at the low income rose from 22.3 percent to 28.3 percent, a 27 percent increase, while that for the high income family rose 72 percent. The overall average tax rates on these real incomes rose 53.7 percent for the low-income family, 72.9 percent for the median-income family, and 72.8 percent for the high-income family. Except at the high income, the biggest share of the increase in the tax burden, on average or at the margin, was due to increases in both the Social Security tax rate and its tax base. At the relatively

Table 7.3

The Federal Tax Burden on Selected 1980 Real Incomes in 1965*

	One-half 1980 Median Income	1980 Median Income	Twice 1980 Median Income
1980 Income	$10,500	$21,000	$42,000
1965 Equivalent	$4,021	$8,041	$16,082
1965 Personal Income Tax	$143	$779	$2,431
Average Tax Rate	3.6%	9.7%	15.1%
Marginal Tax Rate	15.0%	19.0%	25.0%
1965 Employee-Paid Social Security Tax	$146	$174	$174
Personal Tax Plus One-half Social Security Tax			
Average Tax Rate	7.2%	11.9%	16.2%
Marginal Tax Rate	18.6%	19.0%	25.0%
Total Tax Burden			
Average Tax Rate	10.8%	14.0%	17.3%
Marginal Tax Rate	22.3%	19.0%	25.0%

*Assume one-wage earner family, for Social Security tax calculations.

high-income level, almost two-thirds of the overall average
and marginal tax burden increase occurred due to inflation-
induced bracket creep. Even at the 1980 median real income, the jump in the tax burden due to bracket creep was
substantial.

In summary, by 1980 marginal and average tax rates
at all levels of income had risen dramatically from 1965
levels due to rising Social Security costs and resulting tax
rates and its tax base, and to the effects of inflation pushing families into higher average and marginal personal income tax brackets. These forces continued from 1980 to
1984 and, in the absence of the 1981 tax cuts, would have
further boosted the tax burden.

The Adverse Effects of the 1965-80 Trend

The increases in the overall tax burden from 1965
to 1980, especially the rise in marginal tax rates, impaired
the functioning of the tax system. The most obvious adverse effect from the comparison is that on the fairness of
the tax system (see Tables 7.2 and 7.3). Despite the absence of real income changes in the comparison, average
tax burdens rose sharply. This conflicts with the notion
of horizontal equity, that equals should be taxed equally.
Of course, it could be argued that horizontal equity will
not hold over time if the government's relative importance
in the economy changes. But as Table 7.1 indicates, there
was little change in the overall proportion of taxes to GNP
between 1960 and 1980 or between 1965 and 1980. Moreover,
the share of total federal government expenditures in GNP
over these periods changed little. In 1980 it was 22.4 percent, while in 1960 it was 18.4 percent, and in 1965 it was
17.9 percent. This share increased by about 30 percent
from 1965 to 1980, but the overall average and marginal
tax rates on unchanged real incomes increased much more.

The increases in personal income tax burdens did
not result from legislated increases, but rather arose largely from bracket creep. Nonetheless, the distribution of the
taxes was allowed to change markedly. Average and marginal tax rates rose more the higher was real income, so
that the burden of taxation shifted upward toward those
with relatively high incomes. This was especially the case
for the marginal tax rate. This pattern of change suggests
that the tax system became more progressive, holding real

incomes constant; but the changes in average tax burdens were more similar as income rose, especially for the median and twice-median income households where the rise in the average rate was nearly identical. Thus, while the marginal rate changes appear to suggest a trend toward more progressive taxation, this is correct only at the margin, and apparently not for actual average tax burdens at various income levels. Indeed, the general shift toward an increased burden of Social Security taxes in the aggregate (Table 7.1) suggests that the aggregate tax burden has become more regressive.

The allocative and macroeconomic goals of tax policy were also not well served by bracket creep and Social Security. In particular, the rise in marginal tax rates on unchanged real incomes reduced incentives to supply and augment the supply of resources in the U.S. economy. Recall that these increases in marginal tax rates were much larger for most taxpayers than the rise in average tax burdens. A tax system is more efficient if, given the average tax rates, the marginal tax rate is lower. Thus, increases in marginal tax rates that are not accompanied by boosts in revenue, or the average tax rate given income, are inefficient. Movements toward efficiency require reductions in marginal tax rates, given the average tax rate. Such movements are possible when the tax base is broadened, for example, and marginal rates are cut. From 1965 to 1980 (and continuing to 1984 as shown below), however, the tendency has been the opposite due to the expansion of Social Security taxation.

Finally, the adjustability of taxes due to price-level changes has been perverse, from the viewpoint of macroeconomic objectives, during periods of aggregate supply shocks such as the oil price shocks of 1974-75 and 1979-80. In each instance, nominal GNP was little affected by higher energy costs, but real GNP--or productivity from existing resources--fell sharply, and this was matched by a higher level of prices. Despite the reduction in real income, the share of taxes in GNP or nominal income was virtually unchanged so that relative to real income, the tax burden (again on average and at the margin) rose prior to 1987. But the tax system was designed to have the tax burden fall when real incomes fall, given prices, in part to cushion households somewhat from the adversity of falling real income. Thus, when there are supply shocks, the taxation of nominal incomes results in bracket creep that worsens the decline in disposable income rather than alleviating some of the decline. Of course, with a progressive tax system, this problem was exacerbated.

THE EFFECTS OF THE 1981 TAX ACT
ON THE BURDEN OF PERSONAL TAXATION

Had no income tax rate changes been approved, inflation from 1980 to 1984 would have pushed all families into higher tax brackets. Coupled with existing provisions for Social Security taxation in 1980, these increases would have raised the average and marginal tax burden substantially, even if the purchasing power of family income (real income) had been unchanged. These effects are shown in Table 7.4.

Income in Table 7.4 equals the 1980 levels adjusted for the 26 percent increase in the general level of prices (consumer price index for all urban consumers) from 1980 to 1984; since income rises at the same rate as prices, no real income gain occurs. The 1980 tax tables are used to compute the personal tax liabilities. The Social Security tax calculations include both the rate increase to 13.7 percent (6.7 percent for employee-paid and 7.0 employer-paid components) and the 46 percent rise in the tax base to $37,800, provided under the 1977 and 1983 Social Security Act amendments.[5]

Despite unchanged real incomes, the families in Table 7.4 would have been subject to substantial jumps in their tax burdens from 1980 to 1984 under the 1980 tax law. Compared with 1980, the total tax burden, measured by taxes per dollar of income (shown at the bottom of Tables 7.2 and 7.4), would have risen by 17.8 percent for the median income family (28.5 percent divided by 24.2 percent = 1.178), 17.3 percent for a two-wage-earner family, and over 22 percent for the low-income and one-worker high-income families.[6]

Bracket creep, the taxation of purely inflation-induced changes in wages, would have raised the average tax rate for the personal income tax by over 20 percent in most cases. The rise for the lowest income level, from a 4.3 to a 7.0 percent average tax rate, would have been a staggering 63 percent increase. Even marginal tax rates would have risen sharply despite the unchanged real income. The change from Table 7.2 to Table 7.4 indicates

Table 7.4

What the 1984 Federal Tax Burden Would Have Been under the 1980 Personal Income Tax Law: No Change in Real Income

	One-half 1980 Median Income	1980 Median Income	Twice 1980 Median Income	
			One Wage Earner	Two Wage Earners
1984 Income	$13,230	$26,460	$52,920	$52,920
Personal Income Tax	$923	$3,906	$14,249	$14,249
Average Tax Rate	7.0%	14.8%	26.9%	26.9%
Marginal Tax Rate	18.0%	28.0%	49.0%	49.0%
Employee-Paid Social Security Tax	$886	$1,773	$2,533	$3,546
Personal Tax Plus Employee-Paid Social Security Tax				
Average Tax Rate	13.7%	21.5%	31.7%	33.6%
Marginal Tax Rate	24.7%	34.7%	49.0%	55.7%
Total Tax Burden*				
Average Tax Rate	20.7%	28.5%	36.7%	40.6%
Marginal Tax Rate	31.7%	41.7%	49.0%	62.7%

*Includes personal income tax and employee- and employer-paid Social Security tax.

that total marginal tax rates would have risen by 12 to 15 percent under 1980 tax laws. These relatively large percentage increases are associated with much smaller changes in the marginal tax rate for the personal income tax of 2 to 6 percentage points and a 1.44 percentage-point increase in the marginal tax rate for Social Security (12.26 percent to 13.7 percent).

Accounting for Higher Real Income

Of course, average and marginal tax rates would have actually increased more than the comparison of Tables 7.2 and 7.4 indicates because of typical real income increases and the progressive personal income tax system. From 1980 to 1984, real GNP per capita rose about 8 percent, or slightly less than 2 percent per year.

If each of the families in Table 7.4 had experienced similar growth in their real income, their incomes would have been 8 percent higher than those shown in Table 7.4 and their tax burdens would have been higher as well, given the progressive personal income tax. The overall average tax rates in Table 7.4 would have risen by 2.5 percent to 4.2 percent above those shown in Table 7.4.

For the 1980 median-income family shown in Table 7.4, the personal income tax average rate—the component of the tax system most sensitive to real growth—would have risen from 14.8 percent to 15.7 percent, a 6.1 percent rise due to 8 percent real growth.[7] At relatively low incomes, the average tax rate is most sensitive to income changes because marginal tax rates exceed average tax rates by the greatest amount; 8 percent real income growth for the low-income families in Table 7.4 would raise their personal income taxes much more, so that the average tax rate would rise from 4.3 cents per dollar of income to 7 cents per dollar, an 11.4 percent rise in the average tax rate. Such real income growth would have raised the average tax rate for the high-income family in Table 7.4 by about the same percent as that for the median-income family. None of the families shown in Table 7.4 would have moved into higher marginal tax brackets due to typical real income growth from 1980 to 1984 under the old tax law.[8]

THE 1981 PERSONAL INCOME TAX RATE REDUCTIONS

To offset the escalating tax burden due to inflation and the rise in marginal tax rates—which reduced incentives to earn additional income through work, saving, or investment—Congress approved a 23 percent cut in all personal income marginal tax rates to be phased in fully by 1984. For the purposes here, the major components of the 1981 tax act were a 23 percent cut in all marginal tax rates, phased in as a 5 percent cut in 1981, 10 percent in 1982, and 10 percent in 1983, and "indexing" of bracket incomes and personal exemptions beginning in 1985.[9]

Other Provisions of the Economic Recovery Tax Act of 1981

There were other important changes in the 1981 tax act, especially the adoption of the accelerated cost recovery system, extended investment tax credits, and reductions in tax rates on business income. These changes have been highly successful in stimulating business investment and productivity growth, as intended, and are not examined here.[10] Two other nonrate provisions had important effects on personal income taxes: the extension of tax-deferred income treatment through IRAs and the all-savers certificates (July 1981 to November 1982), and an earned income credit for two-wage-earner families.[11] These are not formally analyzed here. Another important change was to end the differential tax treatment of capital income for relatively high-income families. In 1980 marginal personal income tax rates on income from capital rose from 54 percent to 70 percent, as taxable income rose from $60,000 to $215,400. This distinction was dropped in 1982, so that all taxable income was subject to the same marginal tax rate.

The Effects of the 1981–84 Rate Reductions

With the rate reductions included in the 1981 tax act, the three families shown in Table 7.4 wound up in 1984 with the tax burden shown in Table 7.5.[12] Compared with what they would have been (Table 7.4), taxes were

Table 7.5

The 1984 Federal Tax Burden for Selected 1980 Real Incomes

	One-half 1980 Median Income	1980 Median Income	Twice 1980 Median Income	
			One Wage Earner	Two Wage Earners
1984 Income	$13,230	$26,460	$52,920	$52,920
Personal Income Tax	$711	$2,994	$10,958	$10,958
Average Tax Rate	5.4%	11.3%	20.7%	20.7%
Marginal Tax Rate	14.0%	22.0%	38.0%	38.0%
Employee-Paid Social Security Tax	$886	$1,773	$2,533	$3,546
Personal Tax Plus One-half Social Security Tax				
Average Tax Rate	12.1%	18.0%	25.5%	27.4%
Marginal Tax Rate	20.7%	28.7%	38.0%	44.7%
Total Tax Burden*				
Average Tax Rate	19.1%	25.0%	30.5%	34.4%
Marginal Tax Rate	27.7%	35.7%	38.0%	51.7%

*Includes personal income tax and employee- and employer-paid Social Security tax.

reduced substantially. For the personal income taxes considered alone, the cuts in average and marginal tax rates
were close to the target. Average tax rates fell by 22.9 to
23.6 percent for the three family incomes. Similarly, marginal tax rates fell by 21.4 to 22.4 percent.

But the results shown in Table 7.4 never actually
occurred. A comparison of Table 7.5 with the Table 7.2
tax burdens, the actual taxes paid in 1980, indicates the
effect of the 1981 rate changes on actual tax burdens, with
no real income changes. Again, focusing only on the personal income tax liability, it appears that tax burdens
were reduced. For the median-income family, the average
personal income tax rate fell from 11.9 percent in 1980 to
11.3 percent in 1984, a 5 percent reduction; the marginal
tax rate fell from 24.0 percent in 1980 to 22.0 percent in
1984, an 8.3 percent cut. These changes are shown in
Table 7.5. For all three groups, the marginal tax rates
fell, but by far less than the 23 percent observed when
comparing Tables 7.4 and 7.5. For 1980 median-income
taxpayers and higher income families, average personal income taxes declined, but, again, by much less than 23 percent. At the relatively low-income level, however, the
average tax rate actually rose from 4.3 to 5.4 percent, a
25.6 percent increase.

It should be emphasized that the modest declines in
the personal income tax rates from 1980 to 1984 shown in
Table 7.6 were fortuitous. They occurred primarily because inflation was not high enough to entirely erode away
the gains from the personal income tax cuts for some families. The 6 percent average inflation rate over the four
years was well below the 7.8 percent average rate projected
by the administration in 1981. Even that forecast was
viewed as a "rosy scenario" at the time; for example, the
Congressional Budget Office projected a 9.8 percent average
annual inflation rate for the four years.[13] Instead of the
26 percent rise in prices and income that occurred due to
inflation since 1980, these forecasts envisioned 35 and 45.3
percent increases, respectively. Either outcome would have
led to higher average and marginal personal income tax
rates for most families in 1984 than they faced in 1980,
despite the 1981 tax cuts and unchanged real incomes.

When the Social Security tax boosts since 1980 are
taken into account, however, even the modest gains cited
above generally disappear. At the bottom of Table 7.6,
the measures of the total tax burden indicate that average

Table 7.6

Changes in Tax Burdens from 1980 to 1984 for Selected Incomes: No Real Income Growth*

	One-half 1980 Median Income	1980 Median Income	Twice 1980 Median Income	
			One Wage Earner	Two Wage Earners
Personal Income Tax Rates				
Average	25.6%	-5.0%	-7.2%	-7.2%
Marginal		-8.3	-11.6	-11.6
Personal Income Tax Plus Employee-Paid Social Security Rate				
Average	15.2	-0.6	-2.3	-3.5
Marginal	-6.3	-4.7	-11.6	-9.0
Total Tax Rate				
Average	15.1	3.3	2.0	-0.6
Marginal	-2.1	-1.7	-11.6	-6.5

*Percent change; excludes "deduction for a married couple when both work."

tax rates generally increased and that marginal tax rates fell only slightly for 1980 median- and low-income families. Only two-wage-earner, high-income families appear to have received a slight reduction in their average tax rate. One-wage-earner families at the same income level fared worse, on average, because the rise in the average tax burden due to Social Security tax hikes was larger for families that earned more than the maximum Social Security tax base in 1980.

Changes in the Actual Tax Burden

The assumption of no real income growth used to derive the tax rates in Table 7.5 is appropriate for assessing the tax cut effects alone. Actual tax changes from 1980 to 1984, however, include not only the effects of inflation on income and the tax law changes, but also the effects of real income changes on income. Families typically earned higher real income in 1984 than in 1980 and also paid higher tax rates because of the progressive income tax.

Representative actual tax burden changes for the 1980 median-income families are shown in Table 7.7. There, nominal income (from Table 7.2) has been raised 8 percent to reflect the rise in per capita real GNP over the 1980-84 period. The table provides a comparison of 1980 and 1984 tax burdens assuming this typical growth.

Table 7.7 shows that the average personal income tax rate rose from 1980 to 1984 for 1980 median- and low-income families. When the higher 1984 Social Security taxes are included, the overall average tax rate rose for every group shown. Marginal tax rates generally declined somewhat over the period.[14]

It is clear that the rise in the tax burden from 1980 to 1984, despite the enacted tax rate reductions, fell disproportionately on low-income groups.[15] In Table 7.7, the rise in the overall average tax rate is smaller at higher incomes, raising the possibility that some high-income families actually paid lower average tax rates in 1984 than in 1980. Indeed, there is a "break-even" 1980 income level of $55,537, where the 1984 average tax rate under the assumptions above equals that paid in 1980. Only about 6 percent of tax returns had an income in excess of $50,000 in 1980. More important, these returns totaled about 15.9 percent of all taxable income. Moreover, the tax reductions

Table 7.7

1980 to 1984 Changes in Tax Burdens for Selected Incomes: Real Income Gain of 8 Percent

| | One-half Median Income | | | 1980 Median Income | | | Twice 1980 Median Income | | | | | |
| | | | | | | | One Wage Earner | | | Two Wage Earners | | |
	1980	1984[a]	Percent Change	1980	1984[a]	Percent Change	1980	1984[a]	Percent Change	1980	1984[a]	Percent Change
Personal Income Tax Rates												
Average	4.3%	6.0%	39.5%	11.9%	12.1%	1.7%	22.3%	22.0%	-1.3%	22.3%	22.0%	-1.3%
Marginal	16.0	14.0	-12.5	24.0	22.0[b]	-8.3	43.0	38.0	-11.6	43.0	38.0	-11.6
Personal Income Tax Plus Employee-Paid Social Security Rate												
Average	10.5	12.7	21.0	18.1	18.8	3.9	26.1	26.4	1.1	28.4	28.7	1.1
Marginal	22.1	20.7	-6.3	30.1	28.7[b]	-4.7	43.0	38.0	-11.6	49.1	44.7	-9.0
Total Tax Rate												
Average	16.6	19.7	18.7	24.2	25.8	6.6	29.9	31.0	3.7	34.6	35.7	3.2
Marginal	28.3	27.7	-2.1	36.3	35.7[b]	-1.7	43.0	38.0	-11.6	55.3	51.7	-6.5

[a] Excludes "deduction for a married couple when both work."
[b] Income is $23 below next personal income tax bracket, where the marginal tax rate rises 3 percentage points.

from 1980 to 1984 for these taxpayers were generally quite
small either as a percent of 1980 average tax rates or in
absolute percentage–point reductions. The largest tax reductions were about two percentage points for 1980 incomes
from about $80,000 to $100,000, where, under the assumptions above, the average tax was about 40 to 42 percent
in 1980.

The 1981–83 Tax Rate Cut Myths

Public discussion of the 1981 personal income tax
cuts has been dominated by two pervasive myths. The
first is that the tax rate reductions led to lower personal
income taxes for high–income families but little reduction
in taxes for low–income families. The second myth is that
personal federal taxes fell from 1980 to 1984.

Table 7.6 clarifies the source of the conflicting
claims that 1981 tax changes either resulted in greater
benefits for those with higher incomes or reduced marginal
and average tax rates equally.[16] Both the personal income and overall average tax rate changes in Table 7.6
indicate that the tax increases shown there fell disproportionately on lower–income families. The differential impact
of the tax cuts shown in Table 7.6, however, does not
arise from the tax rate changes since 1980; indeed, the
comparison of Tables 7.4 and 7.5 shows that average and
marginal tax rates were lowered by about the same percentage across income levels by the tax cuts enacted. The
discriminatory tax changes shown in Table 7.6 arose from
bracket creep and Social Security tax hikes, increases that
fall disproportionately on lower–income families. Fortunately, the greatest culprit, bracket creep, was largely eliminated by the 1981 tax act, though not until 1985.[17]

The second myth is that the tax changes contributed
to a surge in the deficit in late 1981 and 1982 and to the
magnitude of recent and prospective deficits.[18] Table 7.7
clearly indicates that, for representative families, the average tax burden rose from 1980 to 1984. Thus, personal tax
rate cuts alone are not a likely candicate as a source of
the increased federal deficit. While personal taxes as a
percent of income did decline slightly at very high incomes,
these reductions did not fully offset the generally larger
increases in tax liabilities of lower–income groups that
earn the larger share of income.

Federal revenues would have been larger and the deficit correspondingly smaller in 1984 had the 1981-84 personal income tax rate changes not occurred. A comparison of Tables 7.2 and 7.4 shows that 1984 revenues would have been about 22 percent larger under the old tax schedule. For fiscal year 1984, actual personal income taxes amounted to about $300 billion; this would have been about $85 billion larger under the 1980 tax rates. This "loss," however, was more than offset by the effect of inflation alone on federal tax receipts.[19] The apparent decline in the size of taxes relative to GNP was largely due to the cyclical decline in the economy and to cuts in business taxes.

THE INDEXATION PROVISION OF THE 1981 TAX ACT

The 1981 tax act provided for the indexing of bracket incomes and personal exemptions used in computing federal taxes beginning in 1985, based upon inflation over the previous year. The specific formula used to compute this inflation adjustment factor is the rise in the average consumer price index (CPI) for all urban workers from the year ending in September two years earlier to the previous year ending in September.

For example, since prices, as measured by the average CPI, were 4.1 percent higher during October 1983 to September 1984 than during October 1982 to September 1983, the bracket incomes and personal exemptions for 1985 income taxation will be about 4.1 percent larger than in 1984.[20] Thus, the personal exemption will rise from $1,000 to $1,040 per exemption, and the maximum taxable income that is subject to a zero marginal income tax rate for joint returns will rise from $3,400 to $3,540.

Table 7.8 shows the 1984 and 1985 tax schedules for married taxpayers filing joint returns. The difference shows the effects of the indexation provision in the first year. Although these changes may seem trivial, over a few years indexation will have substantial effects on taxes and tax burdens.

Indexation and the Effect of Inflation
on Personal Taxes from 1980 to 1984

Perhaps the simplest way to see how indexation will work in the future is to look at what would have occurred

Table 7.8

Federal Income Tax Schedules, Married Filing a Joint Return,
1984–85

1984		1985	
Taxable Income	Tax*	Taxable Income	Tax*
0– 3,400	0	0– 3,540	0
3,400– 5,500	0+11%	3,540– 5,730	0+11%
5,500– 7,600	231+12	5,730– 7,910	241+12
7,600– 11,900	483+14	7,910– 12,390	503+14
11,900– 16,000	1,085+16	12,390– 16,660	1,130+16
16,000– 20,200	1,741+18	16,660– 21,030	1,813+18
20,200– 24,600	2,497+22	21,030– 25,610	2,600+22
24,600– 29,900	3,465+25	25,610– 31,130	3,607+25
29,900– 35,200	4,790+28	31,130– 36,640	4,987+28
35.200– 45,800	6,274+33	36,640– 47,680	6,530+33
45,800– 60,000	9,772+38	47,680– 62,460	10,173+38
60,000– 85,600	15,168+42	62,460– 89,110	15,790+42
85,600–109,400	25,920+45	89,110–113,890	26,983+45
109,400–162,400	36,630+49	113,890–169,060	38,134+49
162,400+	62,600+50	169,060+	65,167+50

*The percentage at the right in this column is the mar-
ginal tax rate applied to taxable income in the range indicated.

had it been adopted in the recent past. Suppose that in
1981 Congress had adopted indexation to adjust for increases
in prices beginning in 1980, instead of passing the 1981–84
personal income tax reductions and delaying indexing until
1985. What would the effect have been on taxes paid in
1984?

The comparison of Tables 7.2 and 7.4 shows these
effects. Average personal income tax rates rise from 4.3,
11.9, and 22.3 percent to 7.0, 14.8, and 26.9 percent, respectively, for the three families shown, despite no change
in real income. These rates, which represent increases in
the average tax rate of 62.8, 24.4, and 20.6 percent, respectively, are due to bracket creep, that is, the taxation
of purely inflation-induced income increases at marginal tax
rates (bracket rates), instead of at average tax rates.

The effect of indexation is shown in Table 7.9. With indexation tied to <u>current</u> prices, the tax code would have raised the taxes shown in Table 7.2 by 26 percent from 1980 to 1984, simply matching the rise in prices and leaving the three groups of taxpayers with unchanged marginal tax rates or average tax rates. Such indexation would have raised the personal exemption to $1,260 from $1,000 and increased the bracket incomes (which were the same in 1980 as those shown on the left in Table 7.8) by 26 percent.

Table 7.9

An Illustration of the Effect of Indexation on Taxes from 1980 to 1984

1984 Tax (with Indexation, Using 1980 Tax Law)	One-half 1980 Median Income	1980 Median Income	Twice 1980 Median Income
Income	$13,230	$26,460	$52,920
Personal Exemption	5,040	5,040	5,040
Taxable Income	$ 8,205	$21,449	$47,938
Personal Income Tax	$ 572	$ 3,156	$11,801
Marginal (Bracket) Rate	16%	24%	43%
Average Tax Rate	4.3%	11.9%	22.3%

Note that indexation does not lower tax burdens. Instead, it leaves 1984 tax burdens unchanged from 1980 taxes, since real income is unchanged. Since both the average tax rate and real income are unchanged, after-tax real incomes are the same in Table 7.9 as in 1980. Indexing ensures that the inflation-induced increase in nominal income in each case is taxed at an unchanged average tax rate, instead of the higher marginal tax rate.

The 1981 Indexation Provisions Adjust for Past Changes in Prices

Because the indexing formula under the 1981 tax act is lagged, the results shown in Table 7.9 are only illustrative. Under lagged adjustment, tax schedules would have been adjusted to reflect the 40.2 percent price increases from 1979 to 1983 (8.8 percent annual rate of inflation) instead of the 26 percent increase from 1980 to 1984 (6 percent per year) used in Table 7.9. The difference reflects the fact that, from the period October 1978 to September 1979 to the period October 1979 to September 1980, the average price level rose 13.5 percent, while from calendar year 1983 to 1984, it rose only 4.2 percent. This discrepancy would have led to indexing of 1980 income tax tables that exceeds the inflation-induced rise in incomes from 1980 to 1984.

Table 7.10 shows what the personal income tax burdens in 1984 would have been if the 1981 tax act indexation provision had been implemented for 1981. A comparison of these tax burdens with the 1980 tax burden on the same real income shown in Table 7.2 indicates that the lag can have a large effect when inflation in the base-year period (1980 in this case) exceeds that in the most recent year of the calculation (1984).

Table 7.10

The 1984 Federal Personal Income Tax Burden with Lagged Indexation from 1979–83: No Real Income or Tax Rate Changes

	One-half 1980 Median Income	1980 Median Income	Twice 1980 Median Income
1984 Income	$13,230	$26,460	$52,920
Personal Exemption	($5,608)	($5,608)	($5,608)
Personal Income Tax	$399	$2,843	$10,689
Marginal Tax Rate	14.0%	21.0%	37.0%
Average Tax Rate	3.0%	10.7%	20.2%

Under such lagged indexation, tax burdens would have fallen from those shown for 1980 incomes. In effect, the 1984 indexation calculation in Table 7.10 compensates for 1980 inflation, but not for 1984 inflation. Thus, tax

burdens move down toward their 1979 levels on unchanged
real incomes. Lag in indexing results in average tax
rates falling from 4.3, 11.9, and 22.3 percent, respectively,
to 3.0, 10.7, and 20.2 percent, respectively. The 30.2 percent decline in the average tax rate of the low-income family exceeds the 10.1 percent decline for the 1980 median-
income household and the 9.4 percent decline for the high-
income household, because the bracket creep from 1979 to
1980 that is being offset is largest for low-income households.

The 1979 average tax burden for the unchanged real
incomes shown was 1.8 percent for the low-income household, 10.6 percent for the median-income household, and
19.9 percent for the high-income household. Thus, the lag
in indexation does not allow the 1979 tax burdens for these
households to be restored. The marginal tax rates shown
are the same as in 1979 for unchanged real incomes, with
one exception. At the same real income in 1979, the low-
income household would have faced the same (14 percent)
marginal tax rate in the tax tables, but would have qualified for an earned income credit in 1979. This credit would
have reduced its average tax rate from 2.8 to 1.8 percent
but boosted its marginal tax rate by 12.5 percentage points,
making it 26.5 percent.

Indexation that adjusts bracket incomes and personal exemptions to current prices tends to ensure that
average and marginal tax rates are unaffected by inflation. Thus, taxes rise in line with income unless real income changes. Such contemporaneous adjustment is costly
to administer, however, so indexation schemes are usually
tied to past price increases. Under the 1981 tax act provisions, tax tables and personal exemptions are adjusted
to inflation over the year ending in the previous September.
In the examples in this section, lagged indexation of 1980
tax tables nearly maintained average and marginal tax
rates at their 1979 levels in 1984, because 1979-80 price
increases were included in the adjustment, while 1983-84
price increases were not.

FUTURE TAXES UNDER INDEXING

The central features of tax changes under indexation
should be clear from this analysis. First, indexation ensures that purely nominal income gains are taxed at existing

average tax rates rather than higher marginal tax rates. Thus, bracket creep is largely eliminated and tax burdens do not change significantly unless real income changes. Of course, federal income taxes will continue to grow faster than incomes because the tax system remains "progressive" for real income gains. As the tables throughout this chapter show, the tax paid per dollar of income (the average tax rate) rises as incomes rise in any year.

Second, due to the lag in inflation adjustment, some bracket creep can occur. If the inflation rate from 1984 to 1989, for example, raises incomes at the same percentage rate as the bracket and personal income adjustments based on 1983 to 1988 inflation, then families with unchanged real incomes from 1984 to 1989 will be subject to the same personal tax burdens (on average and at the margin) as in 1984. If the 1988–89 inflation rate exceeds the 1983–84 inflation rate, then tax burdens will rise on unchanged real incomes, even with indexing. On the other hand, if inflation from 1984 to 1989 is less than the increase in prices from 1983 to 1988, then real tax burdens will be somewhat smaller in 1989 than in 1984 for unchanged real incomes.

To examine the impact of indexing in 1985, actual 1984 taxes shown in Table 7.5 must be compared, taking account of the tax rate reductions in the 1981 tax act. These taxes are shown again at the top of Table 7.11. In the lower two panels, 1984 incomes are increased by an assumed rise in prices from 1984 to 1985 of 4.7 percent.[21] In the middle panel of Table 7.11, taxes are computed for 1985 income without indexation, using the 1984 tax schedule shown on the left and the $1,000 per person personal exemption. At the bottom of the table, 1985 taxes use the rate schedule on the right and the increased personal exemption level of $1,040.

The relatively small impact of indexing in 1985 <u>alone</u> is shown. Without indexation, the three families would face tax increases in 1985 of $87, $274, and $945, respectively. With indexation, taxes increase from 1984 to 1985 by $41, $159, and $570, respectively. The differences in the tax increases may not seem large in magnitude, but indexation keeps the average tax rate on the unchanged real incomes from rising. Without indexation, the tax per dollar of income would have risen 7.4 percent at the low income, 4.4 percent at the middle income, and 3.9 percent at the high income. The low-income family will face the same personal income tax burden in 1985 as in 1984. The middle- and

Table 7.11

The Effect of Indexation in 1985 on Three Unchanged Real
Incomes

	One-half 1980 Median Income	1980 Median Income	Twice 1980 Median Income
1984 Taxes			
1984 Income	$13,230	$26,460	$52,920
Personal Exemptions (4)	4,000	4,000	4,000
Tax	$ 711	$ 2,994	$10,958
Bracket Rate	14%	22%	38%
Average Tax Rate	5.4%	11.3%	20.7%
1985 Tax (4.7 Percent Inflation and No Indexation)			
1985 Income	$13,852	$27,704	$55,407
Personal Exemptions (4)	4,000	4,000	4,000
Tax	$ 798	$ 3,268	$11,903
Bracket Rate	14%	22%	38%
Average Tax Rate	5.8%	11.8%	21.5%
1985 Tax (4.7 Percent Inflation and the 1981 Indexing Provision)			
1985 Income	$13,852	$27,704	$55,407
Personal Exemptions (4)	4,160	4,160	4,160
Tax	$ 752	$ 3,153	$11,528
Bracket Rate	14%	22%	38%
Average Tax Rate	5.4%	11.4%	20.8%

upper-income examples show trivial rises in the average tax rate due to slight bracket creep because of the lag in indexation.

After a few years, however, the insulation of federal tax burdens from inflation has a substantial effect on taxes. Even the relatively low 3.9 percent per year rise in the average tax rate for the high-income family in Table 7.11 that would have occurred without indexation in 1985 would cause taxes per dollar of income to double in about 18 years. For the low-income family, the average tax rate would double in less than ten years. Of course, higher rates of inflation would lead to even faster growth of tax burdens than these.

Martin Feldstein, in a defense of indexation, showed both its importance and its expected effects by noting that the repeal of indexing would add "$17 billion in taxes in 1986, $30 billion in 1987, $44 billion in 1988 and even larger amounts in later years."[22] The 1988 tax increase is about $200 per person alive today. Also, this is in addition to the nearly 17 percent projected increase in nominal taxes that will occur under indexation due to inflation and the larger increases in federal taxes arising from expected real income gains. Moreover, Feldstein's projections were based on an assumed inflation rate of only 4 percent. Within ten years, even with this inflation rate, he argues that overall taxes would be 25 percent larger if indexation were repealed and the remainder of the tax law were unchanged. Such estimates are very sensitive to the inflation rate; the estimated 1988 tax increase above due to bracket creep would be nearly twice as much ($80 billion) if inflation from 1983 to 1988 ran at 6.5 percent, the rate that prevailed from 1980 to 1983. Over the period 1981 to 1983, the U.S. Commerce Department has shown that purely inflation-induced income gains raised federal tax receipts by over $120 billion.[23] Thus, indexation may seem like a small technical detail when looked at from the short perspective shown in Tables 7.8 and 7.11. Inflation at the recent pace, however, causes a large difference in tax burdens over a few years time when indexation is not practiced.

The Income Tax Is Not Fully Indexed

It is important to bear in mind, also, that the personal income tax was not fully indexed by the 1981 tax act.

Credits, adjustments, and deductions that have fixed dollar amount ceilings (such as the deduction for a married couple when both work) and other credits (such as that for child care) are not indexed.[24] Thus, inflation can still raise federal income tax burdens on unchanged real incomes, although to a lesser extent than in the past.[25]

For example, the federal tax credit for child and dependent care expenses is a percentage (20 to 30 percent depending on income) of such expenses up to $2,400 ($4,800 for the care of two or more persons). Although inflation will drive up incomes and child care expenses, the nominal limits on creditable child care expenses are scheduled to remain fixed. As a result, once inflation pushes such expenses to the nominal limit, the value of the credit in reducing average tax rates becomes inversely related to future inflation.

Another popular adjustment that reduces average tax burdens and that is not indexed is the individual retirement account (IRA) contribution, under which individuals can deduct up to $2,000 from taxable income. On a joint return, the maximum reduction in taxes for such a contribution is the marginal tax rate (MTR) times $4,000. Relative to income (Y), the maximum reduction in the average tax rate is MTR x ($4,000/Y). Inflation reduces the share of income that is sheltered from taxes because inflation boosts income (Y), without boosting the nominal ceiling. The maximum reduction in the average tax rate due to contributions to an IRA is eroded; the average tax rate for such a household with an unchanged real income will continue to rise after 1984 to reflect this reduced real benefit.

FINDINGS

The adjustability of the income tax is typically regarded as a desirable feature of the U.S. tax system. The personal income tax, moreover, is progressive, so that as income rises (falls), taxes rise (fall) more. This feature of the tax system is desirable because: it provides automatically for the financing of the variable demands for government expenditures; it is fair since when income is relatively high (low), the tax burden is higher (lower); and it promotes economic stability. But the personal income tax has been based, until recently, on nominal or dollar income. As a result, changes in prices (and factor

payments) arising from inflation or price level changes
have resulted in undifferentiated adjustments of taxes.
Thus, with unchanged real incomes, nominal income growth
associated with price level changes has resulted in rising
average and marginal tax rates. These changes are sharply at odds with the desirable properties of an optimal tax
system. First, they are unfair because they violate the
principle of horizontal equity; in this case, families with
otherwise equal abilities-to-pay face different tax burdens
over time, with tax burdens being higher the higher are
prices. Second, by raising marginal tax rates, bracket
creep has resulted in reduced growth in resource supplies
and greater inefficiency in the use of existing resources.
These changes have impaired the achievement of allocative
and macroeconomic objectives of tax policy.

In addition to bracket creep, individual tax burdens
have been raised by ballooning tax rates and the tax base
for social insurance. Such taxes are inherently regressive
because the tax base is capped at a maximum level of
wage and salary income in each year. Moreover, such
taxes are proportional to income at income levels below the
cap so that, for real income changes, they do not provide
the vertical equity or stabilizing influences that a progressive tax would allow. Of course, to an extent, this pro-
portionality allows some of the adverse effects of bracket
creep to be avoided. Further, because such taxes have a
smaller tax base than the personal income tax (due to income caps and the exclusion of nonlabor income from the
tax base), they require higher rates than would otherwise
be the case to raise a given amount of revenue. Higher
tax rates for a given amount of revenue reduce the efficiency of the tax system.

These two forces--bracket creep and Social Security
tax boosts--substantially raised the income tax burden, on
average and at the margin, for nearly all families from
the mid-1960s to 1980 despite the more limited expansion in
the share of federal government expenditures or taxes in
GNP. In an attempt to reverse this trend, Congress reduced average and marginal personal tax rates by about
23 percent in 1981, with the reduction phased in from 1981
to 1984. In addition, Congress provided for indexation of
the personal income tax to begin in 1985.

The power of bracket creep and Social Security
boosts was sufficiently large from 1980 to 1984, however,
that few families realized lower tax burdens in 1984 than

in 1980. Indeed, most families faced sharply higher tax burdens in 1984 than in 1980. Since bracket creep and Social Security taxes are regressive, raising average and marginal tax rates relatively more at relatively low incomes, the pattern of actual tax burden changes from 1980 to 1984 reflects the largest increases at relatively low incomes and smaller increases at relatively high incomes.

Beginning in 1985, the personal income tax is indexed so that further boosts in marginal and average tax rates due to bracket creep are largely eliminated. Some components of the personal income tax have not been indexed, however, and the indexation provided is based on past price level changes so that bracket creep is not totally eliminated. While indexation will end the most insidious (automatic) source of the upward spiral in marginal tax rates and average tax burdens since the mid-1960s, it will not offset the increases that have occurred from 1965 to 1984. Moreover, the tax base and tax rates for social insurance will continue (under existing legislation) to rise sharply over the next 35 years, so that further tax reform will be required if marginal tax rates are to be returned to their mid-1960s levels or even kept constant. This increase will be matched by benefits received.

NOTES

1. For a more detailed consideration of the fiscal functions of government than that provided below, see Musgrave and Musgrave (1976). Most public finance textbooks provide similar discussions.

2. In 1980 the median family money income was $21,023. The median measure indicates the level at which one-half of all families receive more income and one-half receive less. The average size family in 1980 contained 3.27 members and the average number of wage earners per family was 1.63. The range of income in 1980 considered here encompasses most families. In 1980 18.9 percent of families had incomes below $10,000 and 13.5 percent of families had incomes in excess of $40,000. See Statistical Abstract of the United States (1982-83), pp. 432-34.

3. Social Security taxes are measured as a percent of "income." The employer-paid portion, however, is deducted before the income is measured. As a percent of wage earnings up to the maximum tax base, the employer-

paid tax is $t/1+t$ on average and at the margin, where t is the statutory rate on wage "income." Whether an increase in the employer-paid Social Security tax is borne from nominal take-home wage reductions or by product price increases is not important here. In either case, the real wage, the purchasing power of wages, is reduced. For discussions of this "incidence" issue, as well as thorough discussions of the tax system and its effects, see Pechman (1983) and Musgrave and Musgrave (1976).

4. See Joines (1981), for example, for a discussion of the differential taxation of capital and labor income.

5. Social Security taxes have an unusual feature in 1984 only, which does not affect the total burden of taxation, but does affect the calculations of the mix of the tax liability. Under the 1983 amendments, the Social Security tax rate in 1984 is 14 percent, instead of the 13.4 percent established in 1977 for 1984 or the 13.7 percent used here. The employee-paid portion of 7 percent is actually levied at a 6.7 percent rate, with the remainder (0.3 percent) paid from personal income taxes through a "tax credit" to Social Security funds. For purposes here, the Social Security tax in 1984 is 6.7 percent paid by employees, and the employer-paid component is 7.0 percent.

6. These percentage increases in the tax burden measure the rise in taxes as a percent of income, cents paid in taxes per dollar of income, on average. Similar calculations can be made for the marginal tax rate. Besides providing a meaningful measure of change in the tax burden, percentage changes in the average tax rate provide a convenient approximation to percentage changes in nominal taxes. The latter is roughly the sum of the percentage change in nominal income and the percentage change in the average tax rate. Some analysts emphasize percentage-point changes in taxes; for example, a rise in the average or marginal tax rate from 5 to 10 percent is viewed as a 5 percentage-point rise instead of a 100 percent increase in taxes per dollar of income. The data for such calculations are provided in the tables, but the percentage-point calculations are not important here.

7. The rise in average tax rates with unchanged marginal tax rates arises from the fact that additional income is taxed at the marginal tax rate, which exceeds the average tax rate. It is also this discrepancy that gives rise to bracket creep for purely inflation-induced increases in nominal income.

8.   A $21,023 income in 1980--increased 26 percent
for inflation and 8 percent for real growth--yields a 1984
income of $28,608, slightly above the income necessary to
move into a new bracket.   The conclusion in the text holds
for this family due to rounding.   This family would have
jumped one bracket due to inflation (from a 24 percent
marginal income tax rate to a 28 percent rate) and another
bracket due to typical real income growth (from a 28 percent rate to 32 percent).

9.   The 23 percent cut arises because the tax rate
was cut to 95 percent of its initial level, then 90 percent
of this level, then 90 percent of that rate; the final tax
rate is (.9)(.9)(.95) or 77 percent of its original level, a
23 percent cut.   Differences due to rounding largely account
for the departure from 23 percent for the marginal and
average personal income tax rate reductions examined.

10.   See Meyer (1983) and Tatom (1981).   Also, see
the Economic Recovery Tax Act of 1981 for details of other
nonrate provisions affecting the personal income tax.

11.   In 1984 personal income taxes can be reduced by
contributions of up to $2,000 to IRA or deferred income
plans that were not allowed for many taxpayers in 1980.
As a percent of income, these benefits are, in the limit,
equal to the marginal tax rate times $2,000 divided by in-
come.

The new deduction for married couples when both
work is limited to 10 percent of the lower income up to
$30,000.   The benefit subtracts the marginal tax rate times
a maximum of one-half of income for a two-wage-earner family.   The maximum reduction in the average personal income tax rates in Table 7.3 are thus (0.05 x 14 percent)
0.7 percent at the lowest income, (0.05 x 22 percent) 1.1
percent at the median-income level, and (0.05 x 38 percent)
1.9 percent for the high-income family.

12.   The marginal personal income rate for the low-
income family here masks the marginal tax burden at lower
incomes.   For incomes between $6,000 and $10,000, the
earned income credit declines at a 12.5 percent rate on
additional income.   Thus, for a family of four, the marginal personal income tax rate is 12.5 percent for incomes
from $6,000 to $7,400, 23.5 percent from $7,400 to $9,600,
and 24.5 percent from $9,600 to $10,000.   At $10,000 the
marginal personal income tax on additional income drops to
12 percent and remains there until income reaches $11,600,
where it rises to the indicated 14 percent.

Thus, at the margin, the tax burden on families with incomes from $7,400 to $10,000 exceeded that of 1980 median-income families. The situation is even worse for a head of household with one dependent, where the marginal personal income tax rate of 23.5 percent begins at an income of $6,000 and rises to 26.5 percent as income approaches $10,000. Bracket creep falls most heavily on persons in these brackets because of both the large difference between marginal and average tax rates at low incomes and the complicated and nonindexed earned income credit.

13. See Congressional Budget Office (1981), p. 4.

14. Without rounding the 1980 median income down by $23, the marginal personal income tax rate of this group would have risen from 24 to 25 percent, and the overall marginal rate of this group would have risen from 36.3 percent to 38.4 percent. The maximum marginal tax rate of 50 percent of earned income was achieved at $60,000 of taxable income in 1980 and at $162,400 in 1984. The latter is equivalent to $128,889 in 1980 prices. At earned taxable incomes above this level, the marginal tax rate has been unchanged from 1980 to 1984.

15. Business Week (1984) notes that between 1980 and 1984, changes in the distribution of personal disposable real income were such that the top quintile (20 percent of income recipients) gained, while the bottom quintile lost, both by about 8 percent. Families in the second lowest quintile lost close to 2 percent, while those in the third quintile registered a slight gain of about 1 percent. In the fourth quintile, the gain was about 3.5 percent. This pattern reflects the effects of tax changes, spending cuts, and the business cycle, with a large share arising from the different increases in the overall average tax rates included in the analysis.

16. These distributional changes have been noted by Conyers (1984) and Heller (1984), for example.

17. Proponents of the view that taxes were cut are often leading opponents of indexing. See Silk (1984) and Heller (1984), for example.

18. See Walter W. Heller (1984). He attributes the rise in the deficit to the "huge tax cut" or the "biggest tax cut ever." The alternative cyclical view of recent deficits, which owes much to Heller for its popularization, is developed in Tatom (1984). Hershey (1984) and Harris Bank (1984) echo the frequent claim that personal tax cuts

occurred from 1980 to 1984. See Meyer and Rossana (1981), Meyer (1983), McKenzie (1982), and Tatom (1981) for discussions of the absence of tax reductions due to bracket creep.

19. For example, the Bureau of Economic Analysis (1984) indicates that cyclically adjusted receipts rose $121.9 billion due to inflation alone in 1981–83. Data for 1984 are not yet available.

20. It is "about" 4.1 percent in 1985 or the similarly calculated inflation in the future, because the act calls for rounding the bracket incomes and personal exemptions to the nearest $10.

21. The latter was found assuming a steady 5 percent annual rate of increase of the CPI from October 1984 to December 1985. The 5 percent inflation rate was chosen arbitrarily; the changes in average tax rates, with or without indexation shown, are not very sensitive to the inflation assumption for 1985.

22. Feldstein (1983).

23. See Bureau of Economic Analysis (1984).

24. An example of a rise in the average tax rate, due to fixed nominal adjustments to income or taxes, is the loss in the earned income credit for the low–income family discussed above. In 1979, on the same real income as those used, such a household faced an average tax burden that was 1 percentage point lower due to the availability of the earned income credit (1.8 percent instead of 2.8 percent). Inflation–induced bracket creep removed the availability of this credit by pushing nominal income above the $10,000 ceiling, where the credit becomes unavailable. From 1979 to 1984, this accounts for most of the rise in the household's average tax rate from 1.8 percent to 3.0 percent, despite the indexation shown.

25. In addition, interest income is overstated during periods of inflation, and the indexation of tax brackets and personal exemptions does not address this problem. Interest rates contain an inflation premium that compensates for lost purchasing power, primarily of the initial amounts loaned. These payments maintain the value of capital and, hence, are not income, though they are taxed as such under the federal income tax. The higher is inflation, the larger is this component of interest income and the larger are taxes on unchanged real incomes. For a discussion of this problem, see Tatom and Turley (1978).

REFERENCES

Bureau of the Census. Statistical Abstract of the United States: 1982-83 (103d edition). Washington, D.C., 1982.

Bureau of Economic Analysis. Survey of Current Business (August 1984), p. 9.

Business Week. "The Reagan Tax Cuts: Were the Supply Siders Right?" (May 28, 1984), pp. 68-69.

Congressional Budget Office. "An Analysis of President Reagan's Budget Revisions for Fiscal Year 1982." Staff Working Paper, Congress of the United States (March 1981).

_____. "Effects of Major Changes in Individual Income and Excise Taxes Enacted in 1981 and 1982 for Households in Different Income Categories." Staff Memorandum (March 1984), processed.

Conyers, John, Jr. "What Recovery?" Washington Post, October 3, 1984.

Economic Diary. "Who Is Better Off Under Reagan—And Who Isn't." Business Week (October 22, 1984), p. 14.

Economic Recovery Tax Act of 1981: Law and Explanation. Commerce Clearing House, August 1981).

Feldstein, Martin. "Why Tax Indexing Must Not Be Repealed." Wall Street Journal, March 1, 1983.

Harris Bank. "A Taxing Development." Barometer of Business (September/October 1984).

Heller, Walter W. "The Unavoidable Issue." Wall Street Journal, October 26, 1984.

Hershey, Robert D., Jr. "The Reagan Economic Legacy." New York Times, October 28, 1984.

Joines, Douglas H. "Estimates of Effective Marginal Tax Rates on Factor Incomes." Journal of Business (No. 2, 1981), pp. 191-226.

McKenzie, Richard B. "Supply-Side Economics and the Vanishing Tax Cut." Federal Reserve Bank of Atlanta Economic Review (May 1982), pp. 20-24.

Meyer, Stephen A. "Tax Cuts: Reality or Illusion?" Federal Reserve Bank of Philadelphia Business Review (July/August 1983), pp. 3-16.

Meyer, Stephen A., and Robert J. Rossana. "Did the Tax Cut Really Cut Taxes?" Federal Reserve Bank of Philadelphia Business Review (November-December 1981), pp. 3-12.

Miller, Glen H., Jr. "Alternatives to the Current Income Tax." Federal Reserve Bank of Kansas City Economic Review (September/October 1984), pp. 3-16.

Musgrave, Richard A., and Peggy B. Musgrave. Public Finance in Theory and Practice (2d ed.). McGraw-Hill, 1976.

Pechman, Joseph A. Federal Tax Policy (4th ed.). Brookings, 1983.

_____. Options for Tax Reform. Brookings, 1984.

Silk, Leonard. "Federal Deficit and Indexation." New York Times, October 26, 1984.

Tatom, John A. "We Are All Supply-Siders Now!" this Review (May 1981), pp. 18-30.

_____. "A Perspective on the Federal Deficit Problem." this Review (June/July 1984), pp. 5-7.

_____. "The 1984 Personal Income Tax Cuts: A Retrospective Look at Their Effects on the Federal Tax Burden." this Review (December 1984), pp. 5-17.

_____. "Federal Income Tax Reform in 1985: Indexation." Federal Reserve Bank of St. Louis _Review_ (February 1985), pp. 5–12.

Tatom, John A., and James E. Turley. "Inflation and Taxes: Disincentives for Capital Formation." this _Review_ (January 1978), pp. 2–8.

U.S. Department of Treasury. _Tax Reform for Fairness, Simplicity, and Economic Growth_. Treasury Department Report to the President, November 1984.

Wall Street Journal. "All Supply-Siders Now." November 6, 1984.

_____. "Tricklenomics." April 11, 1984.

8

The Underground Economy in the United States and Western Europe

Ann D. Witte

We have all read accounts in recent years of a large and growing informal, subterranean or underground economy in various (if not all) developed economies. Indeed, concern with this phenomenon has not been limited to the popular press, but has extended to the financial press, congressional committees, executive branch agencies, and the academic community in the United States and Western Europe. Is this simply an example of fascination with the novel, or does it represent an important new phenomenon in developed economies with mixed economic systems?

The simple answer to this question is that it represents a bit of both. To adequately explain this, it is necessary first to describe what is meant by subterranean, informal, and underground economy. Unfortunately, this is not easy to do. The definition of this economy varies from author to author and, more importantly, with the particular issue the author is considering. We will discuss the issue of definition at some length later. Here, we will merely note that this economy is usually defined to consist of all market activity[1] that is not recorded in the national statistics or not properly reported to national tax authorities.

The first thing to note about this definition is that it relates to activity that is unrecorded by some national authority. Thus, we know that unrecorded activity became of potential policy significance only after there were comprehensive attempts to measure and tax market activity. These attempts are largely a twentieth-century phenomenon. Well-developed systems of national accounts[2] and comprehen-

sive tax administration[3] emerged largely in the World War
II period. Thus, we would not be at all surprised if unrecorded activity had been of concern at least for the last
30 to 40 years.

Actually, there have been two periods of interest in
unrecorded activity. The first was of limited length and
was concerned with unrecorded activity caused by the high
tax rates, rationing, and other government regulations during World War II and immediately thereafter. Cagan noted
that there was an unusually high ratio of currency to total
liquid assets in the United States during World War II.
Using a technique that will be described later, he concluded
that it is "plausible to attribute three-fourths or even all
of the wartime increase in the demand for currency to income tax evasion" (Cagan 1958: 13).

Indeed, if one looks at the ratio of currency to demand deposits, one finds unusually high ratios in the immediate period following World War II and in the second
half of the 1970s. It was the rapid growth of the currency ratio in the 1970s that led researchers to suggest
that unrecorded activity was again becoming important in
the U.S. economy.[4] Gutmann (1977) estimates that the increase in currency supported unrecorded activity of $176
billion in 1976, approximately 10 percent of GNP in the
United States in that year.[5]

In Europe concern about large and growing amounts
of unrecorded activity also occurred in the 1970s and was
also stimulated by statistical oddities. In Italy the oddity
was a surprisingly low and falling labor force participation rate. According to the Organization for Economic Development statistics, the official participation rate in 1975
was 35.5 percent in Italy, 42.3 percent in France, 44.4
percent in the United States, and 46.4 percent in the United
Kingdom. Further, the participation rate in Italy has
been falling since the late 1950s: in 1959 it was 44 percent, in 1971 36.2 percent, and in 1977 33.7 percent.[6] Researchers estimated that much of the fall was due to people
working in unrecorded activities and that moonlighting in
unrecorded activities was pervasive in Italy. Considering
both of these factors, the hidden economy in Italy was estimated to be between 14 and 33 percent of officially measured GNP during the 1970s.

In Belgium, Denmark, France, and Germany, the
oddity was the growth of the "residual error" between estimates of income that used national income account data and

estimates that used data from tax returns. The size and growth of this discrepancy led to estimates of unrecorded activity of 6 percent of measured GNP in Denmark in 1974–75, 8.9 percent of GNP in the Federal Republic of Germany in 1968, 20 percent in Belgium in 1970, and 23 percent in France in 1965.

These discoveries at approximately the same time suggest that the phenomenon may well reflect a major structural change in the U.S. and Western European economies. However, many reports about unrecorded activity also appear to have been stimulated by an attraction to the "new idea" and by the growth of conservative opinion, which found that this unrecorded activity could be used to buttress arguments for less government regulation, lower levels of social services, and lower tax rates. Indeed, some individuals see increasing amounts of unrecorded activity as a sign of a tax debacle and so call for a thorough reform of our tax system. We will attempt later to discern the likely amount of unrecorded activity in a number of Western European countries and the United States, and the rate at which this activity grew during the 1970s. We will then discuss the degree to which this phenomenon represents a major structural change in the mixed economies of the West, and the degree to which it can be called a tax debacle. Finally, we will suggest areas for future research and present a summary and conclusions.

WHAT IS UNRECORDED AND UNOFFICIAL ACTIVITY AND WHY ARE WE CONCERNED?

As noted in the introduction, what definition of unrecorded economic activity is used depends upon the issue of major concern. To date, the major concerns have been: losses in tax revenue; effects on economic and social indicators; effects of government regulation and high marginal tax rates on behavior; and effects on the way in which people organize their social and economic lives. We will consider each of these concerns and the definition most appropriate for addressing it below.

Perhaps the major and certainly most direct concern about unrecorded economic activity comes from its effect on tax revenues. The fear that increases in such activity have led to major decreases in tax revenue has caused many to speak of a tax debacle. The nations of Western

Europe and the United States now have broadly based taxes
on incomes and either a value-added or a sales tax. Unrecorded economic activity largely escapes these taxes, and
hence is of direct concern to those responsible for collecting taxes. For example, much recent research on unrecorded activity has been sponsored by taxing authorities.
In the United States, the Internal Revenue Service (IRS)
has produced two reports that attempt to estimate directly
the amount of unreported income.[7]

The IRS divides unreported income into a "legal"
and "illegal" sector. Its definitions of earnings in these
two sectors are:

> Legal sector earnings include incomes from
> regularly established enterprises or occu-
> pations, and from legal activities that are
> sometimes called irregular because they
> take place in informal settings. Examples
> of these legal earnings are unreported in-
> terest and dividends, unreported tips, and
> unreported earnings of independent con-
> tractors and other individuals. (Coates
> 1983: 4)

> "Illegal sector" incomes are those derived
> from organizing, financing, producing, and
> delivering illegal goods and services re-
> lated to drugs, gambling, prostitution, and
> so on. (Coates 1983: 5)

Note that these definitions are interested only in income
which is not properly reported to taxing authorities. Thus,
the taxing authorities are interested in incomes from transfer payments (such as alimony and stolen funds) and capital gains, as well as incomes earned directly from supplying labor, capital, or natural resources for productive
purposes (that is, factor incomes in economic jargon).
Note also that this definition carefully divides unreported
income into a legal and illegal sector. The taxing authorities feel that their major responsibility is to ensure high
levels of reporting on legal incomes. They generally see
their role as secondary to that of federal, state, and local
criminal justice authorities in dealing with the illegal sector. However, major figures operating large criminal organizations are often more successfully prosecuted, at least

in the United States, on income tax rather than criminal charges.

The latest IRS report (U.S. Department of the Treasury 1983b) indicates that $81.5 billion of federal income tax was lost in 1981 due to underreported legal incomes and $9 billion due to unreported incomes earned in illegal endeavors.[8] Note that the $90.5 billion of total loss was equal to approximately 22 percent of the total federal corporate and personal income taxes collected in 1981. While this level of loss probably should not be considered a tax debacle, it merits the serious concern it has received from both executive and legislative branch personnel.

A second area of concern has been the effects of unrecorded economic activity on economic statistics used to set national policy (such as the national income accounts and unemployment rates). The definition of unreported activity needed to determine the effect of such activity on national statistics is very different than the definition used by taxing authorities; indeed, the definition varies with the particular national statistic under consideration.

Recall from the introduction that discrepancies between national income account estimates of income and tax return estimates were one of the original signals that there were substantial amounts of unreported activity. Given this and the policy importance of the national income accounts, it is not surprising that much attention has focused on the degree to which such national income account measures as gross national product (GNP) and gross domestic product (GDP) are understated as a result of unrecorded economic activity. The natural definition of unrecorded economic activity for the purpose of discerning its effect on the national income accounts is "legal and illegal activities not covered in the various sources of data used to estimate GNP" (Parker 1983: 1). As far as we are aware, the most detailed study of the effect of unrecorded activity on the national income and product accounts (NIPA) has been conducted by the U.S. Bureau of Economic Analysis (BEA). The first thing to note is that NIPA, unlike the accounts of many Western European countries, consciously excludes illegal activity. Thus, in the United States it is only the "legal" portion of unreported activity that may potentially be incorrectly excluded from the NIPA.

To understand the nature of possible understatement in the NIPA, it is necessary to understand the way in which it is constructed. The first important observation is that the BEA, in making its estimates of national income and product, uses information from tax returns, but does not rely upon this type of information exclusively. GNP is estimated in two separate and distinct ways—as the total of all factor incomes and as the total of all final expenditures on goods and services—in order to ensure as many cross-checks as possible. Indeed, it was the discrepancy between the income and expenditure estimates of GDP that suggested to some European researchers that unrecorded economic activity might be an important phenomenon (for example, see Macafee 1982). In general, the final expenditure approach to GNP estimation makes far less use of tax data, and, thus, should understate GNP to a far smaller degree than does the income approach to estimation. The BEA currently estimates that final expenditures were underestimated by only $22 billion in 1977 (slightly more than 1 percent of GNP in that year), while personal income was underestimated by $69 billion (4 percent of personal income in 1977).[9] In evaluating these figures relative to the figures for income that is not properly reported to the IRS, one should realize that BEA uses the results of the IRS in-depth audit program, the Tax Compliance Measurement Program (TCMP), to blow up estimates of income that use data from tax returns.

To get an idea of the problem, it is useful to list the areas where BEA feels incomes and expenditures are understated. On the expenditure side, BEA believes that most understatement is in the area of personal consumption expenditures, such as: food and tobacco; clothing, accessories, and jewelry; personal care; household operations; certain types of medical care; legal services; funeral and burial services; gasoline and oil; auto repairs and other auto-related expenses; taxicabs; and recreation and hotels and motels. BEA believes the largest understatement comes in the area of nonfarm proprietors' income (income of unincorporated businesses), domestic private corporate profits (based on the results of IRS corporate audits), and tips.

Blades (1982) provides estimates of the degree to which GDP is understated in a number of OECD countries. He notes first that many countries make explicit adjustments for undeclared legal production, which average approximately 2 percent of GDP. In Italy there was a major revision of GDP statistics in 1978, largely to include more hidden economic activity. Blades believes that 4 to 4.5 percent of the increase in GDP for 1975-77 that occurred as a result of the Italian adjustments was due to hidden activity. After official adjustments have been made, Blades believes the GDP of Northern European countries, Canada, Australia, and Japan is understated to about the same extent as U.S. GNP (1 percent or so). He feels that informal activity is much larger in Southern Europe, but that the GDP figures in many of these countries include larger amounts of this type of activity due to the statistical adjustments described above.

There has also been much concern that statistics related to labor market status and hours of work may be markedly affected by unreported activity. It was, after all, the falling labor force participation rate that first alerted Italian authorities to the extent of unrecorded activity. In Italy, the institute DOXA-ISFOL estimated that the true labor force participation rate was 39.5 in 1975, when official statistics estimated it was only 35.5 percent. This suggests that 10 percent of the working population was employed off-the-books in that year. The Italian Instituto Centrale di Statistica believes this proportion increased to 13 percent in 1977.[10] Survey work in Norway (Isachsen, Klovland, and Strom 1982) suggests that 18 percent of persons interviewed in 1980 would admit to having performed unregistered work.

How unregistered work affects important national labor statistics depends critically on whether individuals performing unregistered work also have recorded employment. The evidence indicates that most unregistered work is performed on a part-time basis by people who are also employed in registered activity. Thus, their unreported activity will affect hours of work but will not affect either the unemployment rate or the labor force participation rate as they are currently defined in most developed countries, including the United States. To be more precise, while estimates vary, it appears that well over half of the people working in unrecorded activity are also employed in recorded activity and are properly counted as employed, although their hours of work are underestimated. There also appears to be a core of unrecorded workers whose main source of income comes from unrecorded activity. The size and composition of this core vary with the stage of the business cycle and from country to country, but probably consists of 25 percent or more of those working in unrecorded activity. In the United States and Northern Europe, undocumented aliens often comprise a large portion of this core. For example, in the United States we have estimated (Simon and Witte 1982: 58) that in the mid-1970s there were approximately 1 million undocumented aliens working exclusively in unrecorded economic activity. The very high rates of unemployment and low rates of labor force participation among nonwhite teenage males in the United States suggests that this group may provide a substantial number of individuals who work full time in unrecorded activity.

In Europe the number of undocumented workers in the countries of the European Economic Community was estimated to be between 500,000 and 600,000, with perhaps half of these residing in the Federal Republic of Germany.[11] The core workers of the underground economy may well be misclassified and may be counted as either out of the labor force or unemployed when they actually are working in unrecorded activities.

A major portion of those working in unrecorded activity are also receiving various types of social welfare payments (pensions or unemployment benefits). Most of these benefits either require a certain labor market status (such as unemployment) or income below a certain level (such as welfare and some pension payments) for receipt. Many persons receiving these benefits are known to be working either part or full time in unrecorded activity. Like full-time employment in unrecorded activity, this type of employment causes labor force participation rates to be understated and unemployment rates to be overstated. Taking all of these factors into account, we have guesstimated (Simon and Witte 1983) that the labor force participation rate in the United States may have been understated by 1 percent and the unemployment rate overstated by 1 percent in the mid-1970s.

It has been suggested that other economic indicators have been affected by unrecorded activity, but to date less work has been done to discern the precise nature of these effects. For example, it seems likely that the consumer price index is overstated, particularly in the area of personal and household services, repairs, clothing, and some agricultural goods. The effect on the inflation rate, a more important statistic for policy purposes, is far less certain.

In an exhaustive study, Dennison (1978) has suggested that productivity (measured output per unit of input in the nonresidential business sector) was 1.8 percent smaller in 1975 than it would have been if 1967 conditions had prevailed. However, he considered factors other than unrecorded activity. More recently, Feige (1982: 59) has suggested that 65 percent of Dennison's unexplained decline in productivity in the United States during the 1970s was due to the growth in unrecorded activity.

Many political leaders, particularly those with a conservative bent, have seen the underground economy as providing conclusive evidence that the extensive regulations, social welfare systems, and taxes of the modern Western world are too high. They argue for decreased regulation, lower tax rates, and reductions in social welfare payments. Indeed, a number of researchers have suggested that cuts in tax rates will not only have the beneficial incentive effects depicted in the Laffer Curve, but will also surface some unrecorded activity. Unrecorded activity can also be used to support the claim that we have a tax debacle and need supply-side economic policies (see Gutmann 1977, Simon and Witte 1981, and McGee and Feige 1982). If this point of view is correct, the drop in tax rates in the United States and Great Britain in recent years should stem the growth in unrecorded activity.

The most appropriate definition of unrecorded activity for those interested in the effects of regulation and high marginal tax rates is probably all activity escaping broadly based taxes counted on a national income and product account basis. We first used such a definition in preparing a paper for the U.S. Joint Economic Committee's Special Study of Economic Change (Simon and Witte 1980). Indeed, a number of the monetary and transaction approaches discussed below are probably best seen as yielding estimates of the GNP or other national income account statistics for the underground economy.

A final reason for concern about unrecorded activity is more academic and theoretical than of direct policy relevance. A number of researchers (particularly economists, sociologists, and anthropologists) are interested in the effect of unofficial activity on their theories and understanding of human behavior.

For some time Edgar Feige (for example, see Feige 1979) has been suggesting that the poor performance of macroeconomic models in predicting the course of economic activity in Western developed economies during the 1970s is due largely to the rapid growth of unrecorded activity. Feige believes that these models predict quite accurately, and that it is the recorded statistics to which the predictions are compared that are in error.

Sociologists and anthropologists have quite different concerns. They see unofficial activities as important parts of the economic and social life of work places and neighborhoods. Economically, unofficial activity allows families to supplement their earnings, and in times of high unemployment may actually be a major source of income. Further, unofficial activity often humanizes the work environment in large impersonal organizations (see Henry 1978 or Mars 1982). For those who are either not able to or who prefer not to work in such organizations, unrecorded work may provide badly needed employment in less structured environments. For example, many women prefer unstructured, part-time work in their homes (providing child care and personal and household services) while their children are small.

We suggest two definitions of unrecorded economic activity: economic activity the income from which is not properly reported to taxing authorities; and economic activity that is not properly recorded in a particular national statistic. The first definition is most appropriately used by those concerned with raising revenue; the second is most appropriate for national statisticians and macroeconomists trying to predict the course of economic activity.

Further, we suggest that from a social science research perspective we should be concerned about unofficial, not unrecorded, activity. What we are interested in is the relative size and nature of activities carried out in various settings. It does not particularly matter whether the activity is recorded; rather, it is the activities' place in social and economic behavior that is of central concern. For the purpose of social science research we suggest the following definition of unofficial economic activity: economic activity that produces income and product, but is neither condoned by nor carried out in recognized economic entities.

THE EXTENT AND GROWTH OF UNRECORDED AND UNOFFICIAL ACTIVITY

The answer to the above question of how much unrecorded and unofficial activity is there and how rapidly is it growing depends critically on the definition of unrecorded activity one uses. We will consider what is known about unrecorded activity under each definition given above in turn.

Under the first definition, researchers attempt to estimate the amount of income that is not reported to taxing authorities. Both direct and indirect methods have been used to estimate the total amount. The indirect methods have been used for a longer period and we will consider them first.

The indirect method compares the total amount of personal income estimated by national income accountants and the amount of income reported to taxing authorities. The difference between the two may provide an estimate of income that is not reported. These estimates have been made for a number of countries and they vary markedly and in unexpected ways from country to country. For example, there is little unreported income in England, but much in Belgium and France. The explanation for the seeming paradox lies in the fact that the national accounts statisticians in the United Kingdom rely heavily on tax records to obtain their estimates of income. Note also that the size of the discrepancy can vary from year to year and, indeed, appears to indicate that unreported income was less of a problem in the United States and Denmark in the 1970s than in the 1960s. Other information of higher quality makes it appear that this is quite unlikely to have been the case.

Our conclusions concerning this approach are not unlike those of other researchers who have considered it (such as Frey and Pommerehne 1982; Henry 1983). The approach marked a useful beginning for estimating unreported income, but it is probably best used now for obtaining estimates of underreporting of certain types of income (such as dividends and interest in the United States) than to obtain overall measures of unreported income. Further, attempts to use this type of estimate to compare the amount of unreported activity across countries is likely to be fruitless given substantial differences in the methods of estimating national income.

To date, the most comprehensive direct effort to estimate the amount of income that is not properly reported has been made by the U.S. Internal Revenue Service. The IRS produced a report in 1979 that estimated that between $100 and $135 billion of income was unreported on individual federal income tax returns in 1976. Further, they estimated federal income tax revenue losses of between $19 and $26 billion, an amount roughly equal to the federal budget deficit in the early 1970s. There was considerable dissatisfaction with this report within the IRS, in Congress, and outside the government. As a result, IRS contracted with both the Survey Research Center (SRC) at the University of Michigan to estimate income flows in informal markets using a consumer-expenditure sample survey approach, and with Abt Associates to estimate incomes earned in criminally illegal activities. The IRS itself undertook a major reanalysis of its own data bases, particularly data from its TCMP.

These efforts have resulted in new estimates of unreported income and the tax gap in the United States for 1973, 1976, 1979, and 1981. These estimates suggest that unrecorded activity was large and growing rapidly during the 1970s. Perhaps a tax debacle was under way. However, comparing these estimates with national income (recorded total factor payments), it appears that although this activity increased during the 1970s, it did not increase dramatically. Perhaps the situation in the United States is better described as a tax erosion rather than a tax debacle.

It is wise at this point to carefully evaluate the methods the IRS used to obtain its income estimates. These included a wide range of different sources, but we will describe only the major sources here.

Estimates of Unreported Income
Earned in Legal Activities

The single most important source of information for the IRS estimates was the TCMP. The IRS used TCMP data to obtain estimates of unreported income and overstated expenses for individuals and small corporations that file tax returns. Every three years IRS's researchers select a stratified random sample of approximately 50,000 individual tax returns to be intensively audited. TCMP audits are conducted only by experienced examiners who consider every line item on the tax return. IRS used the line item differences between auditor and taxpayer results to estimate unreported income and overstated expenses. Relatively few TCMP auditors' recommendations are overturned on appeal. Thus, it appears that TCMP results are the best direct information we are likely to have for a large number of returns.

In preparing the 1983 report, IRS researchers used TCMP results for 1965, 1969, 1973, and 1976 (1979 results were not yet available). To obtain estimates for 1979 and 1981, IRS made straight-line projections of voluntary reporting percentages (the ratio of income reported on returns to that which should have been reported) obtained from the 1965, 1969, 1973, and 1976 TCMPs to estimate voluntary reporting percentages (VRPs) for 1979 and 1981. Estimates of unreported income and overstated expenses for 1979 and 1981 were then obtained by using information on returns actually filed in 1979 and 1981[12] and the projected VRPs. This means that estimates for these years and, more important, the trends they represent are largely a projection of past trends. They may well not reflect actual trends in the late 1970s. One would not expect tax trends of 1970 to continue to the present.

The IRS has long realized that even the very thorough TCMP audits cannot detect all unreported income. To try to discern the extent to which TCMP auditors could detect unreported income, the IRS carried out a special study in 1977. Researchers collected all information documents (for example, forms 1099 and W-2) for approximately 12,000 of the 50,000 1976 TCMP returns. They used these to discern the proportion of total income of various types that auditors were able to uncover. Using mainly this information, they multiplied all TCMP estimates of unreported income by 3.5 to obtain estimates of the unreported income of filers used in the 1983 report. This procedure assumes that auditors catch $1 out of every $3.50 that is not reported. Needless to say, this procedure is open to question. Further study of the proportion of unreported taxable income auditors can uncover is badly needed.

Estimates of unreported income for individuals who did not file a tax return were obtained by using data files for 1972 and 1977 that contained individual information from the IRS master file (this file contains tax return information), the Census Bureau's Current Population Survey (CPS), and the administrative records of the Social Security Administration (SSA). The CPS, which is used to measure labor force statistics (such as the unemployment rate), is a monthly survey of living quarters in the United States. Living quarters included in the survey are selected randomly, and about 60,000 individuals living in these quarters are interviewed each month. Questions concerning labor market status, occupation, and income are asked. Respondents are assured, and indeed have, anonymity. The first interview is carried out in person, with subsequent interviews being made by telephone.

Records in the three files were matched on the basis of Social Security number. The resulting file is called an Exact Match File. Individuals with SSA or CPS records indicating receipt of income, but no IRS file of potential nonfilers. (It should be noted that the IRS did not receive any information that would directly identify these individuals. Anonymity was maintained.) The income levels and other relevant information for these individuals were checked to see if they indeed should have filed a tax return.

The average Adjusted Gross Income (AGI) of nonfilers as identified by the 1972 Exact Match File was $6,826, while the average AGI of nonfilers in the 1977 file was $12,026. This suggests an extraordinary growth in the number of high-income individuals who do not file returns. Exact Match Files were only available for 1972 and 1977. The IRS obtained nonfiler income estimates for the years used in the report by assuming that the rate of growth in nonfiler income revealed in the 1972 and 1977 Exact Match File occurred evenly over the period. For the 1979 and 1981 estimates, the IRS assumed that this rate of growth moderated. Again, we are left with the conclusion that the information in the IRS report for 1973 and 1976 is the most reliable.

The IRS believes that neither TCMP nor the Exact Match File captures all of the unreported income earned by informal suppliers, illegal aliens, or those in illegal activities. Thus, they commissioned special studies to estimate the unreported incomes earned in these activities. The special study on informal suppliers was carried out by researchers at the University of Michigan's SRC. Based on focus-group discussion, SRC developed a series of questions concerning purchases from informal suppliers, which were added to its monthly Survey of Consumer Attitudes. Informal supplier questions were asked in September, November, and December 1981, with approximately 700 households being interviewed in each of these months. Households were selected randomly on the basis of the last four digits of their telephone numbers, after stratification by area code and central office number. Selection by telephone number excludes the approximately 6 to 7 percent of the population that do not live in quarters with telephones. This population tends to be disproportionately poor and black, and presumably made greater-than-average use of informal suppliers. Thus, the SRC's results are open to some, although we do not believe great, bias for this reason.

The SRC study estimates that informal suppliers had $42 billion worth of sales to consumers, and $25 billion worth of net income from these sales in 1981. It is interesting that the SRC's work indicates that purchases from informal suppliers occur in areas the BEA identified as having recording problems. The areas are personal, household, and automobile care; food; home repairs and additions; and fuel. SRC obtained estimates of the income of informal suppliers only for 1981. The IRS estimated unreported income of informal suppliers for other years by extrapolations based on trends in net nonfarm proprietors' income from the NIPA. Thus, for informal supplier income, our most reliable data are for 1981.

To establish estimates of illegal alien income not reflected in the TCMP and the Exact Match File data bases, the IRS began by surveying existing estimates of the size of the illegal alien population. It concluded that there were between 3.5 and 6 million illegal aliens in the United States in 1979. It next estimated, using social science research, that between 65 and 90 percent of illegal aliens were employed. To obtain earnings for these individuals, the IRS estimated the occupational structure for this population using Immigration and Naturalization Service (INS) and General Accounting Office (GAO) research. Wages for illegal aliens in each occupation were estimated using INS information. It appears that over 50 percent of illegal aliens have taxes withheld and, thus, are not working in unrecorded activity.

Estimates of Unreported Income Earned in Illegal Activities

To estimate incomes earned in illegal endeavors, the IRS commissioned a detailed study by Abt Associates. The structure of illegal production is complex and output is difficult to measure. To measure the production of illegal goods and services, researchers at Abt and the IRS consid-

ered for each illegal activity two different approaches:
the direct measurement of net output (the production approach) and the measurement of final sales (the consumption approach).   In order to estimate the output of the
drug and gambling industries, researchers at Abt and the
IRS used the results of nationally representative sample
surveys to estimate the final consumption of the illegal
product.   To estimate the output of the prostitution industry, a production approach was used.   Since the methodologies used are complex, we will only describe the way in
which the output of the drug industry was measured, as it
is by far the largest and most dynamic of the illegal activities considered.

Estimates of drug use adopt either consumption- or
production-based approaches.   Consumption-based approaches
rely on estimates of the user population, while production-based estimates rely on acreage estimates.   Most researchers who have considered the two approaches believe
that consumption-based estimates are more reliable.

There are a number of possible ways of estimating
the size of the drug-using population: sample survey,
arrest information, treatment program information, and incidence of drug-related diseases (such as drug overdoses
and hepatitis).   All of these sources of information are
subject to biases: surveys are subject to both response
and nonresponse biases; arrests and treatment program ad-
missions are determined jointly by agency and drug-user
actions; and diseases related to drug use are generally as
much a function of dealer and user experience and market
conditions as of the size of the consumer population.
Those who have assessed these alternative sources have
generally concluded that the very careful surveys of users
conducted by the National Institute of Drug Abuse (NIDA)
provide the most reliable estimates of the user population.

NIDA sponsors a national household survey every
two years that asks over seven thousand people about
their previous experience and present use of various illegal drugs.   In order to lower the number of inaccurate
responses, those surveyed are asked to mark their answers
on cards that they seal and drop into mailboxes.   Hoch-
hauser (1979) has reviewed a number of studies that attempt to measure the nature of biases in drug surveys.
He concludes that: reporting of current use is more consistent than recall of past behavior, which tends to underestimate the recency and frequency of use; some respon-

dents, particularly young people, fabricate use; and individuals who consent to respond are different both socially and demographically from those who do not respond. Approximately 14 to 20 percent of the individuals selected for the NIDA survey are not interviewed; however, only about half of those not interviewed refused to participate.

The sampling units in the NIDA survey are individuals over 12 years of age who live in households. The use of this sampling frame probably means that NIDA results do not paint a completely accurate picture of drug use, since it excludes all individuals living in group quarters (such as military barracks and college dormitories) and casual housing (hotels and abandoned buildings). Due to this limitation, NIDA results probably underestimate drug use.

In order to estimate the value of drugs consumed (final purchases under NIDA terminology) in any year, it is necessary to multiply the number of consumers by their average consumption. The result is multiplied by average price to obtain the value of drugs sold in the United States. Researchers at Abt/IRS made estimates of average daily dosage by user type and drug, using a variety of sources including medical evidence of effective dosage, informant reports of drug-user practices, and information from law enforcement agencies. They also report their estimates of dosage as being "somewhat conjectural." Our own evaluation is that they should be seen as informed conjecture. Drug prices used in the Abt/IRS study are the average price paid by agents of the Drug Enforcement Administration (DEA). Since DEA makes frequent and continual purchases, these prices are probably quite accurate.

Before one can obtain an estimate of the output of the drug industry in the United States, three further adjustments are necessary: for drugs sold at retail rather than wholesale price; for payments to foreign suppliers; and for purchase of domestic inputs. When all these adjustments are made, it appears that the drug industry is an important and rapidly growing sector of underground activity. Taxable income from the U.S. illegal drug industry is estimated to have increased from $5.1 billion in 1973 to $23.4 billion in 1981, a more than fourfold increase. Sales of the so-called recreational drugs (cocaine and marijuana) appear to have increased far more rapidly than did heroin sales during this period. However, it appears that even the drug industry produced a relatively small proportion of total unrecorded activity, an estimated 8 percent.

As noted earlier, the prostitution and gambling industries are quite small and relatively stagnant. Gambling is estimated to have produced only an estimated 1 percent of total unreported income, and prostitution less than 3 percent. It should be noted that estimates for both of these sectors are quite controversial and subject to substantial errors.

To summarize, the best estimates indicate that there is a large amount of underground activity in the United States. The IRS estimates indicate that unrecorded income was 12 percent of recorded national income in 1981. We know far less about trends in unrecorded activity; however, it appears it grew somewhat more rapidly than the recorded activity during the 1970s. To maintain historical perspective, it should be noted that the growth in the relative amount of underground activity appeared to have been larger in the late 1960s (remember the flower children and the Vietnam War protests) than during the 1970s.

One conclusion is clear: unreported taxable income is a growing problem, although it may at this point be an exaggeration to say that it represents a tax debacle. With this in mind, it is useful to consider the areas where unreported income has grown most rapidly. For "legal" income, underreporting of dividends, interest, capital gains, and royalty income has grown most rapidly. For "illegal" incomes, it is only incomes from drug sales that have grown extremely rapidly. It is interesting that it is income from sales of the so-called recreational drugs that has grown most dramatically. Perhaps we have a law enforcement debacle in this area.

When one turns attention from unreported incomes to the tax compliance problem, one sees an intriguing pattern. Voluntary compliance rates have been falling during the 1970s for most types of incomes. The decline has been most dramatic for capital gains and royalty income, but rather substantial declines have also occurred for dividend, nonfarm proprietor, and estate and trust income. Voluntary compliance is highest for wages and salaries, but even for this type of income, the compliance rate declined between 1973 and 1981. Compliance rates, as might be expected, are lowest for "illegal" and informal supplier income. However, perhaps surprisingly, they are not zero.

The IRS estimates that 21 percent of informal supplier income was reported, and that varying proportions of "illegal" income were reported (for example, 4 percent of income from marijuana sales and 9 percent of income from heroin sales). Generally, at least some income from illegal sources is reported by individuals extensively involved in illegal activities in order to protect against tax-evasion convictions obtained on the basis of net worth audits.

Other Estimates of Income Escaping Taxation

As far as we are aware, other than the United States, only the Swedish authorities have tried to carefully estimate the amount of income escaping taxation. Using tax audit information and various other central data banks, the Swedish Riksskatteverk estimated that unreported taxable income was betwen 8 and 15 percent of reported taxable income in 1978. Note that the implied voluntary compliance level is comparable to the overall level in the United States in 1979.

Other methods of estimating the size of unreported activity generally attempt to estimate either some portion or all economic activity that occurs outside official channels. These methods can be divided into direct and indirect methods, just as those estimating unreported taxable income can be. It was the indirect methods that were first utilized and have been used most extensively. Hence, we will consider such methods first.

The earliest and still quite popular indirect method of estimating the "GNP" of the "underground economy" relies in various ways on currency outstanding. As noted in the introduction, this method was used by Cagan (1958) to estimate the amount of tax evasion in the United States during World War II. More recently, Cagan's method has been used by Henry (1975), Tanzi (1980), and others to estimate the amount of unreported economic activity.

Actually, methods even simpler than Cagan's have been used. Gutmann (1977) in his original work assumes that there was no underground economy in the 1937-41 period. Thus, the ratio of currency to demand deposits in that period was "normal." Gutmann then attributes the marked increase in this ratio in the United States in the 1970s to the existence of unrecorded economic activity.

Assuming that the extra currency during the 1970s was used for unrecorded transactions, and that the velocity of circulation of currency was the same for unrecorded as for recorded activity, Gutmann arrives at his oft-quoted estimate that unrecorded activity amounted to $176 billion in 1976. Gutmann's method has been severely criticized by many authors (U.S. Department of the Treasury 1979; Simon and Witte 1980; Frey and Pommerehne 1982; and Henry 1983). These criticisms need not be repeated here. It has generally been concluded that Gutmann's method is too simple to provide useful estimates of unrecorded activity, but that his work was useful in stimulating interest in the underground economy.

A number of authors have recently used more sophisticated methods (although similar to Cagan's) to relate currency demand to unreported activity. These authors estimate an equation seeking to explain currency demand using multivariate statistical techniques. One of the variables they see as explaining currency demand is tax rates. Armed with estimates of the effect of tax rates on currency demand, researchers estimate the amount of currency demand that is caused by high tax rates. Making some further assumptions concerning the velocity at which this currency turns over in conducting unrecorded activity, they arrive at the estimate of the tax-evasion component of unrecorded activity. Although this method is still used and is certainly to be preferred to Gutmann's approach, it is not believed to provide very accurate estimates of unrecorded activity (see Henry [1983] for a discussion).

A final method of estimating unrecorded activity was developed by Feige (1979). This relies on a technique that was used to estimate recorded economic activity before the national income accounts were developed. Like Gutmann, Feige takes the late 1930s as a baseline. However, he examines changes in the ratio of total transactions to GNP rather than the ratio of currency to demand deposits. Feige attributes all of the increase in the transaction/GNP ratio since 1939 to growth in unrecorded activity. Making various assumptions about currency turnover, Feige concludes that the "irregular" economy was nearly 20 percent of total GNP in 1976, and that it grew four times as fast as the regular economy between 1976 and 1978. Feige (1980) has refined his estimates and now concludes that there was a dramatic growth in the hidden economy during World War II, followed by absolute decline until 1968.

Since 1968, Feige believes that unrecorded activity has grown rapidly and amounted to 27 percent of GNP in 1979. Most people feel that Feige's estimates are far too high.

As noted in the introduction, researchers have seen traces of unrecorded activity in other statistical irregularities such as labor force participation and utilization of electricity. Sensitivity to statistical irregularities is important and points up areas in need of careful direct study.

The studies commissioned by the IRS are some of the most comprehensive direct studies conducted to date. Recall the SRC's study of purchases from informal suppliers described previously. Techniques similar to SRC's have been used in other countries, particularly in Scandinavia, but have asked questions designed to discern both supply and purchase information. See Hansson (1982) and Isachsen, Klovland, and Strom (1982).

In the United Kingdom, researchers have compared detailed information on individual family expenditures and income obtained in the Family Expenditure Survey to determine the level and extent of participation in unrecorded activity (see Dilnot and Morris 1982). They found that the income and expenditures of between 10 and 15 percent of the families were such as to suggest participation in unrecorded activity. The levels of participation suggested that an amount of income equal to approximately 2-3 percent of GNP was not recorded. The heads of 20 percent of the families participating in unrecorded activity were self-employed, and 70 percent were employed full time. Part-time workers were found to be particularly likely to have some unrecorded income.

FINDINGS

Having reviewed a rather extensive literature, what can we conclude about the size and rate of growth of unrecorded activity in the United States and Western European countries? In arriving at our estimates for some countries, we use techniques we have not yet discussed. The first technique involves a careful examination of tax laws and tax administration made possible by a recent survey conducted by Boidman (1983). Other things being equal, we expect lower levels of unrecorded activity in countries where withholding is pervasive, self-assessment is not extensively used, penalties are high, and examination of returns is extensive. The second technique was developed by researchers at the University of Zurich (Frey and Weck 1983a, 1983b). Their research uses what we have termed the factor approach. Frey and Weck are interested in the relative size and rate of growth in unrecorded activity in developed economies. They feel that most existing methods do not provide adequate estimates, and so they utilize an approach that identifies the factors likely to be associated with unrecorded activity. Giving various weights to these factors, the researchers form a set of indices that gives the relative rankings of different countries in terms of their likely levels and rates of growth of unrecorded activity. The factors they utilize relate to: the burden of taxation and regulation, the labor force participation rate, the unemployment rate, tax perception and tax morality, and hours of work. However, we are not very confident about our estimates for most countries. Although we do not completely agree, we believe it is useful to quote the conclusion of two British researchers concerning various estimates of unrecorded activity: "We review a number of widely cited studies and conclude that they contain virtually nothing of value. The only estimates of the size of the black economy that we believe deserve serious attention are those made for the United States by the Internal Revenue Service" (Dilnot and Morris 1982: 163).

It appears that unrecorded activity has been growing relative to recorded activity, but not dramatically, with the possible exception of the Federal Republic of Germany and the likely exception of Italy. In recent years the tax authorities have reacted to this growth, and it appears likely that it will be less, other things being equal, in the 1980s than it was in the 1970s. The other-things-being-equal phrase is important. One factor that could increase unrecorded activity is low levels of recorded activity. Unrecorded activity appears to thrive in times of economic recession. Indeed, some researchers (such as Ferman, Berndt, and Selo 1978) believe that unrecorded activity provides employment of the last resort for many people.

UNRECORDED ACTIVITY: A STRUCTURAL CHANGE?

We now return to the question with which we began this chapter: Does unrecorded activity represent an important new phenomenon or does it represent simply the latest hot topic? We will attempt to answer this question primarily by referring to the U.S. situation, although many of the comments made apply to Western European countries as well.

To carefully answer this question, one must first consider the nature of unrecorded activity and possible reasons for recent changes in its level and rate of growth. As we have seen, most unrecorded activity consists of the production of legal goods and services. Further, it appears that it is this type of activity and the illegal drug industry that have grown most rapidly in recent years and have been the major source of public concern. It should be noted that we have the most reliable trend data for unrecorded legal activity only for the 1973-76 period. Most of the unreported legal incomes estimates for 1979 and 1983 in the IRS report are based on trends established during the 1973-76 period, during which unreported legal incomes grew on an average annual rate of 13 percent.

There are at least five major reasons for changes in the amount of unrecorded activity: changes in economic conditions (for example, changes in the level of unemployment and inflation); changes in the structure of the economy, the family, and the population; changes in behavior; changes in technology; and changes in the legal and institutional structure. We will discuss possible effects of each of these factors in turn.

Changes in Economic Conditions

Since 1969 our economy has experienced a number of cyclical downturns (1969-70, 1974-75, and 1980-81). Further, until quite recently we have experienced rates of inflation and rates of interest unparalleled in the post-World War II period. Unemployment undoubtedly moved some workers from the recorded to the unrecorded sector. Inflation and high interest rates have stretched family budgets, and thus more households have sent part-time workers into unrecorded activity as overtime and other recorded employment were limited during the 1970s.

While the U.S. economic situation was difficult during the 1970s, the situation in the countries to our south and north has been even worse. Hard times (political as well as economic) in these countries have increased the flow of illegal immigrants, and it is estimated that half of these work in unrecorded activity.

The fact that Italy experienced economic difficulties before the United States and also expressed concern about the growth of unrecorded activity earlier lends some (admittedly circumstantial) support to the contention that unrecorded activity may thrive in difficult economic times. The peak of Italy's postwar growth occurred in 1962, and concern about the growth of unrecorded activity began as early as 1966 and was quite widespread by the mid-1970s.

Structural Changes

The United States has experienced great structural changes during the last 20 years. The female labor force participation rate (the percent of all women who are working or actively looking for work) went from 37.7 percent in 1960 to 43.3 percent in 1975 and to 51.5 percent in 1980. In 1980, the labor force participation rate of mothers with children under six was 56.6 percent. The increased participation of women has been a major drain on the labor supply available for home production. As a result, demand for such things as personal and household service, restaurant meals, and child care has increased markedly. It is exactly in these areas that unrecorded production most frequently occurs.

The fact that more women were working during the 1970s than previously both allowed (due to higher family income) and encouraged (household and family demands) more part-time work. Indeed, the percent of the labor force that was employed part time increased from 9.1 percent in 1960 to 14.1 percent in 1970 and to 14.6 percent in 1980. Some research suggests that part-time workers are more likely to participate in unrecorded production than are other types of employees.

Changes in economic structure may also have encouraged the growth in unrecorded activity during the 1970s. Recent studies (Birch 1970; Armington and Odle 1982) find that most employment growth during the 1970s occurred in small establishments. For example, 55 percent of the employment growth between 1978 and 1980 took place in establishments with fewer than 20 employees (Armington and Odle 1982). It is in small enterprises that most unrecorded activity takes place. Armington and Odle find that a significant proportion of the growing small establishments are branches or subsidiaries of large firms.

NOTES

1. Some authors, particularly sociologists and anthropologists, define the economy to include nonmarket activity such as do-it-yourself activities, housework, and aid between neighbors. For example, see Dow (1977), Henry (1978), and Mars (1982). We define our concern more narrowly for two basic reasons. First, we believe that there is a greater possibility of measuring market rather than nonmarket activities. Second, the major policy concerns associated with unrecorded activity relate only to the market portion of that activity. Those desiring to understand the many ways in which human needs and wants are fulfilled may well be advised to adopt a broader definition. In some of our discussions we consider the relationship between market and nonmarket activities.

2. The first official national income statistics for the United States were published in 1926 by the Federal Trade Commission. The Bureau of Economic Analysis, which is still responsible for national income statistics, was not established until the 1930s. See Henry (1983) for a discussion.

3. Before World War II most tax revenue was raised from taxes on property and foreign trade, and by various excise taxes. Although 50 percent of federal revenue in the United States was generated by the income tax in the 1920s, tax rates were not high and the income tax did not affect most sectors of the population. It was during World War II that tax rates were raised and the coverage of the income tax broadened. Between 1939 and 1945 the number of individual taxpayers increased from 3.9 to 42.6 million. See Haws (1983) for a discussion of the development of the U.S. tax system.

4. See Henry (1976) and Gutmann (1977) for early work using currency approaches to estimate the size of the underground economy. It is interesting that many researchers saw the phenomenon as new rather than as a repetition of a World War II pattern.

5. Both in Europe and in the United States there were also sociological and anthropological studies which revealed surprising diverse and unrecorded ways of earning

money. However, these studies did not produce global estimates of the amount of unrecorded activity and, thus,
did not receive the attention from public decision makers
and the public that the work with statistical discrepancies
received. For examples of the sociological and anthropological work, see Dow (1977) and Henry (1978).

6. This discussion of Italy is taken from Tanzi
(1982). Dallago (1983) provides an excellent summary of
work on unrecorded activity in Italy.

7. See U.S. Department of the Treasury, Internal
Revenue Service (1979, 1983b).

8. Estimates of incomes from illegal endeavors
were made only for illegal drugs, illegal gambling, and
female prostitution. Thus, the tax loss figure for illegal
incomes provided by the IRS is understated. In a report
sponsored by the IRS, researchers at Abt Associates provide income estimates for many additional types of illegal
incomes. See Carlson (1983) and Weisberg and Goldstein
(1983).

9. See Parker (1984).

10. This information is taken from Frey and Pommerehne (1982).

11. See De Grazia (1982, p. 31) for a discussion.

12. This is not strictly correct. The IRS used information on a random sample of filed returns (Statistics
of Income [SOI] program data). As SOI data were not
available for 1981, the IRS had to project filed returns as
well as VRPs data for this year.

9

The President's 1985 Tax Reform Proposal: An Economic Assessment

Jay Mauer

Efforts to achieve major reforms of the federal tax system have been mounted, with varying degrees of success, over the postwar years. However, none of it has enjoyed the intensity of support at the presidential level and within the U.S. Congress that is now evident in the 1985 tax reform drive. The political forces and personalities behind this drive raise the likelihood that major tax changes will successfully emerge from these efforts.

Three problem areas have acted as driving forces to tax reform. First, there has been the persistent, long-term tendency toward using the tax system to encourage and support specific economic and political interests. As these measures have accumulated in the tax code, pressures have built for a concerted effort to purge the system of this special-interest legislation. Second, the inflation of the 1970s and early 1980s has introduced severe distortions into the tax system. This led both to serious problems in capital recovery during the 1970s and to an upward drift in the marginal tax rates applied to middle-class taxpayers. Third, there has been an increased frequency of piecemeal tax legislation in recent years that has contributed to a perception of uncertainty surrounding the tax code, interfering with longer-term economic decisions.

It is into this environment that President Ronald Reagan has brought forward his Tax Proposals to the Congress for Fairness, Growth, and Simplicity (herein called the 1985 Tax Reform Proposal). This effort to bring about a major overhaul of the federal tax system draws on ele-

ments from several progenitors: the conservative Kemp-
Kasten FAST bill, the Democratic alternative Bradley-Gephart
bill, and the so-called Treasury I proposal introduced by
the administration in late 1984 without the president's formal support.   With this background, the president's 1985
Tax Reform Proposal spans a wide range of the political
spectrum, ensuring broad congressional support.

Given the widespread dissatisfaction with the current
tax system at the federal level and given the political base
from which the current proposals are drawn, it is clear
that the president's 1985 Tax Reform Proposal must be
seriously considered.   Even if this effort is unsuccessful,
the tax concepts introduced are assured an important role
in shaping future tax reform legislation.

OVERVIEW OF 1985 TAX REFORM PROPOSAL

When viewed in broad perspective, it can be seen
why the 1985 Tax Reform Proposal has gained widespread
political support.   The Proposal, in effect, results in a
substantial reduction in the tax burden on households (individuals) through reductions in personal tax rates, measures to reduce (or eliminate) the tax burden on the poor
(low-income households), and measures to streamline the
tax code.   These tax reductions are estimated by the
Treasury to have a neutral or, on balance, favorable impact on some 70 percent of the individual taxpayers in
the United States.

To retain revenue neutrality, and thus to make up
for the loss of revenues from the household sector, the
Proposal raises the tax burden on U.S. corporations.   Un-
derstandably, this latter feature has been a source of
particular consternation within affected segments of the
business community.

The effect of the 1985 Proposal on tax burdens must
be viewed from a long-term perspective in recognition that
taxes are ultimately borne by individuals.   Thus, the apparent shifting of the tax burden to businesses should not
obfuscate the fact that, ultimately, the change in the tax
incidence falls on individuals.   We shall suggest, later in
the chapter, which groups and sectors in the United States
are likely to be affected directly by these tax changes.
However, a full analysis of the incidence of the higher
taxes on groups within the nation is beyond the scope of
this chapter.

TAX CHANGES AFFECTING THE HOUSEHOLD SECTOR

From a quantitative standpoint, three tax changes are proposed that will reduce the tax liability for the household sector: reductions in marginal tax rates; the increase in the zero bracket amount (ZBA, also known as the "standard deduction"); and increases in personal and dependency exemptions. These reductions are partially offset by a number of loophole-closing measures, the most important of which is the repeal of the state and local tax deduction. These and other changes are discussed in turn below.

Marginal Tax Rate Reduction

Under current law, the taxes on individuals vary from a minimum rate of 11 percent to a maximum of 50 percent. In all, there are 14 separate tax brackets; the progression of the rates for each class of taxpayers is adjusted annually for inflation as measured by the consumer price index for all-urban consumers (CPIU). Under the 1985 Proposal, the 14 tax rates would be replaced by three rates: 15 percent, 25 percent, and 35 percent. The income subject to these rate brackets would continue to be indexed.

The effect of the Proposal would be to reduce the aggregate tax liability for individuals by 7 percent. The percentage reduction in taxes is greater for the lower-income and upper-income households. The tax burden for households with incomes below $20,000 (in 1986) would fall approximately 18 percent. A like reduction is projected for households filing joint returns in excess of $120,000.

Increase in the ZBA

For nonitemizing taxpayers, no tax is imposed on income up to the ZBA or standard deduction. Under the 1985 Tax Proposal, the ZBA would be raised for taxpayer categories as follows for 1986:

	Current Law	1985 Proposed	% Gain Under Proposal
Single returns	$2,480	$2,900	17
Joint returns	3,670	4,000	9
Head of household	2,480	3,600	45

As under current law, the Proposal would adjust the ZBA
for inflation.

Increased Personal and Dependency Exemptions

Under current law, each taxpayer is entitled to a
personal exemption of $1,040 and to exemptions for each
dependent of $1,040. The 1985 Proposal would raise these
exemptions to $2,000 beginning in 1986. As is the case
currently, these exemptions would be indexed for inflation.

Repeal of the State and Local Tax Deduction

Present provisions permit individuals who itemize to
deduct taxes paid to state and local governments. However, it must be recognized that those who itemize tend to
be high-income taxpayers. Two-thirds of all taxpayers do
not itemize deductions. As a result, this group is not entitled to deduct state and local taxes. Even itemizing taxpayers may receive little benefit from the deduction unless
they reside in high-tax states. Under this rationale, the
1985 Tax Reform Proposal would repeal the state and local
tax deduction for individuals. The effect of this measure,
if adopted, would be to offset in part the reduction in tax
liabilities for households described above. With opposition
from New York, California, and other high-tax states, this
provision has become one of the more hotly debated aspects
of the Proposal.

Other Provisions Affecting Households

In addition to the repeal of the state and local tax
deduction, the 1985 Proposal would change a broad number
of provisions in the federal tax code affecting individuals.
Quantitatively, the more important of these measures are
as follows: include in income a portion of employer-provided
health insurance; repeal of income averaging; revisions in
capital gains treatment; modification of deferral arrangements under retirement plans; simplification; and repeal of
the second-earner deduction.

Summary: Household Sector

The revenue effects of the provisions described above have been estimated by the U.S. Treasury. The economic assumptions underlying these estimates are: real GNP growth over the 1986–90 period of 4 percent per annum; inflation, 5 percent per annum; and real rate of return, 4 percent. The inflation and real return assumptions are about in line with the current consensus forecast by business economists. The economic growth projection, however, is above the prevailing consensus forecast.

The Treasury's projections are presented in Table 9.1. As seen in the total change line, the 1985 Proposal results in a reduction in tax revenues for households of over $130 billion over the five years to 1990.

BUSINESS SECTOR TAX CHANGES

A reduction in the corporate income tax rates is more than offset by a number of changes that have the effect of raising tax revenues, on balance, from the business sector. In contrast to the tax changes affecting households, the business tax changes contained in the 1985 Proposal introduce a number of major departures from the principles embodied in the present tax code. These include a change in the capital recovery system, which replaces the Investment Tax Credit (ITC) and the Accelerated Cost Recovery System (ACRS) with a new and less favorable capital recovery approach called the Capital Cost Recovery System (CCRS). Tax revenues from businesses are also substantially enhanced through the imposition of a Depreciation "Windfall" Recapture Tax. These measures are described in greater detail below.

Reduction in Corporate Income Tax Rates

Under the 1985 Proposal, the corporate income tax rate would be lowered to 33 percent from the current rate of 46 percent. This action is rationalized on the basis that it reduces the value to corporations of preferences in the tax code for particular forms of investment. The corporate rate reduction is the principal provision in the proposal for providing tax relief to the business sector.

Table 9.1

1985 Tax Reform Proposal: Individual Revenue Gains/Losses ($ billions)

	Fiscal Years					
	1986	1987	1988	1989	1990	Total
Revenue-Reducing Measures						
Marginal tax rate reduction	-11.1	-49.5	-60.6	-66.7	-72.7	-260.6
Increase zero bracket	-4.4	-6.2	-6.6	-7.1	-7.6	-31.9
Increase exemptions to $2,000	-18.8	-39.1	-42.1	-45.1	-48.0	-193.1
Net Revenue Reducing	-34.3	-94.8	-109.3	-118.9	-128.3	-485.6
Revenue-Raising Measures						
Repeal state and local tax deduction	4.5	33.3	34.1	37.0	40.0	148.9
Include part of health insurance in taxable income	2.4	3.5	3.7	3.8	4.0	17.4
Repeal income averaging	1.0	3.9	4.3	4.6	4.9	18.7
Capital gains	.6	2.9	4.6	5.0	5.4	18.5
Repeal of ITC	1.7	4.8	5.6	6.4	7.2	25.7
Modify retirement plan deferral arrangements	1.1	1.8	2.1	2.4	2.8	10.2
Simplification	1.3	6.0	6.6	7.0	7.6	28.5
Repeal second-earner deduction	1.6	7.1	7.7	8.3	9.0	33.7
Other	2.2	5.5	8.6	15.4	20.5	52.2
Net Revenue Raising	16.4	68.8	77.3	89.9	101.4	353.8
Total Change	-17.9	-26.0	-32.0	-29.0	-26.9	-131.8

Source: President's Tax Proposals to the Congress for Fairness, Growth, and Simplicity.

235

Deduction for Dividends Paid

The double taxation of dividends has long been a feature in the federal tax code. The 1985 Proposal would permit partial relief from double taxation by allowing corporations a deduction equal to 10 percent of dividends paid to their shareholders. Under this treatment as deduction, this relief would be provided only when the income from which the dividends are paid is actually taxed at the corporate level. The dividends-paid deduction, therefore, would not be available with respect to corporate distributions from so-called tax preference income.

Indexing of Inventories

Another significant departure from the principles of the current tax code is the indexing of inventories to adjust for inflation. Under the 1985 Proposal, businesses would be permitted the option of using an indexed FIFO method of inventory accounting, which would be based on a federal government price index. About two-thirds of the inventories in the United States are currently under (unindexed) FIFO accounting, resulting in an overstatement of income tax liability during inflationary times. Indexing inventories would substantially reduce this tax system bias.

Investment Tax Credit Repeal

Under current law, the ITC is provided for taxpayers' investments in equipment (and certain structures). The credit is equal to 10 percent of qualified investment placed in service (6 percent for three-year property). The tax basis of the depreciable property in turn is reduced by 50 percent of the amount of such credit. In effect, the ITC provides an incentive for these forms in investment. Under the 1985 Proposal, the ITC would be repealed.

Accelerated Cost Recovery System Replaced by the Capital Cost Recovery System

The ACRS system of depreciation was established in the Economic Recovery Tax Act of 1981. Under this system, all "recovery property" is assigned to an asset class with a specified recovery period and depreciation schedule. In contrast, the pre-ACRS depreciation rules required taxpayers to recover an asset's original cost, less salvage value, over its estimated useful life. For most assets, ACRS allows much faster cost recovery than was obtainable under the previous law.

The 1985 Proposal would replace ACRS with a new system--called CCRS--which returns to the "useful lives" principle that was embodied in the pre-1981 tax code. In addition, the CCRS system introduces a procedure to adjust depreciation allowances for inflation by means of a basis adjustment.

A comparison of the effect on the cost of capital for comparable asset classes under CCRS and the combined programs of ACRS and ITC is provided in the next section of this chapter.

Depreciation "Windfall" Recapture Tax

This provision in the 1985 Proposal would require that businesses treat as taxable income 40 percent of the corporation's "excess depreciation" taken between 1980 and 1986. These additions to taxable income would be spread over a three-year period. For purposes of this provision, "excess depreciation" is defined as amortization deductions under current law, minus those that would have been allowed during this 1980-86 period using the straight-line depreciation method. This windfall-recapture provision has been the focus of much criticism on the grounds that it is a retroactive tax.

Other Provisions Affecting Businesses

Additional changes included in the 1985 Proposal that affect businesses include: a range of items to more "accurately" measure income by better reflecting the "time value of money"; and international issues. Income-measurement proposals incorporate requirements that production costs be capitalized on a more comprehensive basis, that limitations be introduced on the cash method of accounting, and that deductions be repealed for additions to bad debt reserves and to reserves for mining and solid-waste reclamation.

Among the international issues, the most important is the proposed per-country limitation on the use of foreign tax credits. Under this change, the amount of income tax paid to a foreign country that may be claimed as a foreign tax credit in any year will be limited to the U.S. tax on income from that country. Current practice calculates this limitation on an overall basis. That is, the amount of credit currently available is the aggregate of income taxes paid to all foreign countries, and foreign-source taxable income is the aggregate of all taxable income from outside the United States.

Summary: Business Sector

The net revenue effects of the proposed changes affecting business and described above are summarized in Table 9.2. As seen in the table's total change summary line, federal tax revenues derived from the business sector are estimated to rise to a cumulative $118 billion over the five years to 1990.

ECONOMIC EFFECTS OF THE 1985 TAX REFORM PROPOSAL

The economic implications of the 1985 Proposal can be addressed by focusing on its impacts on several key economic indicators. The comments in this section are directed toward summarizing work that analysts have reported.[1] These study results differ, as one might expect given the range of methodologies employed. Moreover, more analytic effort appears to have been directed toward the Treasury I proposal released in December 1984 than toward the president's 1985 Proposal, though the differences between the two proposals are modest and confined mainly to the capital recovery area. Conclusions based on the Treasury I analysis in other areas should be applicable, by-and-large, to the 1985 Proposal.

This section will examine the economic efforts of the 1985 Proposal. We will see that the most important effects are primarily sectoral in nature, in contrast with macroeconomic. On reflection, this conclusion is not surprising. Revenue neutrality is one of the stated objectives of the proposed legislation. At the same time, tax reform is by

Table 9.2

1985 Tax Reform Proposal: Business Revenue Gains/Losses ($ billions)

	Fiscal Years					
	1986	1987	1988	1989	1990	Total
Revenue-Reducing Measures						
Corporate tax rate reduction	-10.0	-26.9	-36.1	-39.2	-42.0	-154.2
Deduction for dividends paid	--	-3.4	-6.2	-7.2	-8.0	-24.8
Indexing inventories	--	-2.4	-4.5	-4.5	-4.5	-15.9
Net Revenue Reducing	-10.0	-32.7	-46.8	-50.9	-54.5	-194.9
Revenue-Raising Measures						
Repeal ITC	14.0	25.6	29.4	33.3	37.4	139.7
CCRS replacing ACRS	.3	-.7	2.3	8.7	15.4	26.0
"Windfall" recapture tax	7.6	19.4	20.4	9.1	--	56.5
Income measurement	3.3	6.9	10.3	13.6	15.0	49.1
International issues	1.3	3.4	4.1	4.6	5.0	18.4
Other	2.4	4.2	4.6	5.5	6.9	23.6
Net Revenue Raising	28.9	58.8	71.1	74.8	79.7	313.3
Total Change	18.9	26.1	24.3	23.9	25.2	118.4

Source: President's Tax Proposals to the Congress for Fairness, Growth, and Simplicity.

nature a matter of changing the burden of taxation within the economy and society. As indicated earlier, the broad effect of the Proposal's measures is to reduce the tax burden on the household sector. Revenue neutrality is, in turn, achieved by raising taxes on the business sector.

With this tax reform configuration and given our current economic setting, the business sector is particularly vulnerable to economic forces arising from tax system changes. One critical dimension in this regard is the impact of the proposed legislation on the capital recovery system. A related dimension is the effect on the international competitive position of the United States. This section will first compare the capital recovery implications of CCRS and ITC/ACRS. Then, the international effects of the proposed legislation are identified. Finally, with this as background, the Proposal's implications for several domestic sectors are examined.

Comparison of CCRS and ITC/ACRS

In evaluating the economic effects of the 1985 Tax Reform Proposal, we will argue that it is critical to assess its impact on the nation's capital recovery system. For this assessment, it is possible to compare the effects on business costs and cash flows of CCRS in the Proposal with the ITC/ACRS capital recovery system under current law. The comparison is complicated by the fact that CCRS incorporates inflation indexing, while this feature is not provided under ITC/ACRS. For purposes of this comparison, our focus is the present value of investment allowances under ITC/ACRS and CCRS. This comparison is presented in Figure 9.1, which shows the treatment under the two plans for representative assets in each of the CCRS asset classes. As indicated in the figure, the ITC/ACRS system provides more generous treatment than the 1985 Proposal for all five equipment asset classes under conditions of inflation up to 10 percent (8 percent for the public utility asset class). In the case of factory structures, CCRS would provide about the same tax deductions as ITC/ACRS at today's inflation rate.

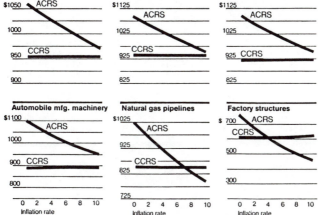

**Present Value of Depreciation Plus the Deduction
Equivalent of the ITC Per Thousand Dollars of Investment**

NOTE: Allowances are discounted at an interest rate equal to a 5% inflation rate plus a real interest rate of 4%.
SOURCE: Morgan Guaranty Trust Company

Figure 9.1.   Comparison of Investment Allowances

The U.S. International Competitive Position
and Historical Perspective

As indicated above, the costs borne by U.S. firms will be higher in comparison with current tax provisions whether considered from the standpoint of the overall 1985 Proposal (including the windfall profits tax and subsidiary provisions) or from the more limited standpoint of the valuation of investment allowances.

If the Proposal is enacted, this rise in costs will result in a reduction in international competitiveness. An indication of the extent of the erosion in the U.S. competitive position can be gained by a comparison of the after-tax cost of capital in the United States relative to the cost in other nations, as presented in Figure 9.2. Under current law, the after-tax cost of capital in the United States is among the lowest of the major industrial countries; under the 1985 Proposal, it would be among the highest.

After-Tax Cost of Capital Index*	UNITED STATES		CANADA	FRANCE	WEST GERMANY	JAPAN	UNITED KINGDOM
	Current Law	1985 Proposal					
EQUIPMENT	57	73	59	68	71	67	66
PLANT	76	81	80	77	90	75	76

*Index is present value of after-tax cost of capital based on asset cost = 100 in local currency terms; assumes inflation = 5% and real discount rate = 4%.

Figure 9.2.   After-Tax Cost of Capital for Manufacturing

Should it be adopted, the Proposal would raise business costs in the economy as a whole on balance. The replacement of ITC/ACRS with CCRS would impose unusually large cost increases on capital-intensive companies. Recognizing that the capital-intensive companies are predominantly represented in the manufacturing (internationally traded goods) sectors, this increase in costs would have the effect of reducing, pari passu, the international competitiveness of U.S. manufacturing firms.[2]

A decline in international competitiveness will have both trade and investment implications for the U.S. economy. These will come at a time of already severe international competitive pressures on U.S. manufacturing companies from the dollar's protracted rise over the past five years, as shown in Figure 9.3. The effect of the dollar's rise over this period can be seen on the pattern of import and export flows, as shown in Figure 9.4.

A further erosion in competitiveness will result in further increases in imports to the United States, a continued pattern of "no-growth exports, and a shift in U.S. direct investment to off-shore locations as companies attempt to get into more favorable production cost environments. The consequence of these developments will be a further loss of jobs in the United States, which will tend to be

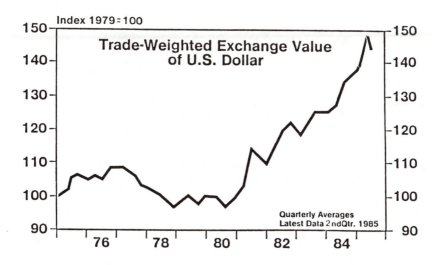

Figure 9.3.   The U.S. Dollar Has Strengthened by More
Than 40 Percent Since 1980

Figure 9.4.   Soaring Imports, No-Growth Exports

concentrated in those industries and states that have not yet fully recovered from the 1981–82 recession, and that continue to be held back by the strong dollar.

From a national standpoint, the substantial loss of international competitiveness since 1980 has resulted in substantial job losses. Econometric studies have estimated these job losses to be in the 2 million range.[3] These losses have been concentrated in a number of the nation's basic manufacturing industries. Moreover, these industries tend to be concentrated in the nation's Midwestern region. In 17 states, as listed in Figure 9.5, total employment has yet to recover to the levels that prevailed in late 1979 despite the general increase in employment for the nation as a whole. When the manufacturing sector alone is considered, fully 41 states have yet to regain their 1979 employment levels, as seen in Figure 9.6.

Business Fixed Investment

Against the backdrop of the pressures currently facing the U.S. economy, plant and equipment investment in the United States can be expected to be substantially affected. This conclusion is borne out by all of the tax reform analyses. Business fixed investment that is strictly domestic in character will tend to be discouraged by the higher cost of capital. Manufacturing businesses that are subject to international competitive pressures both in export markets and at home in the U.S. market will also be under substantial pressure from the overvalued dollar to expand their production facilities outside of the United States. It has been estimated that the combined effect of these pressures will be to reduce business fixed investment approximately $65 billion, or roughly 10 percent from the base case. This deviation from the baseline is expected to be greatest in the 1987–88 period.[4]

Personal Consumption

There is broad agreement in the tax reform analyses that the reduction in tax rates for households will spur consumer spending. When compared to the base case, these consumption effects peak in the 1987–88 time frame. The analyses suggest that consumer spending will be higher by

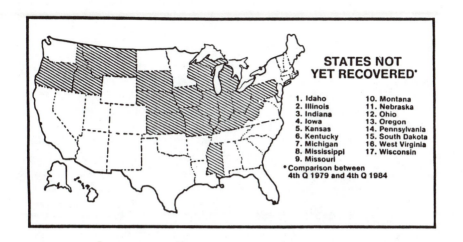

Figure 9.5. Total Employment Still Below 1979 Levels in 17 States

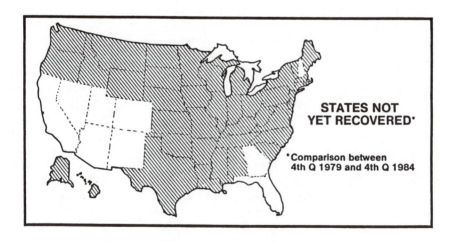

Figure 9.6. Manufacturing Employment Still Below 1979 Levels in 41 States

$25–30 billion, or approximately 1 percent above the base-line during this period.

Residential Housing

The deductibility of property tax payments and interest payments on home mortgages provides a subsidy to homeownership under current law, which is reflected in housing demand and has become capitalized into home prices. The 1985 Tax Reform Proposal preserves the full deductibility of mortgage interest for the taxpayer's principal residence. However, the Proposal also severely limits the deductibility of mortgage interest payments for second homes and eliminates the property tax deduction. Moreover, on primary residences, the lower marginal tax rates reduce the value of the mortgage deduction, likewise contributing to weaker residential housing demand. The transitional effects of the Proposal toward the residential housing sector are greatest in the period 1986–88. During this period, new housing activity is projected to fall by 5 percent relative to the base case. Home prices will also be affected. Using the median home price compiled by the U.S. Commerce Department as a gauge, home prices are projected to decline 5 to 10 percent from the base case according to the tax reform analyses surveyed.

Labor Force Growth

One of the rationales for the personal tax rate reductions included in the 1985 Proposal is the belief held by supply-side economists that lower taxes on households will call forth greater work effort, with implications for faster economic growth. The presumption is that lower marginal tax rates would increase the number of low-to-middle-income family "second earners" who would be willing to join the labor force. In this regard, it is useful to survey the tax reform analyses to determine their projections of labor force growth. The consensus is that the extent of these supply-side effects should be regarded as modest. Over a ten-year time span, for example, the studies suggest that the labor force would rise approximately .5 percent faster than the base case.

Interest Rates, Inflation, and Economic Growth

Over the five-year transitional period to 1990, the Proposal's revenue neutrality assures only minor net effects on interest rates, inflation, and economic growth. The fall in business investment is partially offset by a rise in consumer outlays. However, as we proceed into the 1990s, the Proposal's antigrowth elements begin to play a more important role in shaping the economy. The shift of income from the corporate sector toward the low-saving household sector will contribute to a lower saving and investment path, with negative implications for productivity growth and, therefore, the U.S. economy's long-run trend rate of economic growth. This bias, assuming a stable monetary policy, will contribute to inflation, long term. Finally, a lower supply of savings in the economy and somewhat higher inflation rate suggest a somewhat higher path for interest rates.[5]

AN ALTERNATIVE APPROACH

The major structural difficulty with the 1985 Tax Reform Proposal is its effort to balance tax revenue losses toward the household sector with tax revenue gains at the expense of the business sector, with resultant negative effects on business investment. An alternative approach would be to allow households no overall tax reduction through the adoption of a form of border-adjustable consumption tax or a modified form of the Value-Added Tax (VAT).[6]

Under these tax systems, the amount of the tax on specific export products is rebated at the border, permitting those goods to be exported more competitively in international trade. Under the General Agreement on Tariffs and Trade (GATT), a country may adjust the price of an exported item by the amount of indirect taxes, but not for direct taxes such as income taxes and Social Security taxes. At present, because border tax rebates occur under the VAT, goods from the EEC have a competitive advantage over goods produced in the United States, which bear the cost of high income and payroll taxes, a very important point.

Tax revenue given up in the achievement of fairness and efficiency toward the household sector under the 1985

Proposal could be replaced by instituting a modest national consumption tax on the order of 1 or 2 percent, with exemptions on appropriate purchase classes such as food, clothing, medicines, and so forth. A modification in this direction would not require reducing investment incentives under current law, would be biased in favor of the saving-investment process, and would be beneficial from the standpoint of the nation's international competitive position.

SUMMARY AND CONCLUSIONS

This chapter has reviewed the major features of President Reagan's 1985 Tax Reform Proposal. The broad outline of this Proposal is to reduce tax rates applicable to households and to recoup revenues through raising taxes on the business sector. These combined measures have the effect of preserving (approximate) revenue neutrality for the proposed legislation overall.

Under these conditions, the Proposal has its greatest effects on specific economic sectors over the period to 1990; the macroeconomic effects of higher interest rates and inflation and lower economic growth are projected to emerge in the longer term--effectively in the 1990s. The sectoral effects of the Proposal are seen to be most worrisome toward the nation's international competitive position and, through that channel as well as directly, on business plant and equipment spending. The residential housing sector is also projected to be negatively affected. Consumption spending will be stronger under the Proposal.

Finally, an alternative approach--the border-adjustable consumption tax--is suggested, which would permit the substantial overhaul of tax provisions affecting households without imposing onerous revenue-raising measures on the business sector.

NOTES

1. R. Brinner, "Tax Reform II," Data Resources U.S. Long-Term Review (Summer 1985): 27-39; D. Hodes and L. Mauer, "U.S. Tax Reform: Capital Recovery and International Direct Investment," Business Economics, September 1985, forthcoming; R. Brinner, J. Abraham, R. Gough, and J. Rosan, "The Treasury Tax Proposal: Steps Toward Neu-

trality," Data Resources U.S. Review (January 1985): 15-25;
L. Taub, "The Treasury Tax Proposals," Chase Econometrics
U.S. Macro (December 1984): 1-27; J. Jasinowski, "An Econo-
metric Analysis of the Treasury's Tax Reform Proposal,
Using the Wharton Econometric Model," National Association
of Manufacturers, January 1985.

2. Traditional theory in economics suggests that
over the long run, an increase in the cost structure of
one country relative to its trading partners will set into
motion forces that bring about a fully offsetting depreciation in the exchange rate for that nation. This view is
called the purchasing power parity theory. While this
theory may be applicable over very long periods of time--
decades perhaps--it has been clear since the late 1970s
that broad macroeconomic forces can also be powerful determinants of exchange rates. Thus, high real interest
rates in the United States in recent years have contributed
to the dollar's progressive strength, resulting in as much
as a 40 to 50 percent overvaluation when judged on a
purchasing parity basis.

The forces that contribute to high real interest
rates in the United States are expected to continue for the
foreseeable future. Foreigners' asset preferences, specula-
tion aside, are also unlikely to shift dramatically against
the dollar. Therefore, these forces can be expected to
dominate the dollar exchange rate for some years to come.
Under these circumstances, the cost increases associated
with the 1985 Proposal will not be fully offset by a decline in the U.S. dollar's foreign exchange value. At
least over the next five years, we can expect the higher
business costs associated with the Proposal to be absorbed
in the form of a deterioration in U.S. competitiveness.
This erosion in competitiveness will be felt by U.S. companies both in export markets and in their domestic markets.

3. R. Brinner, "Report to the Joint Economic Committee," Data Resources Incorporated, March 1985.

4. Several studies suggest this as the appropriate
order of magnitude. As noted in Hodes and Mauer, "U.S.
Tax Reform," analyses using the major large-scale econometric models tend to underestimate the full negative investment effects since these models make no allowance for
swings in net direct investment activity by U.S.-based and
foreign multinationals.

5. While these results are expressed quantitatively in several of the tax reform analyses, a qualitative identification of indicator direction seems most appropriate, given that the effects pertain primarily to the "out-years."

6. The VAT is presently in use in all of the member nations of the European Economic Community and approximately 12 other nations outside of the socialist bloc. Japan, however, is not a member.

10

Concept of Income Realization and Deductible Costs

Glen W. Atkinson

One of the major concerns that led to the initial popular support of current efforts to reform the federal income tax system is the widespread belief that the system is unnecessarily complicated, and that these complications have caused inequitable treatment among different classes of taxpayers and market inefficiency. The issues of simplification, fairness, and efficiency, while treated separately for analytical purposes, are interrelated. As people seek to avoid taxes by taking advantage of the complex structure, it results in people with the same amount of income being treated differently. Such maneuvers cause resources to be used differently than they would be in the absence of tax planning. In addition, it is widely believed that too much of our time and talent is used in tax planning and calculation rather than in other more productive efforts, and that those income units with the most discretionary income can take fuller advantage of tax-planning schemes to avoid tax liabilities. Thus, it is widely assumed that tax simplification is required to improve the fairness of the system and to remove obstacles to efficient use of resources.

The prospects for simplifying the tax base depend in large part on establishing a workable definition of income, which in turn depends on a determination of what should be included in taxable income, and what costs of earning income should be recognized. These issues will be treated at length below, but prior to that it should be noted that in this chapter I am not concerned with the

rate structure. Whether we have a flat tax or a progressive rate structure with few or many brackets has little
to do with tax simplification. The problem most taxpayers
have is determining their legal taxable income. Once this
is done, a tax table is used to compute the tax liability
regardless of the rate structure. For instance, the corporate income tax has fewer rate brackets than the personal income tax, and yet it is probably more complex
than the personal tax. There are other valid reasons for
preferring one rate structure over others, but changing the
rate structure will not get at what seems to concern a
majority of the taxpayers. However, the overall rate
structure can be lowered if the base is broadly defined,
and lower marginal rates will likely lead to less effort to
avoid taxes, and thus a more neutral tax. This seems to
be the driving force behind current reform efforts.

In addition, we are attempting to establish a measure of taxable income for households, unincorporated business firms, and corporate enterprises. Households and unincorporated business firms are subject to the personal income tax. However, since business income is allowed to
deduct more expenses for earning income than is the case
for labor income, business firms will generally use more
supplemental forms to establish their costs. Fuel to operate
a machine is treated as a business expense, but breakfast
for the construction worker, which is his fuel, is not. It
is argued that breakfast is not discretionary spending,
whereas the machine will only be operated if it can produce net income for the owner. Consequently, discretionary
spending is more likely to be considered an expense in the
tax code than mere life-sustaining activities. A lunch at
a business convention in Hawaii is deductible, but lunch
out of a lunch pail is considered a consumption expenditure that generates satisfaction. The public disdain for
the three-martini lunch is understandable. Owners of
sports teams can argue that business deductions for ball
games are in the national interest, but it is not these
types of "operating" expenses that cause us difficulty in
determining taxable income (Wall Street Journal, July 17,
1985, p. 33). Although these abuses receive much coverage
in the news, the fundamental issues of expense deductions
are how to deal with capital assets and the timing of income.

The tax on corporate income is actually a tax on
net income, and could be more accurately defined as a

corporate profits tax. It is a tax on profits retained in the firm as well as dividends paid out. Dividends received then are subject to the personal income tax. Proposals to eliminate the corporate tax and to integrate the corporate and personal tax will be discussed below.

It is my contention that the authors of various income tax reform proposals have promised more tax simplification than they can deliver, and the public is bound to be disappointed. This is not only because interest groups will be lobbying to mold the package for their benefit, but also because income is a complex concept in our complex, evolving economic society. Two-thirds of the personal income tax returns do not make use of personal deductions now, and the Reagan tax reform proposal would increase this to 70 percent. These taxpayers are led to believe that if their household income can be defined on a W-2 statement and the short tax return, then income of all taxpaying units can be as simply defined. However, it is not just the calculations of personal deductions that complicate the tax structure, but also what should be included in taxable income and how to treat business expenditures, particularly for capital items that will limit any simplification of income taxes. This is further complicated by the dual personal and corporate tax systems.

We will discuss the following topics separately, but it is obvious that these issues are interrelated:

1. Definition of comprehensive taxable income.
2. Treatment of unrealized gains.
3. Relationship between corporate and personal taxes.
4. Treatment of capital expenditures and income.

DEFINING COMPREHENSIVE TAXABLE INCOME

Public finance economists have generally advocated a comprehensive tax base as a way to ensure equity and tax neutrality, but there is less than complete agreement about the definition of a comprehensive base. Moreover, attempts to move toward a comprehensive base sometimes lead to more complication.

The definition of taxable income is not a new topic in economic theory, and the discussion even antedates the concern over high rates and the impact of inflation on bracket creep by several decades. In fact, the work of Irving Fisher to define income preceded the income tax itself. Fisher was concerned with the role of interest rates in relating capital and income, and only later applied his concept to taxable income. According to Fisher, income is the value of services consumed or enjoyment income. Enjoyment or satisfaction cannot be directly measured, but expenditures for consumption can be. Rather than measuring the flow of money to the various factors of production, he thought income could be best measured by expenditures for present enjoyment. He defined money income as all "money received which is not obviously, and in the nature of the case, to be devoted to reinvestment" (Fisher, p. 37). But Fisher went beyond money income to a service-flow concept that includes current consumption plus the psychic imputed income from the enjoyment from consumer durables such as a house and value of uncompensated household labor (Young, p. 40). Thus, Fisher did not include savings in his definition of income, but he did include imputed income accruing to the household. This is because the end purpose of economic activity is the enjoyment of the flow of services from production. Consumer services provide immediate enjoyment, but savings generate future, potential enjoyment and should not be considered income until that enjoyment is realized. For that same reason he concluded that accrued capital gains should not be considered income until those gains are used for present enjoyment.

Such a measure would impose the total tax burden on the household sector and make the corporate tax unnecessary. He also warned that "money income practically never conforms to real income or deficits push money income below real income" (Fisher, p. 39). This concept of income delights those who want to use the tax code to encourage capital accumulation and the postponement of consumption. Therefore, it would not be a neutral tax because it would favor future consumption over present consumption. Moreover, it would not lend to simplification because it is not always obvious what is earmarked for reinvestment, and there would be difficulties in measuring imputed household income.

It should be noted that Fisher was writing before the development of modern macroeconomic theory, and he even believed that national income accounting would be impossible or at least misleading. Macroeconomic theory assumes that savings free up resources, but investment spending has the dual role of creating resources and making use of scarce resources. Hence, taxing only household consumption would distort market preferences in favor of postponed consumption and accumulation. This treatment by Fisher results from his proposition that costs of production are negative income, but labor pain in providing household services, for example, simultaneously creates a flow of enjoyable services. We will return to this problem of matching the flow of costs and income over time at various points below. However, it is favorable treatment of accumulation that modern proponents of a consumption tax applaud.

Nicholas Kaldor advocates the abandonment of the tax on income in favor of an expenditure tax for a different reason—namely, the impossibility of measuring taxable income accurately. However, Kaldor denied that consumption and income are the same concept:

> If we defined income as consumption we
> should still require another term to denote
> as potential income the consumption that
> would obtain if net savings were zero.
> Hence, apart from the trivial question of
> which is the right use of words, it is evi-
> dent that income and consumption (as or-
> dinarily used) do not refer to the same
> thing, but to two different things; and if
> we reserved the term income for consump-
> tion we should still need another term for
> what would otherwise be called income;
> and we should still be left with the prob-
> lem of how to define the latter. (p. 164)

He would define income not as the net yield of capital goods or the stream of services derived from them, but as the value of capital goods due to the time factor. Income is the excess of the things produced in a given time period over the value of things consumed in producing them. But it is the uncertainty introduced by the time factor that makes it possible to measure taxable income from capital appreciation: "The income which is derived over a period of time on capital value at an instant of time is a forward-looking concept. It is the expected rather than realized income, and can only be measured by a single rate of interest if there is no uncertainty" (Kaldor, p. 166). Taxable income should include consumption plus real capital accumulation, according to Kaldor. However, unlike price adjustments that can be accomplished with index numbers, no such index can be constructed for interest because true changes in interest rates are not movements that can be inferred from market data (Kaldor, pp. 175-76). On this point, he agrees with Fisher, who made the following remark:

> The student should also try to forget all former notions concerning the so-called supply and demand of capital as the causes of interest. Since capital is merely the translation of future expected income into present cash value, whatever supply and demand we have to deal with are rather the supply and demand of future income. (p. 51)

Kaldor said much the same:

> When the general level of share values goes up it is not possible to say how far the rise represents increased expectations of profits and how far it represents increased confidence resulting in a lower rate at which expected profits are discounted. Thus, the problem of defining individual income, quite apart from any problem of practical measurement, appears in principle insoluble. (p. 176)

So we have one economist telling us that income is consumption, and another saying it is much more than that, but we cannot define or measure it suitably for income tax purposes. However, both Fisher and Kaldor have caused us to focus on the time problem with respect to capital expenditures and capital income. This is one of the primary reasons simplification will remain so elusive as we attempt to broaden the base.

Most tax economists are aware of the conceptual problems raised by Kaldor. Yet most have remained convinced that only a broad definition of income that includes both consumption and accumulation can provide a fair and efficient tax base, and one that will generate sufficient revenues at low marginal rates. Most discussions of tax reform have been based on broadening the definition of income. In fact, the Reagan proposal would shift the emphasis from household to business income.

The Haig-Simons concept of income has served as a benchmark for these reform proposals. Writing in 1921, Robert M. Haig concluded that the concept of income used in modern tax legislation is the

> increase or accretion in one's power to satisfy wants in a given period in so far as that power consists of (a) money itself, or, (b) anything susceptible of valuation in terms of money, more simply stated, the definition of income which the economist offers is this: Income is the money value of the net accretion to one's economic power between two points in time. (p. 59)

Furthermore, he defines taxable income

> in terms of power to satisfy economic wants rather than in terms of satisfactions themselves. It has the effect of taxing the recipient of income when he receives the power to attain satisfaction rather than when he elects to exercise that power. This should do no violence to our sense of equity, however. The fact that a man chooses to postpone the gratification of his desires is no sufficient reason for postponing his tax. (p. 59)

Henry C. Simons offered a similar definition of income:

> Personal income connotes, broadly, the exercise of control over the use of society's scarce resources. It has not to do with sensations, services or goods, but rather with rights which command prices (or to which prices may be imputed). Its calculation implies estimates (a) of the amount by which the value of a person's store of property rights would have increased, as

between the beginning and end of the
period, if he had consumed (destroyed)
nothing, or (b) of the value of rights
which he might have exercised in consumption without altering the value of his store
of rights. In other words, it implies estimates of consumption and accumulation.
(p. 68)

Both Haig and Simons rejected the Fisher doctrine
that income is only subjective consumer satisfaction. The
Haig-Simons concept of comprehensive income, unlike Fisher
and Kaldor, holds that market data can provide reasonable
estimates for determining taxable income. Haig devotes
considerable space to a discussion of the limits of accounting practice in arriving at the estimates, but concludes
that excluding the estimates of accumulation would distort
the true measure of income more than the imperfect estimates. The Haig-Simons concept recognizes the time problem raised by Kaldor associated with the measurement of
capital income, but capital gains yield economic power,
and are, therefore, income and should be subject to taxation. Haig argues that economists and accountants generally agree on what income is, and that concessions to deal
with the real world problems of estimation should not be
made by denying that an accretion to economic power is
income. Rather, they should be made as "merely concessions to the exigencies of a given situation" (Haig, p. 65).
One concession Haig was willing to consider in face of an
exigency is the postponement of taxation of capital gains
until they are realized (p. 65). Because of the time
period problem, valuations of capital gains will be imperfect, but the taxation of capital income should allow for
the maintenance of capital intact.
The Fisher and Haig-Simons concepts still serve as
the basis of the measurement of taxable income in modern
public finance textbooks. Richard Aronson believes one
important reason for the complicated tax structure is that
the nation has never made up its mind whether it prefers
the Fisher or Haig-Simons concept of income (p. 341). On
one hand, we want a broad-based structure with low rates
that is relatively neutral in market decisions, and we want
that structure to reflect ability to pay, which is usually
meant to be based on economic power as opposed to actual
satisfaction. On the other hand, it is easy to win support

for any measure that promises to give additional encouragement to capital accumulation, which leads closer to the
Fisher concept.

Harvey Rosen states that although most public finance economists endorse the Haig-Simons approach for
equity and market efficiency, there are justifiable reasons
to deviate from the benchmark (pp. 336-39). For instance,
he reminds us that efficiency is enhanced when relatively
high tax rates are imposed on those resources and activities with relatively inelastic supply such as land.

Aronson demonstrates that both the Fisher and Haig-
Simons tax cover all of a person's taxpaying capacity over
a lifetime. The real difference is that the timing of the
tax payment will be delayed under the Fisher system.
However, this depends on the assumption that all receipts
are consumed over the life of the individual (Aronson, pp.
337-40). This assumption is particularly troublesome given
the obviously strong drive to leave a positive estate at
death and our limited taxation of intergenerational transfers of income. This accumulation drive seems to contra-
dict the Fisher notion that the end of economic activity is
consumption. There appears to be a powerful drive for
accumulation for its own sake, as Keynes suggested in his
essay, "Economic Possibilities for Our Grandchildren" (pp.
358-73). This phenomenon, which has important consequences for a democratic society in terms of the concentration of wealth and income over generations, has not received the attention it deserves from public finance economists.

To conclude this section, we have attempted to demonstrate that a reasonable concept of income must be attempted. Traditionally, public finance economists have
favored the Haig-Simons measure as a benchmark for establishing taxable income, but recognize there are sound reasons for deviating from it. The problem for tax policy
and administration is to distinguish the sound from the
spurious reasons. One of the continuing nettlesome issues
in this regard is the treatment of unrealized gains when
there are insufficient market data to establish the value
of the gain.

TREATMENT OF UNREALIZED GAINS

The definition of gross income in the Internal Revenue Code certainly gives initial support to the broadest

definition of income. Section 61(a) states that gross income is "all income from whatever source derived." However, Regulation 1.61-1(a) places some limits on the definition of gross income: "Gross income means all income from whatever source derived unless excluded by law. Gross income includes income realized in any form, whether money, property, or services. Income may be realized, therefore, in the form of services, meals, accommodations, stock or other property, as well as cash."

This provides a rather inclusive definition of income in that it does not limit the form in which payment may be required. However, it is limited in that it does exclude unrealized gains. This appears to some to be an arbitrary distinction for those who support the notion of a comprehensive income tax. For example, one person's economic power would be enhanced by employer-provided meals, and taxable on that value. Another person's economic power could be enhanced by the increase in the value of property holdings, but the tax payment would be postponed until it is realized. This fits neither the Fisher nor Haig-Simons definition. Fisher would include unrealized gains in consumer durables in the tax base, while Haig would include those gains plus appreciation of investment property as it accrues.

Accountants, on the other hand, emphasize the concept of income realization and the proper matching of costs in earning income (Young, p. 42). The courts have also given support to the realization principle as the basis of taxation. The Supreme Court ruled in Eisner v. Macomber that "Income may be defined as the gain derived from capital, from labor, or from both combined, provided that it be understood to include profit gained through a sale or conversion of capital assets" (cited in Young, p. 42).

Thus, both the accounting and judicial approaches require an actual market transaction to determine taxable gain. Compare this to Haig's statement that "the goods and services which are of significance are those which are susceptible of evaluation in terms of money. It is not necessary that they should actually have passed through the process of sale" (p. 58).

The primary reason for relying on the realization principle seems to be the difficulty in establishing accurate values as they accrue. Those who favor the Fisher approach would tax neither realized nor unrealized capital gains, but even those who favor the Haig-Simons definition recognize the difficulty of valuing gains as they accrue. At a conference on comprehensive income taxation nearly a decade ago, Cary Brown and Jeremy Bulow remarked on this difficulty, especially with regard to imperfect capital markets (pp. 243-48). They believe that in a competitive market under conditions of certainty there would be little difficulty in measuring changes in accrued net worth; even relaxing the condition of certainty would not present an insurmountable problem with the use of income averaging. It is only in the case of imperfect capital markets that there would be insufficient and unreliable market data to establish accrued values. Under these conditions, the postponement of the recognition of the gain or loss until realization may be necessary. It seems ironic that the intent is to develop a tax system that will not distort market choices, but it is market imperfections that preclude full development.

The taxation of capital gains as they are realized leads to the secondary question of what rate to tax them. Since 1921 capital gains have been taxed at a preferential rate compared to ordinary income. The major arguments for this preferential treatment are the following. First, a high rate on appreciating values given the realization principle, tends to lock-in investments and deter moving assets to new ventures that favor existing enterprises. Second, high marginal rates promote instability because as asset prices are rising, they are withheld from the market to avoid the tax that forces prices still higher. When asset prices are falling, the reverse is true. Third, it is argued that a tax on capital gains is really a tax on capital rather than income, and precludes the ability of the owner to replace the asset with one of equal value. This violates the principle of maintaining capital intact. Fourth, the gains accrue over more than one year, and it is unfair to treat them as if they were generated in the year realized. Fifth, the funds from the sale are not generally available for consumption, but for reinvestment in other capital assets. Finally, capital gains reflect inflationary increases in value as well as real increases.

Opponents of preferential taxation of capital gains respond by noting that available data do not confirm that the lock-in effect is as great as stated by the proponents. Moreover, the problem could be reduced by subjecting the gains to taxation at the time the assets are transferred through gifts or at the death of the owner. Second, they argue that investors have many motives for holding appreciating assets. The tax treatment is not of much importance for those whose primary motive is income and secure assets. However, for those who are motivated to seek appreciation in the value of their assets, the existing preferential treatment does encourage them to shift out of conservative investments to more speculative ventures. Third, they concede that it is unfair to tax the gains as if they accrued in a single year, but they propose that the problem could be more accurately addressed in a system of income averaging. Moreover, they point out that the averaging system should take into account that the deferral of the tax is an interest-free loan, and therefore an interest charge should be built into the averaging scheme. Fourth, this preference is relatively unavailable to those who have only wage and salary income, and is concentrated at the upper end of salary earnings. Finally, preferential treatment of realized gains is not limited to productive assets, but is available to those who hold assets such as rare paintings and precious metals that primarily obtain their value from scarcity rather than production. A system that could be aimed at new and growing firms--where return is more likely to be in appreciation due to reinvested rather than distributed profits--would meet the aims of the preference more closely. But as Richard Goode has noted, "preferential taxation of capital gains may have done more to foster highly leveraged real estate ventures than to encourage innovative enterprises" (p. 271). Of course, the targeting of preferences would conflict with the goal of tax simplification.

THE REALIZATION PRINCIPLE

A more extensive discussion of the pros and cons of a preferential tax rate for realized capital gains can be found in Dickinson (pp. 499-505). The primary point to be made here is that the adoption of the realization principle, coupled with the preferential tax rate, has introduced a whole new set of complications as we were attempting to avoid the complications of the accrual system. William Andrews has concluded that the problem of unrealized appreciation is the Achilles' heel of the ideal of comprehensive income taxation (p. 280). He agrees that unrealized gains must be included in a comprehensive income tax base. Omitting unrealized appreciation in conjunction with highly leveraged purchases of capital assets can "produce exemptions from income way beyond mere accumulation" (p. 281). He goes on to say that "it is only those without capital, who have to save from income, that are taxed on their accumulation as well as their consumption" (p. 281). Comprehensive income tax reformers, faced with the inability to correctly ascertain unrealized gains, have settled for a second-best solution of taxing only realized gains. This, according to Andrews, has taken us further from the ideal goal. Since we cannot measure unrealized gains, and since the present system is loaded in favor of those who can take advantage of financial manipulations, Andrews would have us forget about attempting to tax accumulation and settle for a tax on consumption instead. He concludes that a well-constructed consumption tax would be simpler to build than a comprehensive income tax. In this, Andrews seems to be closer to Kaldor's position that we cannot measure accumulation, rather than to Fisher's position that consumption is income. This position seems to be clearly second best to a comprehensive income tax in terms of equity since accumulation is so heavily skewed in our population. Perhaps a partial solution would be to treat transfers of assets as gifts and at death as consumption.

Clearly, the taxation of only realized gains in our highly leveraged economy alongside preferential rates violates the ideal of the comprehensive income tax on equity and efficiency grounds. It not only favors those with the discretionary income to play the game, it also distorts market behavior. To some extent it locks in investments; it encourages the shifting of income from ordinary income to capital gains; and it encourages financial schemes over production. The question is do we give up on the ideal or can we learn how to value accrued gains? The halfway measures being used have settled for an accrued base in a way that violates the ideal.

COMPREHENSIVE INCOME TAXATION AND THE CORPORATION

A good deal of the difficulty in constructing a comprehensive income tax arises because our income is generated and received at both the individual and corporate levels.

> Confusion of thought is sometimes caused
> by the fact that the accountant usually
> speaks in terms of a business enterprise
> as a separate entity, while the economist
> usually speaks in terms of the individual
> person. The distinction between gross and
> net income—which occupies so large a part
> of the attention of the accountant—is sum-
> marily dismissed by the economist where
> typical income receiver is the man whose
> expenditures are predominantly for purposes
> of personal consumption. The definition
> and reasoning of the accountant, however,
> are readily fitted to the case of the typical
> economic man if this accounting period is
> reduced to its true economic length.
> (Haig, p. 63)

As we have seen, the time problem is still under a great deal of dispute. In addition, the issue of how to treat the corporate "person" in our tax system has been subject to as much rhetoric as analysis. Our economic and legal thought attributes all action to the individual. Economists are fond of saying that corporations don't pay taxes, only people do, but our incidence studies cannot identify which people pay the corporate income tax. However, we do know people do accumulate and hold accretions to economic power in corporate structures. In 1984 of the $674.8 billion of gross private savings, only $156.1 billion was personal savings. A review of the major principles of economic textbooks discloses that we build an adequate theory of personal savings, but pay little attention to what determines corporate savings, which is the bulk of our savings. Thus, the student who takes only a course or two in economics is left with a distorted view of savings determination in the economy. This shortcoming is partially due to the confusion cited by Haig. Economists have not developed an adequate understanding of collective, cor- porate behavior. We have been blinded by the elegance of our individual behavior models, and have applied them to situations where they have only limited relevance (Field, pp. 49-72).

This treatment has led economists to assert that the corporate income tax has no basis in economic theory. That may indicate that economic theory is lacking in its explanatory power. A typical statement regarding the justification of the corporate income tax was recently made by Arnold Harberger: "There is no sound economic underpinning for the corporate income tax" (p. 162).

In the case of Santa Clara County v. Southern Pacific Railroad, the Supreme Court ruled that the corporation was a person with all the rights and prerogatives of the natural individual under the Fifth and Fourteenth Amendments. According to Robert A. Solo, this decision was a watershed in determining economic organization and the relationship of the market system to political authority: "Like it or not, the capacity for problem-solving through individualized choice as it once existed in the market system was gone, or at least was greatly diminished" (p. 72).

Economic theory must be grounded in the existing legal realities. If our legal and economic thought attributes all action to individuals, then for corporations to survive and prosper, they had to be granted access to the legal system. This was accomplished by the Court's decision to grant them individual status. Legally, the corporation is an individual with a legal rather than biological lifespan. This distinction between biological and legal persons has caused considerable confusion in fashioning a tax structure that is equitable, and does not unintentionally distort market choices. This confusion has been exacerbated by the rhetoric of those who want to use the corporate tax to soak the rich, as well as by those who want a tax structure that would favor accumulation over consumption. The former are obviously stating a political preference, while the latter have been able to camouflage their preferences as economic science. However, a neutral tax would not favor accumulation over consumption any more than it would soak the rich. The task of economic science, once it has been politically established that we desire a neutral tax, is to see that there is even-handed treatment of income. Arguments for redistribution or preferential treatment of accumulation must be judged on their own merits.

A balanced statement regarding this problem is made by Richard Aronson. He claims that a separate corporate income tax is not supported by either the Fisher or Haig-Simons concept. "However, this does not mean that the income a person derives from corporate holdings should not be taxed" (p. 429). Haig and Simons were quite clear on the point that all accretions to economic power in whatever form should be taxed under a comprehensive system, but this does not require a separate corporate tax if we would fully integrate corporate and individual income. It is the separate tax treatment of corporate income that causes the problems. Joseph Pechman defends the corporate tax as a means to safeguard the individual income tax in the absence of effective interaction of the two taxes (p. 177).

Defenders of the comprehensive system do not have to defend the dual-tax system. The present system has several sources of inequality. First, dividends are subject to the corporate tax and the individual tax, which encourages high retained earnings for corporations. This hurts most those who are investing for the current income. In addition to the equity problem, this situation distorts capital markets and directs funds away from new firms. This may be one reason for the high level of corporate savings relative to personal savings. Second, the corporate tax rate applies equally to all owners (ignoring shifting of the tax) regardless of their total household income, and violates the principle of progressive taxation. We have already discussed the issue of not taxing unrealized capital gains. Moreover, 60 percent of realized gains are exempt from taxation entirely, and the remainder are taxed at preferential rates.

One of the reforms most often proposed to remedy this situation is for integration of the two taxes, but it is as often rejected because of administrative problems involved in all integration schemes. Full integration would deal with both dividends paid out and retained earnings, and pose the most difficult administrative problems. Dividends would not be taxed at the corporate level, the dividend exclusion provision at the personal level would be repealed, and all dividends would be taxed at the appropriate marginal tax rate facing the individual taxpayer. The difficulties would arise in the attempt to apportion the retained tax liability of earning to each shareholder. George Break has proposed two methods of dealing with this income (pp. 64-65). One method would be to repeal the corporate tax and place the levy on retained profits by taxing all capital gains and losses on corporate shares as they accrue. Thus, shareholders would be required to value their holdings at the end of each year and would be subject to a tax at full rates on any net gain that had accrued. Of course, full deduction of losses would have to be allowed against ordinary income. His other proposal would be to allocate profits proportionally each year to all common stockholders. They would then include this value in their taxable income and adjust the cost basis of their stock at the same time in order to prevent any later taxation of this income. They could then either claim the income by selling the shares without an additional tax, or leave the funds in the firm and pay the tax with other sources of income. In order to reduce the liquidity problem of the latter option, corporations could withhold taxes at the top bracket that is applied to individual incomes. This would lead to over-withholding for most taxpayers, and would work more smoothly if the top rate for individual incomes is close to the corporate rate. Either approach to full integration would treat all gains as accrued after adjustments for losses and expenses. They would also eliminate the problem of double taxation of dividend income.

Because of the obvious administrative difficulties in treating retained earnings in an integrated system, several plans have been advanced to maintain the corporate tax on retained earning and integrate only dividend income. Again Break offers two solutions: "One would be to allow corporations to deduct dividends paid from their corporate income tax base, just as interest payments on debt are now treated" (p. 65). The other method would be to have the portion of the present corporation tax now paid on earnings to be distributed to be converted into a withholding levy fully creditable by shareholders against tax liabilities payable on dividends or other income. This is actually a withholding scheme similar to that applied to labor income presently. Partial integration would solve the problem of double taxation of dividend income, but would reduce government revenue. It would not address the question of treatment of accrued gains; thus, part of the revenue loss could be made up by taxing realized gains equally with ordinary income. Even this would allow the shareholder the benefit of deferred taxation.

FINDINGS

To sum up this discussion, a comprehensive income tax would not distinguish between individual and corporate income. The corporate tax is now justified to protect the integrity of the individual tax, but the present dual system creates problems of evenhanded treatment, especially for dividend income. Integration of the corporate tax and individual tax would reduce these inequities, depending on the integration scheme adopted. Integration could have the added benefit of treating equity and debt financing on the same tax basis for the corporation, and eliminate the incentive for debt financing. However, to the extent that integration would encourage shareholders to want large dividend payments, the corporation would have to work harder to raise funds for net investment. A properly constructed complete integration system could capture accrued gains. The problem then would be how to tax gains in the noncorporate business sector.

Up to this point, the major concern has been how to define comprehensive income. The problems are how to treat both accumulations of net flows and realized and unrealized gains from capital. A neutral, comprehensive income tax base would include all income, whether used for consumption or accumulation. There are legitimate reasons to deviate from this benchmark. For example, resources with an inelastic supply should be subject to relatively high rates. However, many of the deviations from the ideal are for practical accounting and administrative reasons. Other deviations are due to the fact that we have not settled on whether we prefer the Fisher or Haig–Simons concept of income. Still another reason for difficulties in defining gross taxable income is existence of separate taxation of corporate business and household income. The next section will examine how we do and that we should account for expenses in earning income.

COSTS OF ACQUIRING INCOME

Richard Goode, a leading advocate of the comprehensive tax base, would include all labor and property earnings, gains, gifts, and transfer payments received. The only relief would be limited to personal exemptions and the costs of acquiring income (p. 268). "Most economists (with the notable exception of Fisher) have included the maintenance of capital intact as part of their definition of income" (Parker and Harcourt, p. 1). Deductions of costs are necessary to maintain capital intact. Personal exemptions are allowed, to ensure a minimal level of tax-free

income. Personal deductions have been enacted over the
years for various reasons. Mortgage interest is defended
as a means to encourage home ownership, and medical deductions as a means to subsidize personal health care.
Since they are not a means of maintaining capital intact,
they are beyond the scope of this chapter. However, I
would like to cite a couple of examples to suggest how ir-
rational the base of a tax deduction can be to encourage
or subsidize certain activities. The deduction of mortgage
interest actually benefits most those subject to the highest
marginal tax rates. Those who cannot qualify to buy a
house get no direct benefit, and are the ones who are
least likely then to be able to qualify for other itemized
deductions. Even personal exemptions are not beyond abuse.
Why do we allow a special exemption for the blind and not
for the totally paralyzed? The logic of the progressive
income tax is that the effect of the handicap will affect
tax liability through income-earning ability.

To return to the major theme of this section, expenses in earning income must be allowed for a neutral,
comprehensive tax. There are essentially two kinds of expenditures to consider. First are the short-term operating
expenses such as wages, fuel, and raw materials. This
conforms closely to what economists call variable costs, in
that these costs would not be incurred if production halted.
The other type of costs are for long-life exhaustible capital resources that are fixed for the firm. Linking these
two in certain cases are various contractual obligations
that turn variable costs into fixed costs. An example is
the baseball club that can deduct the salaries of its players as a short-term expense. However, when the club is
purchased, the new owners are buying the value of the
monopoly franchise and the players' contracts. Thus, they
are able to depreciate the value of the contracts on schedule and deduct the expenses of the annual salaries. The
sticky tax question is how much of the value should be
allocated to the appreciating monopoly franchise, as opposed to the players' contracts. Other, less glamorous
examples of contractual values are for crude oil supplies
for refineries and grazing leases on federal government
lands. The examples are cited to show that the distinction
between short-term expenses and capital costs is not neat
and exact.

No one denies that business expenses should be allowed to determine taxable income. The problem for the

determination of legitimate short-term expenses is how to distinguish between consumption and business expense. When is a lunch a legitimate business activity? How much accounting will be required and tolerated to distinguish business from pleasurable use of a company-provided car? Are professional sports and Broadway theatre tickets necessary to earn income? Is education a consumer expenditure or a necessary expense for human capital formation in our technical society? Obviously, our tax code and regulations provide "answers" to all of these questions and more, but it is these answers that, in part, complicate the tax system. Most business expenses are beyond question, but it is those at the margin of consumption and production that are debatable. Moreover, the problems would not be diminished if we switched from an income tax to a consumption tax. Although the discussion of these controversial, marginal business expenses attracts public debate, the more important and complicated concern for tax policy is how to treat long-life capital resources.

DEPRECIATION

One of the most thoroughly perplexing issues in income tax policy and accounting is the provision for the recovery of the use of capital equipment and structures in production. The basic provision for the recovery of capital-consumption costs is the depreciation allowances. In recent years the depreciation allowance has been coupled with an investment tax credit to foster capital accumulation.

Some form of depreciation is required in a neutral tax system to ensure there is not an antisavings bias. Pure economic depreciation would apportion the loss in value of the physical asset over its lifetime as that loss occurs due to physical wear and tear and economic obsolescence. Thus, the firm would have a fund set aside as replacement is needed. There are many problems in designing a system for depreciation that is neutral with respect to consumption and savings, and even more difficult to develop a system that is both simple and neutral with respect to various types of equipment and industries. One of the most difficult problems comes from the use of historical cost in a period of inflation, because the firm would not have adequate funds to replace the asset when needed. This would require financing of replacement capital with current income, debt, or new equity issues, which would obviously violate the principle of maintenance of capital intact. This problem of inflation and depreciation is even more difficult to adjust for in the accounting system if the rate of inflation is itself not stable (Jorgenson and Sullivan, pp. 213-15). A positive tax rate based on an assumption about the future rate of inflation could result in a corporate investment subsidy if the rate of inflation turned out to be lower than the assumed rate. This is, of course, not limited to the corporate sector. According to Joseph Minarik, "in 1981 and 1982 the entire partnership sector of the economy showed a net loss--a development unprecedented in the compilation of IRS partnership statistics" (p. 6). Our zeal to fix a defect in this uncertain world often leads to the creation of a new flaw.

Other problems in accounting for true economic depreciation are making reasonable estimates of economic obsolescence in a technically dynamic economy, abuse of tax shelters in financially leveraged investments, and political ploys to gain a tax advantage. All of this makes it quite difficult to sort out what is required to tax capital income without discrimination, and without granting unintentional tax subsidies.

It has become increasingly popular to argue that any system of depreciation will discriminate against capital formation, and, therefore, we should forget it in favor of immediate expensing (Ture, pp. 47-76). Immediate expensing provides that the capital-consumption allowance can be taken at the time the asset is acquired. Jorgenson and Sullivan assert that "while immediate expensing would amount to the elimination of the corporate income tax, this proposal is superior to alternative proposals that would replace the tax by a corporate income subsidy" (p. 226). Ture's advocacy of immediate expensing is based in part on his belief that "whatever their merits for purposes of reporting company results and conditions, the accounting concept and measure of depreciation do not offer useful guides for depreciation policy for tax purposes" (p. 51). However, Charles Hulten and Frank Wykoff have shown that it is possible to measure economic depreciation using market data, and that there is remarkable agreement among different studies using fundamentally different techniques (Hulten and Wykoff, pp. 81-125). Ture notes the objection to expensing would be to replace the income tax with an expenditure tax, but this does not bother him: "The objection, however, is more a matter of nomenclature than substance. Nothing in the concept of income for income tax purposes requires including in the tax base both the annual return generated by capital and the capitalized amount of those returns" (p. 55). This appears to be tantamount to saying whether or not we include net accumulations in the tax base is simply a matter of nomenclature. In commenting on Ture's paper, Alan J. Auerbach interpreted "his remarks in this vein as simply reiterating that non-zero taxes on capital income are distortionary" (Auerbach, p. 78). Moreover, according to Auerbach, unless Ture would include net corporate borrowing in the tax base, the effective tax rate would be negative tax rates on tax subsidies. Frederic Hickman believes Ture should candidly argue for the formal elimination of the tax on capital income if that is what he desires (Hickman, p. 89). Substantively, Hickman points out that only firms with income from prior investments would benefit from expensing. "Thus we are left with the paradox that the companies for which expensing is most necessary in order to produce a neutral tax would, in fact, not get the value of expensing if it were enacted tomorrow" (p. 90).

The United States does not use either economic depreciation in its pure form or immediate expensing. Instead, since 1954 we have opted for various forms of accelerated depreciation that shorten the life of the asset for tax purposes. While the same amount of tax would be paid over the actual life of the asset, the bunching of the deductions in the early years increases the present value of a new piece of equipment. Accelerated depreciation is defended as a means of adjusting for the impact of inflation on assets depreciated at historical cost, and as a means of coping with uncertain obsolescence. The latter has become a more important consideration as international competition heats up with countries that more directly subsidize private investment.

Accelerated depreciation was introduced into tax law in 1954. Depreciation allowances were further accelerated in the Kennedy tax cut of 1962, which was coupled with the introduction of the investment tax credit. The depreciation schedule was further shortened in 1971 and the investment tax credit was made permanent. It has been estimated that the effective tax was 40 percent from 1971 through 1980. The Reagan Economic Recovery Tax Act

(ERTA) of 1981 reduced the effective rate to 21 percent (Gravelle, p. 304). The Tax Equity and Fiscal Responsibility Act (TEFRA) of 1982 reduced the effects of ERTA somewhat.

The major feature of ERTA was the replacement of depreciation with cost recovery (Ture, p. 63). The accelerated cost-recovery system virtually eliminated the concept of useful asset life and assigned each depreciable asset to one of only four asset-depreciation range categories. In the previous system of depreciation, some attempt was made to approximate the useful life of the asset. Under the accelerated cost-recovery system autos, light-duty trucks, R & D equipment, and certain other personal properties are assigned a tax life of three years. Most other machinery can be written off in five years. Public utility assets are depreciated in ten or fifteen years, and real property is assigned a fifteen-year recovery period. In addition to the reduction in the number of categories, ERTA allowed for acceleration of deduction in the first year in each category. TEFRA reduced this acceleration somewhat while maintaining the reduced number of categories. Accelerated cost recovery has helped to focus attention on what Ture calls the secondary neutrality question, "whether any depreciation system can provide tax neutrality in the sense that the tax alters the value of different types of capital in the same proportion" (p. 55). Jane Gravelle has studied the effects of recent depreciation laws on the taxation of capital assets of different durability (pp. 297–306). She calculated the welfare loss of the misallocation of capital due to the effects of depreciation rules on a heterogeneous capital structure. The results of the study are that ERTA increased the deadweight loss from nonneutral taxation of various assets, but that TEFRA reduced the welfare loss substantially because it reduced the tax burden most on the heavily taxed capital supplies.

The effective tax rate on reproducible private capital was reduced from 29 percent prior to 1981 to 21 percent under ERTA and 25 percent under TEFRA (Gravelle, p. 304). Along with the changes in overall effective rates has been a reduction in tax rates on different types of assets under TEFRA, which has reduced the effect of taxation on the allocation of capital. The ERTA system had reduced the overall rate, thus favoring capital accumulation, while increasing the tax effect on the allocation of capital. Perhaps with additional research a depreciation system can be developed to satisfy Ture's secondary neutrality question. In order to satisfy both neutrality questions, strong efforts must be made to eliminate tax arbitrage, which occurs dramatically when depreciation is allowable for tax purposes on assets that appreciate in value such as real estate, timber, and cattle (Rosen, p. 427).

While it is theoretically possible to design a depreciation system that treats capital income neutrally, the investment tax credit is designed to be a positive investment incentive. The credit is subtracted directly from the tax liability rather than deducted from income, and is determined as a percentage of the amount spent on qualifying new investment goods. It was first introduced in 1962 to deal with the recession. Prior to ERTA, the tax credit was 10 percent on assets with useful lives of seven years or more, 6.66 percent for five-to-six-year assets, and 3.33 percent for three-to-four-year assets. No credit was granted to assets of less than three years. The current law allows a 10 percent credit for property in the five-, ten-, and fifteen-year classes, 6 percent for property in the three-year category.

Peter Fisher argued in a recent article that the combined effect of the accelerated cost-recovery system, investment tax credit, and state tax subsidies to corporations amounts to the American version of an industrial policy that "may well undermine productivity and long-term growth, and hence severely limit the capacity to purchase social peace" (p. 18). A recent study by the Citizens for Tax Justice found that the 50 lowest taxed corporations in their study had an average tax rate of 8.4 percent, but reduced investment by 21.6 percent while increasing dividends by 14.1 percent in the years 1981–83. On the other hand, the 50 highest taxed firms in their study paid an average rate of 33.1 percent, and increased investment by 4.3 percent and dividends by 10.7 percent (McIntyre and Tipps, p. 48). The authors say their findings are evidence that the supply-side assumptions of the Reagan tax policy are incorrect.

Other areas of concern regarding the proper accounting for the deduction of costs are the methods for valuing inventories during periods of inflation, and the bias built into the system that allows interest to be a deductible cost, but not dividends.

CONCLUDING REMARKS

In this chapter we have developed two competing concepts of comprehensive income taxation. The Fisher concept would tax only consumption, and the more generally accepted Haig-Simons concept would tax consumption and accumulation. While it may be desirable to deviate from a pure benchmark for theoretical as well as practical reasons, it was suggested that part of the complication in our tax system is because we have not settled on which of these two concepts we prefer. Only if we understand what comprehensive income is can we develop a neutral tax structure. Other complications result from the treatment of capital gains, the existence of nonintegrated individual and corporate income taxes, and problems associated with depreciation of capital.

The point has been made that the concept of income is controversial and complicated within the economics profession. Therefore the income tax will remain complicated, and those who have suggested a tax form can be designed to fit on a postcard are building up hopes that cannot be realized (see Hall and Rabushka for such a proposal).

Nevertheless, there is room for considerable improvement. For example, the first list of tax expenditures was published in 1967 and noted 50 preferential exceptions to the general rules. The list had grown to 105 by 1983 (Minarik, p. 5). There appears to be a growing sentiment to reduce the number of exceptions and to develop a more neutral tax with respect to the allocation of resources. Such a reform would broaden the tax base and allow for lower rates. But since such a move would reallocate resources, there will be winners and losers. Consequently, we can expect the losers to oppose any such reform. The Wall Street Journal (July 19, 1985, pp. 21-24, 25) reported industry-by-industry which would gain more from a rate reduction than they would lose by reduced preferences under the current Reagan proposal, and those who found the rate reduction would not offset the lost preference. We can expect those industries in the latter group to be all for tax reform.

In this environment the role of the economist as analyst should be enhanced as opposed to the advocate, if we agree that the tax system should be neutral. Even under these conditions we can expect continued controversy with respect to tax policy until we have better answers to some of the questions posed in this chapter and greater willingness to experiment.

REFERENCES

Andrews, William D. 1984. "The Achilles' Heel of the Comprehensive Income Tax." In New Directions in Federal Tax Policy in the 1980's, ed. Charles E. Walker and Mark A. Bloomfield. Cambridge, Mass.: Ballinger, 278-85.

Aronson, J. Richard. 1985. Public Finance. New York: McGraw-Hill.

Auerbach, Alan J. 1984. "Does ACRS Foster Efficient Capital Formation?" In New Directions in Federal Tax Policy in the 1980's, ed. Charles E. Walker and Mark A. Bloomfield. Cambridge, Mass.: Ballinger, 77-78.

Break, George F. 1978. "Corporate Tax Integration: Radical Revisionism or Common Sense." In Federal Tax Reform: Myths and Realities, ed. Michael J. Boskin. San Francisco: Institute for Contemporary Studies, 55-73.

Brown, E. Cary, and Jerry Bulow. 1977. "The Definition of Taxable Business Income." In Comprehensive Income Taxation, ed. Joseph A. Pechman. Washington, D.C.: Brookings, 241-60.

Dickinson, Martin B., Jr. 1983. "Capital Gains and Losses." In The Study of Federal Tax Law: Income, Individuals, ed. Vance N. Kirby and Willard H. Pedrick. Chicago: Commerce Clearing House, 499-599.

Field, Alexander James. 1979. "On the Explanation of Rules Using Rational Choice Models." Journal of Economic Issues 13: 49-72.

Fisher, Irving. 1969. "Income and Capital." In Readings in the Concept and Measurement of Income, ed. R. H. Parker and G. C. Harcourt. London: Cambridge University Press, 33-53.

Fisher, Peter S. 1985. "Corporate Tax Incentives: The American Version of Industrial Policy." Journal of Economic Issues 19: 1-19.

Goode, Richard. 1977. "The Economic Definition of Income." In Comprehensive Income Taxation, ed. Joseph A. Pechman. Washington, D.C.: Brookings, 1-36.

_____. 1984. "The Comprehensive Income Tax: Advantages and Disadvantages." In New Directions in Federal Tax Policy for the 1980's, ed. Charles E. Walker and Mark A. Bloomfield. Cambridge, Mass.: Ballinger, 265-77.

Gravelle, Jane G. 1983. "Capital Income and Efficiency in Allocation of Investment." National Tax Journal 36: 279-306.

Haig, Robert Murray. 1959. "The Concept of Income—Economic and Legal Aspects." In A.E.A. Readings in the Economics of Taxation, ed. Richard A. Musgrave and Carl S. Shoup. Homewood, Ill.: Irwin, 54-76.

Hall, Robert E., and Alvin Rabushka. 1983. Low Tax, Simple Tax, Flat Tax. New York: McGraw-Hill.

Harberger, Arnold C. 1984. "The State of the Corporate Income Tax: Who Pays It? Should It Be Repealed?" In New Directions in Federal Tax Policy for the 1980's, ed. Charles E. Walker and Mark A. Bloomfield. Cambridge, Mass.: Ballinger, 161-70.

Hickman, Frederic W. 1984. "Changes in Capital Cost Recovery Policies: Cost and Benefits." In New Directions in Federal Tax Policy for the 1980's, ed. Charles E. Walker and Mark A. Bloomfield. Cambridge, Mass.: Ballinger, 89-91.

Hulten, Charles R., and Frank C. Wykoff. 1981. "The Measurement of Economic Depreciation." In Depreciation, Inflation and the Taxation of Income from Capital, ed. Charles R. Hulten. Washington, D.C.: Urban Institute Press, 81-125.

Jorgenson, Dale W., and Martin A. Sullivan. 1981. "Inflation and Corporate Capital Recovery." In Depreciation, Inflation and the Taxation of Income from Capital, ed. Charles R. Hulten. Washington, D.C.: Urban Institute Press, 171-237.

Kaldor, Nicholas. 1969. "The Concept of Income in Economic Theory." In Readings in the Concept and Measurement of Income, ed. R. H. Parker and G. C. Harcourt. London: Cambridge University Press, 161-82.

Keynes, John M. 1931. "Economic Possibilities for Our Grandchildren." In Essays in Persuasion. New York: Harcourt, Brace, 358-73.

McIntyre, Robert S., and Dean C. Tipps. 1985. "The Myth of Investment Incentives." Challenge 28: 47-52.

Minarik, Joseph J. 1985. "Tax Reform at the Crossroads." Challenge 28: 4-11.

Parker, R. H., and G. C. Harcourt. 1969. "Introduction." In Readings in the Concept and Measurement of Income, ed. R. H. Parker and G. C. Harcourt. London: Cambridge University Press, 1-30.

Pechman, Joseph A. 1984. "Another View of the Corporate Income Tax." In New Directions in Federal Tax Policy for the 1980's, ed. Charles E. Walker and Mark A. Bloomfield. Cambridge, Mass.: Ballinger, 177-80.

Rosen, Harvey S. 1985. Public Finance. Homewood, Ill.: Irwin.

Simons, Henry C. 1969. "The Definition of Income." In Readings in the Concept and Measurement of Income, ed. R. H. Parker and G. C. Harcourt. London: Cambridge University Press, 63-73.

Solo, Robert A. 1974. The Political Authority and the Market System. Cincinnati: South-Western Publishing.

Ture, Norman B. 1984. "The Accelerated Cost Recovery System: An Evaluation of the 1981 and 1982 Cost Recovery Provision." In New Directions in Federal Tax

Policy for the 1980's, ed. Charles E. Walker and Mark
A. Bloomfield. Cambridge, Mass.: Ballinger.

Wetzler, James W. 1977. "Capital Gains and Losses." In
Comprehensive Income Taxation, ed. Joseph A. Pechman.
Washington, D.C.: Brookings, 115–62.

Young, J. Nelson. 1983. "Determination of Gross Income."
In The Study of Federal Tax Law: Income Tax, Indi-
viduals, ed. Vance N. Kirby and Willard H. Pedrick.
Chicago: Commerce Clearing House, 39–251.

11

Roots of the Existing Federal Corporate Income Taxes

Nathan Oestreich, Jeinie Summer, and John Walker

The corporation is such a useful institution that it was invented thousands of years ago and most cultures use it to this very day. In medieval and early modern Europe, corporations were always involved in what today would be considered governmental functions. Such institutions were often after profit as a modern business is, but they were created by governments to serve some public function. Seligman observed as follows:

> one of the chief sources of royal income in medieval Europe consisted in the so-called "fines for licenses, concessions and franchises." These were payments by individuals or associations for all kinds of special privileges. . . . Similar to these medieval concessions are the modern licenses, especially in the Southern commonwealths, which are conferred on individuals and corporations alike, and in most cases for purely fiscal reasons.[1]

Obviously governments have been extracting substantial sums from businesses, including business corporations, for centuries. In many cases the king understood that the corporation would then pass this burden on to its customers. Such arrangements often had a decidedly exploitative, uneconomic, and (by modern standards) unsavory character. Many early corporations were chartered monopo-

lies in one industry to finance useful behavior somewhere
else. The British East India Company was given a monopoly on British trade with the East Indies to generate
enough revenue to support its commercial operators and
finance a significant part of the British national debt.
Employees of the company made trade agreements with
various Indian states, conspired to overthrow unfriendly
governments, and raised an army to relieve the victims of
the "black hole of Calcutta."[2]

Creation of private monopolies to fund national debt
is apparently an example of crowding-in. Today many
people are worried about the national deficit increasing so
much that it will crowd private debt out of the bond market and so reduce investment. "Crowding-in" is inducing
businesses to invest in lucrative ventures so that part of
the revenues from the investment can fund the debt—that
is, national debt growth induces investment growth. Unfortunately, the businesses created by the British debt
tended to be monopolies.

The Red Cross, the Society of Jesus, the Brotherhood
of Locomotive Engineers, Sigma Chi, the Ford Foundation,
the City of Pittsburgh, Harvard University, and General
Motors are all corporations. In recent years only business
corporations such as G.M. have been considered significant
sources of revenue for the government. Most Americans
think of the corporate income tax as a tax on the net income of business corporations. In colonial America and
during the early years of independence, there were very
few purely business corporations. Corporations were usually semipublic works agencies like canal builders and harbor dredgers, or regulatory and financial institutions like
the First Bank of the United States. In general, the people
were afraid of corporations and legislatures were unwilling
to grant charters of incorporation to groups solely seeking
private profit.[3]

Limited liability, now considered the most valuable
of the characteristics of a corporate charter, was not always part of charters granted by the early legislatures.
Some early charters imposed double, even unlimited, liability on the stockholders and/or officers of corporations.
Charters were rarely issued to companies that were not
obviously serving the public interest. Neither employment
nor economic growth seems to have been associated with
corporations in the first 50 years of independence.[4]

With the development of the railroads, Americans began to build much larger business corporations. They were, of course, a part of transportation, and as such were public utilities just as the canals had been before them. However, the owners and managers of the railroads showed a greater preoccupation with and success at developing private fortunes than the canal builders. They were also forced to deal with the management of very large institutions. Many of their techniques were soon applied to more purely private mining and manufacturing concerns.

These new giant businesses were active in developing the modern corporate charter, which allows most types of business activity to be conducted by the firm wherever it wants to do so. Until late in the nineteenth century, corporate charters severely limited the location and types of activity a corporation could engage in, and often limited the length of the corporation's life.

The original corporate charter of Standard Oil of Ohio limited the company to business and property ownership within the state of Ohio, to be managed within that community for the benefit of the community and the stockholders. To evade that restriction, the company developed the trust that held stock in the various single-state Standard Oils, and voted that stock to produce a concert that acted like one company. The Ohio supreme court found that Standard of Ohio had entered into the Standard Oil Trust, which violated the company charter, and that the purpose of the trust was to create a monopoly, which also violated the charter. So Ohio voided the company's corporate charter.[5]

However, New Jersey, guided by the great business lobbyist J. B. Dill, had amended its incorporation laws to allow new, previously prohibited corporate behaviors, including one corporation owning stock in another corporation or owning real estate in another state and doing business there. So the Rockefellers were protected from the threat of unlimited liability that the Ohio Supreme Court had condemned them to by reincorporating their business in New Jersey. Ohio was forced to let Standard of New Jersey operate in Ohio because the federal law requires every state to respect the institutions of every other state. Other states, notably Delaware, began competing with New Jersey to produce incorporation rules that were particularly favored by big businesses, partially in hopes of increasing revenues from corporate franchise taxes.

This episode demonstrates the importance of limiting business taxation and regulation to national governments. States are too weak and venal relative to modern business corporations to stand up to the heat of self-interest lobbying.

State franchise taxes on corporations were a bookkeeping nightmare in the late nineteenth century. Seligman found that there were 13 different ways of measuring and taxing the value of a corporate franchise by the 1890s.[6] Reading the literature and legislative materials much later, Richard Lindholm showed that there were almost as many arguments for taxing the franchise as there were ways of measuring its value. Fortunately, he was also able to show that all of the arguments had only two roots: privilege, and monopoly and large-scale enterprise.[7]

Corporations did very little of the business in the United States, and even less of the not-public, utility-type business until after the Civil War. As pools, trusts, and other capital-concentrating types of contracts were developed to enable private monopoly and avoid the problems of corporate charters limiting the businessperson's scope of action, those businesses increasingly lobbied for less-restricting charters of incorporation.

States responded first with general incorporation laws, enabling a bureaucracy to issue charters to any business meeting general requirements. Later the scope of activity that was acceptable by corporations was broadened, until the traditional rule that a corporation had to serve the public interest was completely dropped. The end of this development was the charter of the United States Steel Company, which authorized it to do business of any kind, anywhere, anytime.

The states creating these corporations often charged nominal franchise tax rates for the service and hoped that total tax collections would be large because so many businesses would be attracted to incorporate in the state. The inducements worked in the sense that most large businesses, as measured by value, became corporate. Seager and Gulick observed: "With each decade during the last fifty years [ending in 1929] an increasing proportion of the wealth of the United States has been brought under corporate control. . . . we believe that no exaggeration is involved in the statement that more than four-fifths of American business enterprise is now carried on by corporations."[8]

By 1930 almost every line of business included some corporations, and most large industries were dominated by them. Whereas in the first 40 years of independence almost all corporations were banks, insurance companies, and transportation companies,[9] today the corner grocer, the neighborhood restaurant, and even the family physician are often corporations.

American states changed the business corporation in two fundamental ways: they enabled the businesspeople to use them for monopolistic purposes without contributing significantly to the treasury, and they converted the privilege of incorporation into a right exercised by most business. These changes upset a large fraction of the population and led to many fundamental changes in the federal rules governing business in general and corporations in particular. These include the antitrust laws, regulatory agencies like the Interstate Commerce Commission and the Federal Reserve, and corporation income taxes.

Viewed this way, the corporate income tax returns to the corporations the burden of supporting the state in the same manner that the corporate monopolies of the middle ages and the first British Empire had accepted in return for their monopoly rights. The flaw in this evolution is that the general incorporation of most business--whether monopolistic or not--means that many businesses pay taxes to the federal government that are reasonable for monopolies but unreasonable for business in general. This is less serious than it seems since incorporation is a voluntary act. No business needs pay the corporation tax unless it finds the benefits of incorporation are greater than the cost of the tax imposed.

Not surprisingly, federal corporate income taxes first appear in 1894 with a tax on all income, personal and corporate. The Supreme Court that same year voided the tax as an improperly apportioned direct tax, but in its opinion implied that an indirect tax on corporations measured by their net income would be constitutional. In 1898 Congress taxed the corporate franchise by measuring its value according to gross income, and the Court accepted the tax as an excise. In 1909 a corporate net income tax defined as an excise tax was adopted and accepted by the Court. This tax is the direct ancestor of the current corporate income tax. The strange indirect excise measured by direct income was ended by the passage of the Sixteenth Amendment, authorizing the taxation of income from any source without apportioning the tax among the states according to their respective numbers.[10]

The tax began with a rate of 1 percent on net income in excess of $5,000. It was a minor source of federal revenue until World War 1, when the rate began to rise. From 1923 through 1967 the corporate income tax always provided at least 20 percent of federal revenues.[11] It is a very adequate source of revenue for the modern state, as it had been for the medieval and early modern states.

With the end of the Korean War, corporate taxes as a share of total receipts began to decline. This decline is shown in Table 11.1. The erosion of the adequacy of the federal corporate income tax has two principal causes. First, using Keynesian-type arguments, business has finally convinced the government that cutting business taxes will induce investment, which will be good for society as a whole as the multiplier process increases everyone's income. Every president from Eisenhower through Reagan has submitted proposals to Congress for the reduction of corporate taxes to induce investment and economic growth.

Table 11.1

Corporate Taxes as Share of Total Receipts

Year	Federal Corporate Tax Receipts as Percent of Total Federal Receipts	Corporate Profits as Percent of GNP
1943	38.2	12.7
1948	21.3	11.2
1953	29.7	10.8
1958	25.2	9.1
1963	20.2	9.9
1968	18.6	9.6
1973	15.6	7.5
1978	14.9	7.7
1983	6.2	6.1

Sources: Historical Statistics of the United States, Colonial Times to 1970, Part 2 (Washington, D.C., 1975), p. 1105; Business Statistics, 22nd ed. (Department of Commerce, 1980), p. 87; Survey of Current Business, January issues, 1981-85.

Second, since 1968 there has been a serious erosion in the share of GNP going to corporations. This is shown in the third column of Table 11.1. The combination of profits declining in relative importance and the declining effective rates of profits taxes produces the second column, which indicates that the corporate profits tax unless significantly reformed will cease to be a serious source of income for the federal government.

Everyone today accepts the notion that business is important for all of us. But business also controls most of the means of production and gets major special services from government that are not available to the rest of us. Large corporations are virtually immune from involuntary bankruptcy. The pain to us all from the failure of a major employer is so great that we bail them out or merge them into other corporations. This trend is most completely developed in finance, where in recent years the federal banking authorities have acted to save or merge a large number of big financial institutions. But they are letting small banks go broke!

Similar concern for commercial and industrial corporations of great size is less common (the Chrysler and Lockheed cases are clearly exceptions), and there is great suspicion that part of defense purchasing has a "Let's keep the big business profitable at any cost" component. Many consider the TFX contract a federal bailout of a sick General Dynamics and its dependent host Fort Worth. Small businesses, including defense contractors, are regularly allowed to fail.

All of this argues for a tax on corporations related to their size--that is, a progressive rate net income tax where the marginal rates are defined as insurance premiums to the Treasury, which secures large firms from failure. This argument bases the progressive rates not on ability to pay as most income taxes are explained, but on benefits received.

No true friend of American business would advocate letting taxes on business disappear at a time when it is obvious that the government is doing more and more for business. Most of the population has been paying higher and higher shares of their income to the government for the whole of the industrial era. This phenomenon is called Wagners' Law, and is usually related to government spending, not taxing. But spending is predominantly tax financed.

The average gross weekly earnings of nonagricultural workers today is no higher than it was in 1962 when adjusted for inflation.[12] But the average worker's taxes are up. The last time we got a spate of new business taxes was from 1894 to 1907. It was a time of unstable incomes for workers, of government helping corporations, and of massive accumulations of private wealth. To repeal the corporate income tax now is to invite the social retribution that produced both the personal and corporate income taxes.

Economists can derive considerable pleasure from the work of Edwin R. A. Seligman, who outlined most of the principal theoretical and institutional problems associated with corporate and business taxes in general. Much of his analysis was published 14 years before we adopted the tax on corporate net income.[13] He championed net income as the best measure of the worth of a franchise and the only one that did not obviously subsidize some type of behavior other than pure business efficiency.[14] Seligman recognized the problem of allocating the profits of a corporation among the many states a big firm might operate in. He devised a simple formula to allocate the profits and a rule that all firms, foreign and domestic, should be treated the same.[15] That is, he devised what has come to be known as the unitary tax. He showed how large firms such as railroads would rearrange their accounts and investments to make most of their business appear to be in regions with the lowest taxes. He explained that any system of allocating business-taxable capacity among multiple taxing regions could lead to double taxation as each region defined most of the business into its tax base. Simply, he explained why we need a single, nationwide formula allocating all business, domestic and foreign, among the several states.[16] Had American state legislatures and Japanese businesspeople doing business in the United States in recent years paid more attention to the work of Seligman and his students, a great deal of time and pain over the unitary tax could have been avoided.

With most states repealing their unitary formulas, they are increasingly trusting foreign corporations to pay their fair share from goodwill alone. If we ever again decide that foreign business deserves to finance more of American government, for whatever reason, the absence of "acceptable" unitary formulas will make it easy for state legislatures to overtax the foreign businesses. It is useful to remember, in state government parlance, that "foreign" means out of state.

CORPORATE TAX BASE

Seligman's discussion of types of double taxation that can arise with a mixture of corporate and individual taxes in a federation is quite extensive. He opposed all types of double taxation and devised methods to avoid most of them that are acceptable to this day. For example, if we define stocks and bonds issued by a corporation as property and the assets the corporation purchased with the proceeds of the sale of the securities as property, then we have double taxation of corporate assets through the property tax. I have not seen the reverse of this argument: that if we exempt corporate assets from taxation, we should then tax their stocks and bonds as property.

In considering the different treatments of incorporated enterprises and corporations, Seligman asked the following:

> If the corporate franchise, in the sense of the privilege of being a corporation, itself constituted the only justification of a tax, how would it then be possible to tax unincorporated companies in the same way? And yet to exempt the latter would clearly constitute a glaring economic inequality. . . . We may go farther and say from the economic standpoint it is wholly immaterial whether the tax upon any corporation be called a tax on franchise or a tax on business. In an economic sense the franchise tax means nothing at all.[17]

Lindholm, with good reason, argues that the franchise has meaning as a base of taxation where it is associated with public utility or other monopoly elements.[18]

This is important to Seligman because he did the best early work on the shifting and incidence of taxes. It is clear in his analysis that the successful imposition of a tax on a corporation requires it to be on a magnitude corporations would not change if they could. Net income, if maximized before the tax is imposed, is such a magnitude. Yet even an unshiftable tax can be capitalized unless the tax applies to all possible substitutes. So a tax on corporate net income will be to some extent capitalized in the price of the stock of the corporation unless all other sources of investment income are taxed at the same rate. If all possible investments have their yield lowered by the same rate, then the net rate of return falls and the tax is a tax on the owners of business, presumably stockholders.[19]

From this thinking Seligman makes two observations about taxes on corporations that are not general taxes on the holders of capital. First, "In the case of direct taxes the original holder is injured while the future purchaser discounts the tax in the depreciation of the article."[20] Second,

> if only corporate and not other securities
> are taxed, as in France, or if only a few
> classes of corporation are taxed--then the
> taxation of the corporation is not sufficient
> to reach the purchaser. He will practically
> escape, because of the freedom of investing
> in non-taxable securities will enable him
> to discount the tax in the price he pays.
> To tax both corporation and shareholder in
> such a case is not unjust or double taxa-
> tion. To tax the corporation alone would
> in reality exempt the shareholder who pur-
> chased after the tax was imposed. An
> additional tax on the shareholder would,
> thus, not be double taxation.[21]

In the United States we have never had a general tax on wealth or the income from wealth, however held. Consequently investors have always had the option of avoiding taxes by investing in nontaxable or relatively low taxed securities or industries. So analyses using single tax rates for capital have no statistical meaning because we have no such experience.

A decade ago Break and Pechman reported that "the effective corporate tax rate was only 16 percent for miscellaneous minerals . . . but it was 48 percent for tobacco manufacturers, pulp mills, and newspapers."[22] Then as now, the rate on the interest on most state and local bonds was zero percent. And several states had no state or local income taxes. Obviously our taxes in investment income are nonneutral and consequently often capitalized. For important common stocks like those traded on the New York Stock Exchange, conditions for listing are so strict that the stock must be fairly old before it is traded at all. When combined with the enormous rate of turnover of stocks through that market, it creates a presumption that no current owner of such stocks pays any corporate tax.

Who then does pay the tax? Seligman would say the previous owner. For most big board stocks that would mean past generations of stockholders. Do these often long-dead folks need tax relief? How would we give it to them? No one knows the answer.

There have been three major developments regarding corporations and their taxation since Seligman. First is the Berle and Means hypothesis, which if correct means there is no connection between the stockholder and the large, broadly held corporation. The technical analysis of tax shifting would then be more meaningful as an analysis of executive pay, insider buyouts, and green mail.

Second is the development of the Random Walk hypothesis about securities prices. This idea is actually older than Berle and Means's work, but did not become generally known to the profession until the 1950s. Simply stated, it asserts that in a properly competitive market a securities price will exhibit a random walk. A simple walk model is $Pt + R = Pt+1$, where P is the price of some security today, R is a random number, and $Pt+1$ is the price of the same security tomorrow.[23] Unfortunately, tax shifting and capitalization arguments require a functional relation between P and taxes that is not a random one.

Finally is the development of econometric testing of tax shifting in more explicit general-equilibrium models than those used by Seligman and his students. It shows that the corporate tax may be shifted (Seligman would say it must be since it is not a general tax). Unfortunately, most of the studies disagree on where the tax goes when it is shifted. The models used, although mathematically elaborate, are little more sophisticated than the Robinson Crusoe models so popular with Frank Taussig's students early in this century.

For example, in the simplest imaginable economy, Robinson would produce a good that he would consume. Let the output be carrots and the inputs be Robinson's time and effort nurturing the carrots and nature (land, rain, sunshine, the availability of nearby nitrogen-fixing plants, and so forth). A tax could be imposed by nature in the form of a drought.

Robinson could then work harder killing weeds, mulching the soil, or carrying water to keep the carrot crop up. That is, his wages per unit of effort would go down. Robinson could do the same amount of work and get fewer carrots. That is, the drought would increase the price of carrots. He could pray to the rain god and sacrifice some of his old carrots, hoping to get more new carrots. That increases the payment to nature, but if the rains do come, Robinson's gross income is maintained, but not his net income.

General-equilibrium studies try to figure out how much of a tax increase goes to each of the three answers outlined in Robinson's dilemma. But the answers they get depend on the propensity of the scholar to find one choice rather than another more than they do on dispassionate science. Recent criticism of econometrics focuses on thousands of studies of the same thing, finding every imaginable result with "good" statistics. To trust such results, it is necessary to have a good economic-theoretic reason to believe they are true.[24] But microeconomic theory simply says any economic actor will act to change any input or product price it can to shift a tax burden. If no input or output price changes are available, then it must be paid by the firm and the tax is capitalized, that is, the market price of the firm itself must change. So to find a tax shift, we need to look at all the prices that can change to see if they have changed. But we expect most prices in a market system to change continually as many other things (such as preferences and time of day) change; so even if a price change consistent with a new tax occurs, it is not necessarily due to the tax.

The purpose of theorizing is to narrow the scope of an inquiry and focus the mind on the most likely answers to a problem. Price theory has failed to do this for tax shifting. It says look at every possible price change when we need a much narrower suggestion.

CORPORATE TAX SHIFTING

If the work of the theorists on random walks has any validity at all, we will not have any serious tax-shifting answers until a whole new dynamic price theory is developed. The theoretical dilemma goes like this. Competitive prices move in a random manner. Tax-shift theory assumes competitive markets and tests price changes with correlations and regression models. Such models assume a normal distribution. Randomness produces a stable paretian distribution that is very different from a normal distribution, and correlations of variables so distributed have no meaning.

Another old economic idea, revealed preference, gives the best guess available as to the incidence of the corporate net income tax. The people most actively demanding its reduction or repeal are businesspeople and their client politicians. They may think they pay the tax or can gain from capitalizing on its repeal, but evidence that it is a bookkeeping nightmare that no reasonable person can defend is available in great quantity.

So we do not know who bears the burden, nor do we have the economic theory and the statistical tools to find out who bears the burden and how it was shifted to them, if it was shifted. What we do know is people who claim to know the answer to this puzzle have feet of clay.

Who pays the corporate income tax? For such a controversial tax with far-reaching economic impacts on the giants of American enterprise, definitive answers are important. Is the tax paid by stockholders in the form of lower dividends and lower stock prices? Does the consumer of corporate products pay the tax mingled with the retail price of those products? Does labor receive lower wages in the corporate sector? Does the American economy suffer because of reduced investment in industry? Is American industry less competitive in world markets because of the corporate income tax? Does the corporate income tax delay incorporation of emerging business and thereby deter capital formation or raise the cost of capital? Does the tax lead business to depend more heavily on debt financing, increasing the danger of bankruptcy? Who does pay this tax and how is the economy affected by its burden?

Prior to 1960, discussion of the incidence of the corporate income tax followed qualitative and philosophical lines. As early as the end of World War I, the corporate excess profits tax was considered to be a major factor in the increased cost of living by Carter Glass, then Secretary of the Treasury.[25]

In 1934 Carl Shoup contemplated the incidence of
the corporate income tax. Did the tax extend to consumers? Business owners were inclined to pass the tax on to
consumers if possible. In 1943 the chairman of the finance committee of the U.S. Steel Corporation expressed
that opinion when he said, "Corporate taxes are simply
costs. The method of their assessment does not change
this fact. Costs must be paid by the public in prices and
corporate taxes are thus in effect concealed sales taxes."[26]

By the late 1940s concern was also expressed about
the distribution of tax burdens among economic and social
classes. Questions were being asked such as: Should or
could the corporate income tax be used to keep the large
corporation from getting larger?[27] In 1951 Richard Goode,
in pondering the equity of the corporate income tax, wrote:
"The policy implications of the incidence of the corporate
income tax are clear. To the extent that consumers or
wage earners actually pay the tax, the 'double-taxation'
and similar equity criticisms of the tax are not admissible,
for certainly the tax cannot be at the same time a burden
on consumers and workers and a 'double' tax on stockholders."[28]

A working model that would provide quantitative
information was essential for economic analysis of the effect of the tax on prices, wage rates, savings, consumption, investment, and national income.

In the early 1960s quantitative answers came from
both ends of the spectrum. The corporate income tax was
shown to be fully borne by capital in the long run or
more than 100 percent shifted forward to consumers in the
short run, depending on whether the reader subscribed to
a mathematical model developed by Arnold Harberger or
a time-series econometric model developed by Marian
Krzyzaniak and Richard Musgrave.

In university libraries all across the country,
bound copies of the Journal of Political Economy for 1962
will open automatically to page 215 of the June issue.
Harberger had set out to provide a theoretical framework
for the analysis of the effects of the corporate income tax
in general-equilibrium terms, and his article has had a
profound effect on public finance. He concluded that capital bears 100 percent of the burden of the corporation income tax.[29]

What were Harberger's assumptions and how did he
arrive at his conclusions? Harberger assumed that there

are two sectors, corporate and noncorporate, of perfectly competitive firms whose production functions exhibit constant returns to scale. There are two homogeneous factors of production, capital and labor. Demand for the output of each sector is assumed to be a function of relative output prices and total income. There are no second-best considerations. The noncorporate sector was assumed to consist of three industries: agriculture, real estate, and repair services.

The model considered only the long-run effects of the imposition of the federal corporation income tax. That is, the final burden of the tax after the size of plant and equipment, number of firms, and technological methods have all been fully adjusted to the economic conditions resulting from the tax.

The resources of the economy would be redistributed, moving toward a long-run equilibrium in which the net rates of return to capital would be equal in both corporate and noncorporate sectors. Based on these assumptions, Harberger constructed a general-equilibrium model and concluded that if the taxed industry was relatively labor-intensive, labor might bear a higher proportion of the tax relative to its factor share, but otherwise capital would bear a higher proportion of the tax. If elasticities of substitution between capital and labor were equal, capital would bear the full burden of the tax.[30]

The following year, Marian Krzyzaniak and Richard A. Musgrave (K-M) published a study that confirmed the conclusions reached by American business and philosophers during the prior 50 years. In their words, "Surprising or not, we shall find that our statistical results are compatible with the businessman's views."[31]

The K-M study was held to the short-run effects—those that excluded changes in the fixed factors of production. K-M formulated their analysis based on the techniques of multiple regression. The time-series model covered the years between 1935 and 1959 and analyzed the effect of the corporate income tax on the rate of return. The model isolated the functional relationship between tax and profit behavior as it affected the rate of return. A significant correlation between high pretax corporate profits and high corporate tax rates indicated that the tax had been shifted. K-M concluded that the rate of return was increased in response to the tax by short-run adjustments.[32]

The economic literature contains literally hundreds of discussions, extensions, refinements, and attacks on these two pieces of research. Perhaps the most important of these to the corporate portion of the federal tax debacle is an attack on Krzyzaniak and Musgrave's work by Cragg, Harberger, and Mieszkowski (Harberger et al.) in 1967 in which they claimed to show that other relevant factors were responsible for the shifting rather than the corporate income tax rate. Harberger et al. claim to have demonstrated the following:

> unequivocally that the Krzyzaniak-Musgrave procedure, corrected so as to reduce the bias stemming from the proxy role of their tax variables, does not lead to their conclusion of more than 100 percent shifting of the corporate income tax, but rather to the conclusion (previously reached by Harberger) that capital bears approximately the full burden of the tax.[33]

Krzyzaniak and Musgrave rebutted the attack, showing that the variables introduced by Harberger et al. reduced the coefficient of the tax-rate variable, but tripled its standard error and the t-ratio became less than one. This did not indicate zero shifting of the tax, but did suggest that the revised model did not allow one to choose between a hypothesis of zero and full shifting. Harberger also added a dummy variable to account for the war years. According to Musgrave, since the variables suffered from multicollinearity, it was not surprising to find that the value of the coefficients changed and became insignificant. Musgrave omitted the war years, ran the equation, and found that the shifting coefficient remained high and significant and did not differ greatly from that of the total period.[34]

In a subsequent article in this debate, Harberger et al. stated that "our judgment that the pitfalls associated with estimating corporate-tax incidence from time-series data, in K-M fashion, are too numerous and serious for the results to be trustworthy."[35] Harberger et al. had intended to cast doubt on the K-M conclusions, and other authors have kept the debate alive for 20 years.

LAND AS A COST ELEMENT

For example, Ratti and Shome (1977) state that the issue is inconclusive, and go on to test the model-specificity of Harberger's results. They introduce a third factor of production--land--and decide that many of Harberger's conclusions are specific to his model and cannot be generalized in the specific factor model.[36]   Roy Adams (1977) observed that since Harberger's model assumed no economies of scale, the number and importance of corporations would decline. The owners of capital could avoid the tax by altering their form of business organization rather than shifting their capital to the production of another product. Since corporations had not disappeared, either the tax could be shifted or economies of scale were a significant factor that should have been included in the model.[37]

Various authors have added refinements to the Harberger model. Zee (1983) considered a variable labor supply and the work-leisure choice.[38]   Ballentine (1977) modifies the Harberger model to allow for imperfections in the market and utility-maximizing firms.[39]   Ebrill and Hartman (1983) examined Harberger's model, specifically looking at the assumption that the corporate and noncorporate sectors produce different goods. The essential feature of a corporation was concluded to be its ability to raise funds in an organized capital market. The innovative entrepreneur would be encouraged to incorporate to access that capital market, but would delay because of the cost of the corporate income tax. Therefore, the corporate income tax raised the cost of capital.[40]

The authors all conclude that commodity prices will reflect the corporation income tax; the controversy is related to how the return on capital will be affected by the tax. Implications for international trade are considered by Melvin (1979). He argued that the effect of the corporation income tax on the prices of corporate products would influence trade patterns. Melvin assumed that there were no economies of scale, that the tax had no effect on labor, or on return to capital (per the K-M model). To determine the actual effect of the tax, he set out to learn how prices would respond to the tax. He concluded that price changes in the United States ranged from 2 to 16 percent. The tax was reflected in the price of the product, and that effect varied significantly among industries. The largest increases were associated with the most capital-intensive products; those products in which the United States would be expected to have a comparative advantage.[41]

On the other hand, Harberger (1984) reviews the position of American industry in the international marketplace and concludes that more of the tax falls on labor than he had originally thought because the American corporation cannot raise prices in the international market and remain competitive.[42] Again, these conclusions are widely divergent; the tax is determined to be shifted forward to consumers, or back to labor, or it remains with the owners of capital.

IMPLICATIONS FOR TAX REFORM

All of the various models, studies, and theories provide a basis for fascinating economic discussions. But this information, or lack of it, is being used to make decisions with implications for profound impact on the American economy.

Harberger's model has been used as a basis by public finance specialists to formulate tax policy in a number of areas--from a model of fiscal reform in Colombia to considerations of the incidence of local property taxes.[43] Harberger (1966) used his model to measure the welfare loss resulting from the differential taxation of capital employed in the corporate sector.[44] Johnson and Mieszkowski (1970) have used the Harberger model to examine the impact of labor on income distribution.[45] While the model and its applications have made a valuable contribution to economics and public finance, all models are limited representations of reality. Decisions based on models using Harberger's assumptions when other credible studies provide divergent results add bias to otherwise cloudy decision criteria.

The years since 1980 have provided fertile ground to sow the seeds of tax reform. Bradley and Gephardt (H.R. 800, S. 409), Kemp and Kasten (H.R. 777, S. 325), and Heftel (H.R. 1165) have all proposed bills that would drastically restructure the corporation income tax. To illustrate the tendency to accept the conclusions of the Harberger model as fact, the Congressional Budget Office report entitled Revising the Corporation Income Tax (May

1985) concludes that the corporation income tax "reduces the efficiency of the economy by distorting business decisions."[46] Three reasons are given: the tax tends to shift investment from the corporate sector to the noncorporate sector; the tax adversely affects the decision to save because of a lower rate of return; and the tax falls more heavily on industries with long-term investments.[47]

Many reasonable people would agree; but the reasons are all based on the assumption that capital bears the burden of the tax. If the rate of return were pushed up to account for changes in the corporation tax, neither saving nor corporate investment would be affected. Because of uneven real income tax rates, consumers of products produced by heavy industry could be paying higher prices, or labor in the affected industries could receive lower wages. Is the tax shifted and, if so, how much? The authors of the congressional report admit that a consensus has not been reached about how the corporate tax is borne. Indeed, one major objection to the corporate tax is that its burden is not explicit and depends on economic effects that are not clearly understood.[48] This ambiguity does not deter the authors of the study from presenting the remainder of the information as if the Harberger model clearly explained the effect of the tax.

The President's Tax Proposals to the Congress for Fairness, Growth, and Simplicity also follows the conclusions of the Harberger model.[49] As Goode said 30 years ago, if workers or consumers pay the tax, double taxation of dividends is not an issue. Yet, "to alleviate the double taxation of dividends," 10 percent of dividends paid to stockholders would be deductible by the corporation and the corporate tax rate would be reduced to 33 percent.[50]

Discussion to this point has dealt with larger, publicly traded corporations. As was noted earlier, the development of the ability to incorporate as a right rather than a privilege has resulted in smaller, closely held corporations becoming commonplace. Small businesses and professionals alike can incorporate their enterprises.

Substantial differences exist between the two extreme types of corporations. Small corporations are, in many respects, mere extensions of their owners, whereas larger corporations are clearly separate and distinct from their owners. Much of the literature on tax incidence is silent with respect to smaller corporations, yet their existence

and the fact that they pay some corporate tax are unde-
niable.

That the tax statutes affect the two types of corporations differently should not be ignored. As will be
illustrated below, some partial attempts to mitigate these
differences have been made. Whether these efforts represent an attempt to appease or satisfy rather than improve
a cohesive system is for the observer's conjecture.

Definition of a Corporation

Difficulty with the definition of a corporation does
not simply involve economic considerations. Controversy
between the government and taxpayers as to whether certain noncorporate entities should be treated as corporations
for tax purposes has a long and inconsistent history.
Early controversy involved attacks by IRS that professionals who were legally prohibited from incorporating their
practices under state laws could not treat their entities as
corporations for tax purposes and take advantage of the
more favorable retirement-plan contribution limitations.[51]
At other times, the government has been known to argue
that unincorporated entities should be treated as corporations.[52]

Regulations and case law have developed a number
of corporate characteristics that should be considered in
determining whether an unincorporated entity should be
treated as a corporation for tax purposes, known as "association" status.[53] Any entity possessing a majority of
the six major characteristics is to be treated as an "association."

Today, one of the most serious implications of "association" status involves limited partnerships. Whereas
the imposition of the corporate tax may be costly to some
limited partnerships, the most costly effect involves the
fact that partners may generally include their share of a
partnership's liabilities in their tax basis (that is, investment base) in the entity as if money had been contributed.[54] Since the amount of annual partnership operating losses passing through to each partner that can be
deducted is limited to his or her tax basis, this adjustment is of great significance. In effect, partners can deduct losses against capital that was provided by lenders.
Corporate shareholders are not entitled to either the loss

pass-through or the basis adjustment. A corporation re-porting a net tax loss (net operating loss) carries that loss backward and forward to be offset against corporate profits in other years. Obviously, one of the major ad-vantages of the partnership form is the pass-through of operating losses and other tax advantages to be offset against the owners' taxable income from other sources.

Corporate Advantages

For many closely held business organizations, in-corporation has numerous, solely tax advantages, as well as the legal characteristics present under state law. In addition to the creation of a separate tax entity that can accumulate at least some capital at corporate tax rates, the corporation can employ the owners and take advantage of the numerous employee fringe-benefit provisions allowed under the statute. This saving has been substantially reduced recently since Congress has mandated parity be-tween the limits on contributions to corporate retirement plans and those of the self-employed. The other benefits--including employee hospitalization insurance, group term life insurance, and others--can result in substantial sav-ings, but employment costs such as taxes and insurance may also be incurred.

Employee fringe benefits can be valuable planning tools, for both shareholders and other family members em-ployed in the business. Accumulation of earnings at cor-porate tax rates is available only to those groups willing to reinvest portions of the earnings in the business. A group that wishes to distribute the earnings must incur the related costs.

Partnership Advantages

Those groups of owners wishing to distribute all profits or operating at a loss may prefer the partnership form. Although partnership net income passes through, distributions are generally tax-free so long as the partner has an adequate tax basis. Adequate basis exists so long as partnership profits equal or exceed any distributions. Of course, partnerships operating with tax losses pass those losses through to partners who may generally offset those losses against their taxable income from other sources.

Allocations of the partnership income and losses may be allocated to partners in any fashion under the partnership agreement. Two restrictions are placed on this carte blanche privilege. First, members of family partnerships must be fairly compensated for the value of their services before remaining profits are allocated. Second, any "special" allocation must be reflected in his or her liquidation rights.[55]

At-Risk Limitation on Losses

Since purchase money liabilities are included in the tax basis of taxpayers' investments, investors who were able to secure nonrecourse financing were able to deduct losses from operations of such activities without bearing the risk of loss in excess of their investments. Limits have therefore been placed on losses that are deductible by individuals, partnerships, and certain closely held corporations. The deductible amount of such losses is limited to the investment plus liabilities for which the taxpayer is personally liable. This limit does not apply to the rental operation of real estate.[56]

Corporate Elections

Most of the partnership's tax attributes are available to small business corporations through an election that is available under Subchapter S of the Internal Revenue Code. There are numerous differences between the tax treatments of such electing corporations and partnerships. Operationally, the two key differences are the inability of the corporation to make special allocations of income, and the fact that the owner does not include his or her share of any corporate liabilities in his or her tax basis in the corporation. Since any operating losses passing through to the shareholders are deductible only to the extent of their tax basis, this could represent a substantial disadvantage.

Although shareholders may be employed by small business corporations, the amount of tax-advantaged fringe benefits that may be provided for them is severely limited. Under the federal tax statute, they are required to be treated as partners if they own a 2 percent or greater interest in the corporation. This requires that they be treated as nonemployees for fringe-benefit purposes only. Of course, any payroll costs related to FICA, other taxes, and insurance must be incurred.

Partnership Election

The federal tax system has also contained an election by unincorporated business enterprises to be taxed as domestic corporations. This election was fairly short-lived, being repealed effective for years after 1968.[57]

Corporate/Shareholder Transactions

Entities have always been able to accomplish significant tax-planning gains by timing the recognition of income and deductions in transactions with employees and shareholders. Until recently, an accrual-basis corporation could deduct accrued compensation so long as payment was made within two-and-one-half months of its year-end, even if the shareholder was on the cash method and did not include the income until received. Currently, the deduction of the corporation is deferred until the amount is included in income by the payee.[58]

Large Limited Partnerships

Some commentators believe that limited partnerships possess essentially all corporate characteristics, while taking advantage of favorable partnership characteristics. Accordingly, a proposal has been made to Congress to treat partnerships with 35 or more limited partners as corporations. The reasoning for proposing the change was to reduce the ability of entities with corporate characteristics to pass-through operating losses, to provide more extensive and consistent limitations on the deductibility of losses from passive investments, to retard tax-motivated shifts from the corporate sector to the partnership sector, and to make tax administration more efficient.[59] The change was not adopted in the final legislation due to the fact that it was not within the proposed scope of the bill and because such a change has significant policy implications that had not been fully analyzed.[60] From the discussion in this chapter, one would surmise that this concept will be revived and given further consideration in the years to come.

Complexities and Uncertainties

These definitional problems are discussed only with an intention to point out the complexity of the definitional problem and some of the factors in the selection of a business form. The disparity of the treatments of corporations and partnerships (and sole proprietorships for that matter) provides incentives for taxpayers to structure major transactions for tax purposes only. Tremendous costs, tax and otherwise, are incurred in these transactions, and there is no clear indication that the provisions are either fair or effective in achieving their stated goals.

It is also clear that Congress has gone to great lengths to adapt the system to avert many perceived abuses. These changes, like the at-risk rules and others, add complexity to a system that may have major theoretical and conceptual flaws. Frequently, two or more changes will be implemented to avoid a single problem or abuse. Since the changes more often treat a symptom rather than the problem itself, the tax system becomes more complex and burdensome.

DEFINITION OF TAXABLE INCOME

Taxable Income in General

The income tax is, by its nature, a tax on net income. In determining that net income, only those items specifically allowed under the statute are deductible. For noncorporate taxpayers, these include trade or business expenses, investment expenses and other nonbusiness expenses, and a few specified personal expenses. In the corporate area, all deductions are presumed to be related to the business of the corporation. This presumption may seem reasonable where the shareholders and the corporation have separate identities. It may, however, be less reasonable where the corporate stock is closely held and corporate goals more closely parallel individual shareholder goals. In extreme instances, expenditures directly related to the personal benefit of the shareholders--such as the personal use of corporate-owned automobiles or entertainment facilities--have been disallowed as constructive dividends, which are also taxable to the shareholder.[61]

Another difference between corporations and other entities involves the deduction for nonbusiness bad debts. Whereas an individual's nonbusiness bad debts are subject to unfavorable treatment as short-term capital losses, corporate bad debts are not distinguished and are deductible as ordinary deductions.[62]

Special Deductions of Corporations

Several special deductions are allowed to corporations. Two of the most important are the dividends-received deduction and the deduction for organizational costs. The dividends-received deduction is intended to mitigate the multiple effect of the perceived double tax on corporate profits when distributions are made in tiered-ownership situations. The deduction is generally 85 percent of the dividends received; 100 percent in the case of certain related corporations. One of the effects of the deduction has been to encourage investment in corporate stocks by corporations, even when the corporation has outstanding debt, the interest upon which was fully deductible. To curb the perceived abuse, the dividends-received deduction is currently limited or disallowed on debt-financed portfolio stock.[63] This limit applies where the debt is "directly attributable" to the stock investment.

Corporate Minimum Taxes

Corporations with significant tax preferences have been subject to minimum taxes on their preferences in excess of a base amount since 1969. A similar tax has also applied to individuals. During the late 1970s, Congress made substantial changes to the individual minimum taxes, ultimately substituting an alternative minimum tax for the earlier one. In determining the alternative minimum tax, an individual adds his or her tax preferences to other income, and the amount in excess of a base amount after several adjustments is subject to tax at a minimum tax rate of 20 percent.

In order to consistently treat corporations, it has been suggested that a corporate alternative minimum tax be imposed. In 1982 Congress elected not to do so, but chose to tax a percentage (now generally 20 percent) of certain of the tax preferences at regular corporate tax rates. Of course, the percentage of tax preferences that are taxed are not subject to the still existing corporate minimum tax. Currently, the corporate minimum tax of 15 percent is imposed on the amount of tax preferences in excess of the greater of $10,000 or the corporation's regular tax liability.

The tax preferences that are partially taxed under this provision include percentage depletion on coal and iron ore, amortization of pollution-control facilities, amortization of intangible drilling costs and mineral exploration and development costs, certain deferred DISC income, and certain financial institution preference items. Additionally, a portion of any gain on the sale of real property may be converted to ordinary income. The amount converted is generally 20 percent of the excess of the depreciation allowed with respect to the property over the amount that is already ordinary income due to the depreciation-recapture provisions.[64]

Corporate/Shareholder Transactions

Numerous inconsistencies exist in the treatment of corporate shareholder transactions. Such transactions range from commercial transactions such as sales, rentals, and employment to inherently corporate transactions such as dividend distributions, transfers of assets to corporations in exchange for stock and securities, distributions in redemption of stock, and distributions in liquidation of the corporation. Also included are corporate reorganizations of various types. The basic question is which, if any, of these transactions should be subject to tax. Once again, the distinction between small closely held corporations and larger absentee-owner corporations becomes apparent.

In transactions such as employment relationships, sales, and rentals, a corporation and its shareholders are generally recognized as separate entities and the transactions are recognized for tax purposes. Only when it is ascertained that the transaction was not carried out in an arm's-length nature is there risk of reclassification of the payments. Excess payments from the corporation may be classified as constructive dividends, and excess payments from the shareholder may be reclassified as paid-in capital. Obviously, the former is more frequently encountered.

Distributions from the corporation are generally treated as dividends. When property other than cash is distributed, it is the fair market value of the property that is treated as a dividend; any appreciation in the value of the property in the hands of the corporation is generally taxed as if the property had been sold. Clearly, such property distributions rarely occur, and almost always occur in the smaller closely held corporation. Distributions in redemption of stock are also subject to similar rules.

Distributions in liquidation of corporate stock are subject to less comprehensive rules. Whereas an individual generally treats a liquidation as the sale or other disposition of the stock (and takes a tax basis in the distributed property equal to its fair market value), in most cases appreciation escapes taxation at the corporate level. Only deferred gain from installment sales, depreciation recapture, and certain inventory gains (generally, the excess of FIFO over LIFO) are taxed on the final corporate return. It has been proposed to Congress that the rules applying to current distributions be extended to liquidations, resulting in the taxation of any appreciation to the corporation as if the property had been sold.[65]

This is another example of the inherent differences between closely held and publicly traded corporations. To tax the appreciation to the corporation is to treat the entities as totally separate and distinct. To allow the appreciation to go untaxed is to treat the shareholder as a continuation of the corporation's business after liquidation. The two concepts are not at all consistent, and the proposals mentioned above tend to treat the corporation and shareholders as totally distinct at the expense of smaller closely held entities.

To better understand the implications, one should compare the treatment of a corporation to that of a partnership. Generally, neither a partner nor a partnership recognizes gain on a distribution, liquidating or otherwise. Consistently, the partnership's basis carries over to the partner, and the tax on any appreciation is deferred until the partner disposes of the property. Perhaps the more prudent action by Congress would be to make the corporate liquidation a nontaxable event with a carryover basis. Such treatment is already allowed upon the liquidation of most subsidiaries and might be preferable for closely held businesses. The probability of such a proposal being passed, however, is probably low since tax revenues would decline and the tax debacle increase.

Debt versus Equity

The obvious incentives in the tax law to finance as much capital as practical through debt, rather than equity, have tremendous ramifications. First, there are the economic distortions that are present in the investment marketplace. Further, other distortions result from smaller corporations financing predominantly with debt. Second, there is the likelihood that corporate bankruptcy, insolvency, and financial difficulty in general are more prevalent because of this incentive.

It has been suggested that a solution to these problems would be to allow a deduction to the corporation for dividends paid to shareholders. A diluted version of this idea has been proposed as part of the president's tax reform proposal, in which a deduction equal to 10 percent of dividends paid would be allowed to domestic corporations.[66]

This proposal must be evaluated carefully. First, it is an attempt to eliminate the double tax, which may in fact not exist with larger corporations as was discussed earlier. Second, as the treatment of shareholders becomes more consistent with that of creditors, to whom is corporate management responsible? Do payments to shareholders represent an expense to the corporation as do interest payments?

Other Primarily Corporate Provisions

Numerous other tax provisions that apply primarily to corporations are not discussed herein because their complexity is prohibitive and they are not as germane to the issues at hand. Provisions typically discussed in this context are the depreciation provisions, the investment tax credit, the deductions and credit for research and experimentation, and other primarily business provisions.[67]

Large Corporations

Generalization to large corporations on most of these issues is sometimes difficult. Whereas some of the incentives discussed may apply less to larger corporations, others, such as the incentive to use debt financing, apply equally.

Summary

This discussion is intended to review several of those provisions related to inherently corporate problems and several that represent specific attempts to solve other problems and prevent abuses. The complexity and burden caused by these amendments to the present system, which represent "patchwork," are obvious. As was discussed earlier, whether they treat the symptom or the problem is unknown. Perhaps there are more basic flaws in the system.

FINDINGS

This discussion has reviewed the history of the corporate entity and the tax on its income or existence. The incidence of the tax, the characteristics of the entity, and the determination have been discussed with an aim to articulate the level of complexity and burden.

Numerous incentives are provided in the statute that may or may not have been intended by Congress. Some of the incentives that have been discussed are:

1. Taxpayers are frequently induced to incorporate if they can benefit from the separate entity or from employee status. Enterprises expecting operating losses typically are better off if unincorporated.
2. Corporations gain some advantage by investing investment funds in incorporated enterprises. Limitations are placed on this advantage for debt-financed stocks.

3. Corporations are encouraged to raise capital in debt markets rather than in equity markets.
4. Corporations are encouraged to make cash distributions as opposed to property distributions to shareholders.
5. Other incentives and disincentives are also present related to corporate as opposed to noncorporate form of existence.

In 1943 Henry Simons stated that "tax law should not subsidize or artificially promote incorporation."[68] Others have followed in making this suggestion, and the bigger question is whether any of the incentives in the system were intended or are appropriate. Did the Congress properly anticipate the incentives and did they deem them appropriate?

Uncertainties also exist as to the impact of this tax. First, the divergence in the way the tax affects larger corporations as opposed to smaller corporations is not certain. Second, it is unclear who bears the burden of the tax. Extensive literature, as was reviewed, addresses the tax on larger corporations. Commentators are far from reaching consensus on the issue. Uncertainty also exists with respect to smaller corporations that often compete with unincorporated enterprises.

Several solutions have been considered over the years and are available. Conceptually, the most simple of the alternatives is the repeal of the tax and a pass-through of net profits and losses from corporations to the shareholders. Essentially, the corporation would be treated as a conduit much like a partnership. Distributions would generally be tax-free, whether in liquidation or otherwise.

Corporations would necessarily need to increase their distributions to cover the tax on the shareholders. This payment could easily be in the form of tax withholding. The mechanics have been proposed in many forms and the most efficient structure could be selected.

CONCLUSION

Although the profits would still be taxed, the taxpayers would conceptually be on a par with other noncorporate taxpayers. The ability of the corporation to shift the tax burden on consumers or labor should be roughly equivalent to the ability of other taxpayers to shift the tax on other forms of business income.

As a less preferable alternative, the pass-through could be utilized only for smaller corporations. This would remove many of the incentives provided in the current system.

Neither of these suggestions should be viewed as a cure-all. Although many of the incentives to enter major transactions for tax purposes only would be removed, corporate tax compliance would not be significantly reduced. In fact, record keeping will be increased in many respects. It is the reduced transactions costs and the removal of the "entity level" tax that make the suggestions appealing.

Of course, any such proposal must be dealt with in light of political realities and the massive educational task needed to achieve its general acceptance. The general public must be made aware that corporate profits, like their own, are subject to taxation.

In 1946, H. Christian Sonne concluded that the corporate tax should be repealed. He concluded his report on the issue as follows: "And so it may be with the corporation tax! It is wrong in principle; it is unhealthy; but our system has lived with it for so long that it may be wise to remove it only gradually over the years, until the country can adjust."[69] Similar arguments could be presented today. Perhaps the political climate is too much to be overcome. The educational process may be a slow one, occurring over many years.

The actions of President Reagan on this issue are indicative of the existing uncertainty. He has been quoted as telling corporate executives that some day the corporate tax should probably be repealed. Months later, however, he has proposed a tax package that would reduce corporate tax rates, but increases the effective tax on corporations by way of other changes. Apparently, the corporation is viewed as an effective "collector" of tax revenues.

In short, the corporation income tax suffers from a number of maladies, is not as productive as it once was for the Treasury, and there is no consensus as to what is wrong and how it should be cured. It is evident that lawmakers have formulated changes in the corporation tax without knowing who pays and what the economic impacts will be. Labor and consumers can be convinced that the stockholders pay the tax. Corporate managers would continue to attempt to shift the tax burden as efficiently and effectively as possible. This lack of information provides the political climate to perpetuate the tax debacle.

NOTES

1. E. R. A. Seligman, Essays in Taxation (1985), pp. 181–82.

2. R. R. Palmer, A History of the Modern World (1954), pp. 293–95.

3. R. W. Lindholm, The Corporate Franchise as a Basis of Taxation (1944), p. 47. This elegant work is the inspiration for much of this section.

4. Curtis P. Nettels, The Emergence of a National Economy 1775–1815 (1962), pp. 293–95.

5. H. R. Seager and C. A. Gulick, Jr., Trust and Corporation Problems (1929), pp. 53–58.

6. Seligman, p. 184.

7. Lindholm, p. 244.

8. Seager and Gulick, pp. 21–22.

9. Seager and Gulick, p. 17.

10. O. Bennett and I. Lippincott, Public Finance (1949), p. 610.

11. Historical Statistics of the United States, Colonial Times to 1970, Part 2 (1975), pp. 1106, 1109.

12. Economic Report of the President (1985), p. 277.

13. Seligman, pp. 136–264.

14. Seligman, pp. 180–92.

15. Seligman, pp. 237–41, 262.

16. Seligman, pp. 199–202, 262.

17. Seligman, p. 192.

18. Lindholm, pp. 244–46.

19. Seligman, pp. 254–58.

20. Seligman, p. 255.

21. Seligman, p. 256.

22. G. F. Break and J. A. Pechman, Federal Tax Reform (1975), p. 91.

23. P. H. Cootner, The Random Character of Stock Markets (1964).

24. M. McAleer, A. R. Pagan, and P. A. Volker, "What Will Take the Con Out of Econometrics," American Economic Review (June 1985), pp. 293–307.

25. Annual Report of the Secretary of the Treasury, 1919, pp. 23–24.

26. Speech by Mr. Enders M. Vorhees, reported by the New York Times, October 10, 1943.

27. William J. Schultz and C. Lowell Harriss, American Public Finance (Prentice-Hall, 1949), pp. 249-69.

28. Richard B. Goode, The Corporation Income Tax (Wiley, 1951), p. 45.

29. Arnold C. Harberger, "The Incidence of the Corporation Income Tax," Journal of Political Economy (June 1962), pp. 215-40.

30. Harberger, p. 230.

31. Marian Krzyzaniak and Richard A. Musgrave, The Shifting of the Corporation Income Tax: An Empirical Study of Its Short-Run Effect upon the Rate of Return (Johns Hopkins Press, 1963), p. 3.

32. Krzyzaniak and Musgrave, pp. 63-65.

33. John G. Cragg, Arnold C. Harberger, and Peter Mieszkowski, "Empirical Evidence on the Incidence of the Corporation Income Tax," Journal of Political Economy (July/August 1970), pp. 768-73.

34. Marian Krzyzaniak and Richard A. Musgrave, "Corporation Tax Shifting: A Response," Journal of Political Economy (December 1967), pp. 811-22.

35. John G. Cragg, Arnold C. Harberger, and Peter Mieszkowski, "Corporation Tax Shifting: Rejoinder," Journal of Political Economy (July/August 1970), pp. 774-77.

36. Ronald A. Ratti and Parthasarathi Shome, "The Incidence of the Corporate Income Tax: A Long-Run, Specific Factor Model," Southern Economic Journal (July 1977), pp. 85-97.

37. Roy D. Adams, "The Demise of Corporations in Harberger's Incidence Model," National Tax Journal (March 1977), pp. 91-92.

38. Howell H. Zee, "Tax Incidence in a Two-Sector Model with Variable Labor Supply," Southern Economic Journal (July 1978), pp. 240-50.

39. G. Ballentine, "Non-Profit Maximizing Behavior and the Short-Run Incidence of the Corporation Income Tax," Journal of Public Economics (February 1977), pp. 135-46.

40. Liam P. Ebrill and David G. Hartman, "The Corporate Income Tax, Entrepreneurship, and the Noncorporate Sector," Public Finance Quarterly (October 1983), pp. 419-36.

41. James R. Melvin, "Short-Run Price Effects of the Corporate Income Tax and Implications for Interna-

tional Trade," American Economic Review (December 1979), pp. 765–74.

42. Arnold C. Harberger, "The State of the Corporate Income Tax: Who Pays It? Should It Be Repealed?" Chapter 8 in New Directions in Federal Tax Policy for the 1980's, ed. Charles E. Walker and Mark A. Bloomfield (Cambridge, Mass.: Ballinger, 1983), pp. 161–81.

43. Charles E. McLure, Jr., "General Equilibrium Incidence Analysis: The Harberger Model after Ten Years," Journal of Public Economics (February 1975), pp. 125–61.

44. Arnold C. Harberger, "Efficiency Effects of Taxes on Income from Capital," in Effects of Corporation Income Tax, ed. M. Krzyzaniak (Detroit: Wayne State University Press), pp. 107–17.

45. H. G. Johnson and Peter Mieszkowski, "The Effects of Unionization on the Distribution of Income: A General Equilibrium Approach," Quarterly Journal of Economics, pp. 539–61.

46. Revising the Corporate Income Tax, Congressional Budget Office, May 1985 (U.S. Government Printing Office), p. xiv.

47. Revising, p. xiv.

48. Revising, p. 49.

49. The President's Tax Proposals to the Congress for Fairness, Growth, and Simplicity, May 1985.

50. Revising, p. 7.

51. See, for example, the landmark decision in Kintner v. Comm., 216 F. 2d 418 (CA-9, 1954).

52. See, for example, Morrissey v. Comm., 296 U.S. 344 (1935) and Outlaw v. U.S., 494 F. 2d 1376 (Ct. Cl., 1974).

53. Reg. Sec. 301.7701-2(a) (2).

54. See IRC Section 752.

55. See IRC Section 704.

56. See IRC Section 465.

57. See repealed Subchapter R, IRC Section 1361.

58. See IRC Section 267(a)(2).

59. S. Print 99-47, The Subchapter C Revision Act of 1985: A Final Report Prepared by the Staff, Senate Finance Committee, May 1985.

60. S. Print 99-47, p. 72.

61. Constructive dividends also occur in other contexts, such as rental arrangements, employee compensation arrangements, and so forth.

62. See IRC Section 166.

63. IRC Section 246A.

64. IRC Section 291.

65. S. Print 99-47, p. 24.

66. President's Tax Proposals, p. 119.

67. Joseph A. Pechman, Federal Tax Policy, 3rd ed. (Washington, D.C: Brookings, 1977), pp. 123-80.

68. Henry C. Simons, Federal Tax Reform (University of Chicago Press, 1950), p. 125.

69. H. Christian Sonne, "How Should Corporations Be Taxed?" How Should Corporations Be Taxed? (Tax Institute, Inc., 1946), p. 30.

INDEX

ABOUT THE EDITOR AND CONTRIBUTORS

RICHARD W. LINDHOLM is emeritus professor of finance and dean of the business school, University of Oregon.

GLEN W. ATKINSON is professor of economics, University of Nevada, Reno.

JIM BATES is a member of the House of Representatives from the 44th Congressional District, California.

STEVEN E. CRANE is assistant professor, department of economics, Marquette University.

BETTE K. FISHBEIN is researcher at the Institute for Social and Economic Studies.

HOWARD GENSLER is dean, Northrop University School of Law, Los Angeles.

DAVE GERRIE is chief of staff for Congressman Jim Bates.

LEONARD M. GREENE is a mathematician, economist, and business executive.

JOHN L. MIKESELL is professor and chairperson of the faculty of economics and finance, Indiana University.

JAY MAUER is assistant professor of economics and finance, St. John's University, New York.

FARROKH NOURZAD is assistant professor, department of economics, Marquette University.

NATHAN OESTREICH is associate professor, school of accountancy, San Diego State University.

JEINIE SUMMER is assistant professor, department of accounting, Portland State University.

JOHN TATOM is assistant vice president, Federal Reserve Bank, St. Louis.

DOUGLAS Y. THORSON is chairperson, economics department, Bradley University.

JOHN WALKER is professor of economics, Portland State University.

ANN D. WITTE is professor of economics, Wellesley College.